Editor: Deb Mulvey
Contributing Editor: Clancy Strock
Assistant Editors: Mike Beno, Mike Martin,
 Kristine Krueger
Art Director: Sue Myers
Photo Coordination: Trudi Bellin,
 Mary Ann Koebernick
Production Assistants: Ellen Lloyd, Julie Wagner,
 Dena Ahlers

© 1992, Reiman Media Group, Inc.
5400 S. 60th St., Greendale WI 53129-1404
All Rights Reserved. Printed in U.S.A.
Second printing

Reminisce Books
International Standard Book Number: (10) 0-89821-723-7
International Standard Book Number: (13) 978-0-89821-723-0
Library of Congress Catalog Card Number: 92-60979

Cover photo by Harold M. Lambert

For additional copies of this book or information on other books, write: *Reminisce* Customer Service, P.O. Box 5294, Harlan, IA 53593-0794; call toll-free 1.800.344.6913. Visit our Website at *Reminisce.com*.

Contents

This book is dedicated
to our parents and grandparents...
the young adults who refused to be
defeated by the Great Depression.

Prologue

By Clancy Strock, Contributing Editor, Reminisce Magazine

This book is the chronicle of a remarkable era in our history—the Great Depression. It also is the story of a remarkable generation of people born just about the time the 20th century began, somewhere between the presidencies of McKinley and Teddy Roosevelt.

We are their sons and daughters, grandchildren and great-grandchildren. Much of who and what we are was shaped by them.

It was their fate to be afflicted by wars, plagues, famines, epidemics, droughts and floods of near-Old Testament proportions. Yet they did much more than survive. These ancestors of ours stubbornly and bravely endured, sustained by their Bibles, their patriotism and their determination that things could be made better than they were.

What a Change They Saw

Theirs was the generation that went from outhouses to outer space, from kerosene lamps to computers, from straw mattresses to supersonic jets.

They made do during the bad times and adjusted to monumental changes in the world around them. They persevered through it all, anchoring their happiness and fulfillment on the belief that *family* was what mattered most.

Stop for a moment and think about their lives, these pioneers of the 20th century:

As they reached their late teens, they marched away to fight in World War I, "The War to End All Wars." What it really turned out to be was a barbaric battle of rat-filled trenches, poison gas and perpetual mud that shattered minds as well as bodies. More than 116,000 Americans died

and another 204,000 were wounded —many to live out their maimed lives in veterans' hospitals.

Tough Times at Home

Meanwhile, back on the home front, 500,000 of their neighbors, parents and children died from the worst influenza outbreak ever.

So Johnny came marching home and married the girl he left behind and started a family and settled down to earn a living. And just

> "We didn't know we were poor...but our parents knew it."

about the time things seemed to be going pretty well, the Great Depression hit.

Soon 35% of all Americans were out of work. Banks closed. Insurance companies failed. Businesses locked their doors. On top of that, the great droughts of 1934 and 1936 burned out the heartland, and entire states were turned into the Dust Bowl.

Those of us who were children in those years often say, "We didn't know we were poor." True enough. *But our parents knew,* and the pain of broken dreams and raising their children in poverty never left their hearts. Not for as long as they lived.

Nevertheless, these were *tough people* and somehow they made it through those bad years. Made it through—and then wept as their sons and daughters went off to yet another war.

They endured the frightening weeks when no mail arrived. They watched their neighbors hang gold stars in their windows, and prayed that Western Union wouldn't bring

the dreaded telegram, beginning: "The War Department regrets to inform you...", to their own house. That message was received by 405,000 parents and young wives.

A Second Chance?

Eventually it ended, and these ancestors of ours watched their children start their own families. I cherish a photo of my own mom and dad sitting close together on the sofa, beaming upon their first grandchild—my firstborn. Like so many of their generation, they felt they had a second chance and could make up for those Depression years, when they wanted to do more for their own children but couldn't.

But Fate wasn't through with them yet. All too soon they sat numbly as these beloved grandchildren were sent off to *another* war in a place called Vietnam.

Loved Ones Sent to War

Think of it! Look at life through my mother's eyes—a husband-to-be, a son and a grandson all wrenched from her and sent to places she had to look up in a world atlas.

I have another snapshot. It's of me in my Army uniform, facing Dad as I said good-bye before going overseas. It was the first time in my whole life I ever saw him cry. It wasn't until years later when I had sons of my own that I understood his tears.

What a generation! They were tougher than Vermont granite. You have to wonder what depths of faith could possibly have kept them going. Theirs was a self-reliance and grim courage that sometimes bent, but never broke.

It wasn't until much later, when they reached their 70s and 80s, that →

you could read the stories of their lives in their faces. There was a permanent sadness around eyes that had shed too many tears and seen too much misery. There was a stern set to mouths that had sometimes gone years without a lot to smile about.

Loved Their Country

Through it all, they were patriots. My dad asked to be buried with a flag over his casket. And I remember the day my mother, visiting me in Philadelphia, touched the Liberty Bell. She held her fingers on it for a full 10 seconds, as though 2 centuries of history were flowing through her like an electric current. She turned with tears in her eyes and said, "This is the most wonderful experience of my life."

As their lives progressed, incredible changes were swirling about: The first automobile they'd ever seen, a telephone in the house, electricity, the radio, running water and refrigerators, the extermination of diphtheria and polio and several other killer diseases. Heart transplants. Travel by air. Television. The list goes on and on, topped by watching a man plant his feet on the moon.

There aren't too many of that glorious, indomitable generation with us these days. Alas, we, their children, thought too late about capturing their memories. Too much of what they knew and felt is gone beyond recall.

Let's Remember Them

But it's still not too late to remember them with awe. They *were* the 20th century in America. We could do a lot worse than carry their strength, vision and indomitable courage with us as we step into the future.

This book is their story, sometimes told in their very own words, sometimes by their loving children and grandchildren.

This is the true story of how things were in the Great Depression.▶

READY TO RIDE! Clancy Strock grew up on a farm in northern Illinois during the Great Depression. In the 1933 photo above, he looks mighty pleased aboard his faithful steed, "Lindy," so named for the hero aviator of the day. As a child, Clancy remained unaware of the hardships of the Depression, and he says his hardworking parents are due the credit for that.

As Contributing Editor of this book, Clancy takes a look back at those years, and, from the objective distance of 6 decades, provides keen insight into not only the trials of the Depression, but the joys that strong people searched for, and found, during those years.

A much-loved contributing editor and columnist for *Reminisce* magazine, Clancy has since passed away. His heartfelt and humorous perspective on the past remains a timeless treasure.

CHAPTER ONE

'When the
Banks Closed,
Our Hearts
Opened...'

RUN FOR YOUR MONEY: Widespread rumors drove many depositors to withdraw their life's savings before the banks closed. Others chose to wait...and lost everything they had.

When the Banks Closed, Our Hearts Opened...'

I was 9 years old in the Depression days when the banks closed in our little Illinois town. I believe Roosevelt called it a "bank holiday." Some holiday.

You might wonder why a third grader would have any memory at all of a financial event. What could a kid have to lose?

Well, I lost my life's savings. It amounted to something on the order of $8 and change, as best I can remember. But it was pretty serious to me then. Fact was, the bank had closed and I was wiped out.

A Lesson in Thrift

The only reason I even *had* a savings account—rather than the bicycle I really wanted—was because the bank and our school promoted a savings program. It was supposed to teach us the virtues of thrift.

It had taken me quite some time to amass my fortune, small though it was. I carefully kept track of my money, dropping it dutifully into the little bank that my parents had given me.

Then, on every Monday morning throughout the school year, I would bring my saved-up nickels and dimes (or whatever I happened to have in my pockets) to school.

Sometimes it was the savings from my bank. Other times it was money I'd earned doing chores over the weekend. Still other times, it was a handout from a benevolent aunt or charitable uncle. Or maybe a birthday gift from Grandpa and Grandma.

My deposits were recorded each week in my trusty passbook. The entries seemed to fill the book fast, but my savings grew slowly. Twice a year the accrued interest (no princely sum, either, at the 3% rate common in those days) was entered.

Never Became Junior Tycoon

Watching my savings and interest accumulate, it slowly entered my mind that my chances of becoming John D. Rockefeller were somewhere between slim and none. By my calculations, it appeared that my personal fortune might pyramid to as much as $50 by the time I graduated from high school. It seemed like scant reward for a childhood of deprivation. To me a nickel saved was, well, a Clark Bar not enjoyed.

Then came the day the banks closed. Preposterous! A bank was a place with guards and expensive furniture and brass bars in front of the tellers and an enormous steel door guarding a vault where, insofar as I knew, my $8 was under safekeeping.

I was wrong. And now I was ruined.

Eventually "my" bank reopened. The first depositors to be repaid were us schoolkids. Whether this was an uncommon stroke of public relations genius or simply a case of paying off the smallest depositors first is something I never found out.

As you might suspect, my money did not go back into the bank. I put my life's assets into a mason jar, which I hid above some rafters high up in the corncrib. For years I had considerably more faith in mason jars than I did in banks.

Given the course of economic events in more recent times, it appears I may have been wise beyond my years.

—*Clancy Strock*

With Spading Fork and Popcorn, They Survived

WHEN THE Great Depression first began, it was devastating for those who lost their jobs and their homes. Federal relief programs did not exist, and President Hoover refused to ask Congress for them or to approve any relief initiatives Congress itself proposed.

Bank runs and failures increased. In 1931, more banks closed to prevent massive withdrawals. My mother and aunt each had a small inheritance in a bank that closed. My mother lost all her money; my aunt lost several thousand dollars.

As the Depression deepened in 1932, jobs were few and far between. More than 10 million Americans were out of work. Congress had promised World War I veterans a bonus payment for their service but never delivered. Many of those veterans organized themselves as the "Bonus Army" and marched on Washington, pleading, "Give us a bonus or give us a job."

Hobo Population Grew

When breadwinners could no longer find work, the burden was so great that some men actually abandoned their families in hopes that charities would provide some assistance to help their loved ones get by.

Many became part of the hobo population, riding boxcars from place to place and looking for work. They slept in barns, abandoned buildings, makeshift shelters, and "hobo jungles" close to the railroad tracks. Those who were lucky enough to find work would send for their families to join them.

By Gloria D. Crail
Fort Madison, Iowa

Others were never heard from again.

My father "rode the rails" looking for work. He'd take any kind of job to make a few dollars to feed and clothe his family. He usually came home on weekends, or as soon as he finished whatever short-term job he had found.

Many times I woke up late at night or early in the morning to the smell of fresh-perked coffee and cigarette smoke, and I knew that meant Dad was back home!

Most of our backyard was planted in a garden throughout the 1930s. The

---

*"Dad would take
any kind of job
to help his family."*

---

garden wasn't plowed with machinery, either; it was dug with a spading fork and tended with hands and a hoe.

We always planted lots of popcorn, and we three younger children usually had the job of shelling it. After that, we'd shift the corn from pan to pan as we blew off the chaff. Then we'd pop it on top of the old cookstove and season it with bacon drippings and salt. It was a delicious Sunday-afternoon treat.

Raised Their Own Food

The Concord grapes in our arbor gave us delicious fruit and jam. Rhubarb was used for pies and sauces. We also ate rhubarb raw, dipped in a little

sugar. Our family picked wild gooseberries and blackberries, and gathered other fruit from my grandfather's farm. I especially remember the delicious fresh cherry pies!

In fall we gathered hazelnuts, hickory nuts and walnuts. My father and older brother shelled the black walnuts and spread them on the roof of the shed to dry.

Dawn of a New Era

Not all Americans had to struggle as we did. For those fortunate enough to keep their jobs or find new ones, life went on as usual. People who owned small businesses found life more difficult, because collecting outstanding bills was almost impossible. A few of the rich folk carried on as though nothing had happened, but many used their resources to help those who were less fortunate.

A new era dawned when President Roosevelt took office in 1933. When his inaugural address was broadcast over the radio, it gave new hope to millions of people. "The only thing we have to fear," the President said, "is fear itself—nameless, unreasoning, unjustified terror which paralyzes needed efforts to convert retreat into advance."

HARD TIMES forced many newly unemployed men to sell apples on street corners to support their families. Those who still had jobs, or simply a nickel to spare, did their part to help by buying the street vendors' produce.

Neighbors Pitched in After Family Lost Farm

MY FAMILY will never forget the day the banks closed.

My parents were farmers, and one day Mother hurried to the bank and deposited a check for about $1,200 just before closing. The check was for a year's crop, and mother kept out only $5 for groceries. In a few minutes the bank closed...for good.

The $5 was the only money my parents had left, but the story doesn't end there. My brother, who was 6, came home from school and went to his room to change clothes. The closet was dark, and he decided to strike a match. You can imagine the rest. My brother got out safely, but the house burned to the ground.

The family moved in with relatives temporarily. One day Dad and Mother looked up and saw a caravan of cars coming, led by a car with a mattress tied on top.

Their friends and neighbors were bringing whatever items they could spare from their own households to help them set up housekeeping again.

Not long after that, Mother received word that her mother wanted her to come for a visit. When she arrived, she found a quilting party in progress in her honor. The ladies spent the day making quilts to replace those that Mother had lost.

The helping hands that assisted my parents encouraged them to keep farming, and they stayed at it for many more years.

—*Singer Lane, Redding, California*

'Depression Hit Us Like a Tornado'

By Cecile Culp
De Soto, Kansas

EVERYONE had their radios tuned to the news when the bottom dropped out of the stock market. They listened closely that day, and for many days to come.

The wealthy were hit first, but it wasn't long before the Depression came sweeping through our little town of Lenape, Kansas like a tornado. The banks went broke and closed their doors. It was hard to believe the money we'd saved there was really gone.

My father owned a general store, the kind where the sugar and beans came in barrels and were weighed out on scales. I remember standing on the store's porch, watching the Union Pacif-

ic freight train roar through. Men filled the boxcars, sitting side by side, all seeking a new life somewhere, anywhere. Some men traveled by walking the tracks; others walked the roads.

Many of these men came into the store to ask for food. My father always fed them. As I watched those men, driven by the forces of self-preservation, I thought about how lonely they must be, alone and remembering the loved ones back home who were depending on them.

Soon there were bread lines—hungry people standing in lines a block long just to get a bite of food. Some of the missions offered one free meal a day, but they soon ran out of money, too.

Meanwhile, more businesses were closing. Smokeless factories carried "for rent" signs, and the doors were closed.

My father's store began to look like a gold mine with all the food lining the shelves. Some of my friends' families had been hit hard; they thought we were rich, and that we had all the food we wanted.

Little did they—or I—know that my

father was having sleepless nights just like everyone else. He, too, was being swept up by the great waves of the Depression and was about to go under. The whole world seemed to be sliding into a great dark place. In 1933, my father had to close the store.

We moved to some property my father owned, and the Depression continued... until the bombing of Pearl Harbor. Just after the United States declared war on Japan, news came that an ammunition plant would be built near us. It seemed to go up overnight, and it was huge! We had never seen anything so large before.

Men flocked to the town by the carload. There was hardly room to walk on the sidewalk. My aunt owned a restaurant in town, and it got so busy that people didn't even have room to sit down. They ate their food standing up, out on the streets, under shade trees and in their cars.

The men who came to work at the ammunition plant had nowhere to sleep, either. Some slept in their cars, and all the sidewalks were filled with cots for them. The plant ran day and night.

The employment problem had vanished. Everyone had jobs, and money began to flow again. There was a wildness in the air, spirits were high, and everyone felt relieved and free. The Depression was over.

BREAD LINES sometimes stretched out for blocks. This crowd lined up for bread at the McAuley Mission under the Brooklyn Bridge in New York City in 1931.

'I'll Take the Cash...'

I WAS TEACHING in a small town, and got my monthly paycheck on Good Friday.

I didn't get to the bank until Saturday, and the cashier asked if I wanted to deposit the check or just take the cash. I said, for no particular reason, I would take the cash.

I was lucky to have a month's pay in my hands, because the banks closed that Monday!

—*Inez M. Warren*
Syracuse, Nebraska

Children's Efforts Made a Difference

By James S. McLellan
Greenville, Maine

MEMORIES of the Great Depression vary with each of us, depending on where and how we lived. I was living on a small farm near Clinton, Maine, where we had a few cows and a large woodlot.

Unlike many families in the city, we never knew what it was to be hungry or cold. We had little or no money, but neither did any of our neighbors on the surrounding farms, so we never felt we were suffering.

Like all farm children, my sister and I were expected to do whatever we could to help out around the farm. In the

> ## "We never knew what it was to be hungry or cold."

early years, we weeded the garden, helped keep the wood box filled up, washed dishes after all our meals and did other small chores.

There was never any thought of being paid for what we did, and there was no such thing as an allowance. We accepted that what we did was part of making a living.

Kids Felt Lucky

Children who had enough to eat and clothes to keep them warm felt lucky; most of us knew families in towns and cities who had much less.

At age 8 I started helping to milk the cows, and was so proud when I was able to turn the separator to remove the cream! Mother made our own butter,

LITTLE HELPERS Margaret Ann and Flora Belle Rhoades did their part to fill the family coffers by selling tomatoes at a roadside stand in Rossville, Indiana in 1931.

and I helped with that, too. The butter was traded in town for staples like salt, flour and sugar. Little money ever changed hands.

Fresh Trout for Dinner

I liked to hunt and fish, and after selling Cloverine salve to buy a .22-caliber rifle at age 12, I helped fill the family larder with a variety of game including grouse, snowshoe hares and squirrels. We had a trout stream near our home, and I often brought home enough trout for dinner.

That was on days when it was raining too hard to work outside. I don't remember that it ever rained too hard to fish!

A $60 Windfall

About the same time, I began trapping fur-bearing animals to raise a few extra dollars. During Christmas vacation when I was 13, I trapped ermine that sold for more than $60. What a windfall! To give you an idea how much money that was for a kid to earn, my father had two hired men who were helping him cut pulpwood for paper. Those men were paid $20 a month plus board.

By age 15, I was hunting for larger game, like deer. The gun, steel trap and fishing pole were not recreational tools; they were what helped us put food on the table.

The Depression was still with us when I got married. I don't know whether I was stupid or brave back in those years, but after we paid the preacher, my young wife and I had only $5 to start our married life. But we also had supreme faith in ourselves and the future.

As we look back now on those long-ago years, we realize they weren't all that bad. We not only survived; we may well have become better and stronger people for the experience.

She Sold Shellfish by the Seashore!

TO MANY PEOPLE, the life I lived in the late 1920s and early '30s would seem to be one of hardship and privation, but I thought I was having a wonderful time!

Of course, there were times I might have agreed—like when my sister and I were out on the mud flats outside our small town on the Oregon coast, digging clams by lantern light in the fog.

But there was a great deal of satisfaction in lugging those buckets of clams home to our mother. She'd help us clean the clams and pack them into quart jars, and then we'd sell them to hotels and restaurants.

We also caught Dungeness crabs in ring nets from a pier and sold them for 10¢ to 15¢ apiece. It was pretty tough work for girls of 11 and 13. We'd catch the crabs day and night, whenever the tide was right, then boil them in a 5-gal. tin can over an outdoor fire and sell them from a roadside stand in front of our little three-room shack.

As we grew older, we earned money in other ways. We made fudge and sold it to mill workers at lunchtime. We made flowers from beads and sold them door-to-door. We kept our eyes peeled for every scrap we could find of brass, copper and aluminum, which brought a few extra dollars from the junk dealer.

Mostly, though, it was the clams and crabs that saw us through those Depression years, and I always remember them with a smile. —*Saxon Morris, Cave Junction, Oregon*

READ ALL ABOUT IT! Newsboys of 3 the era earned their own spending money. Some gave their earnings to their parents to help with household expenses.

Extra! Extra! Newsboys Earned Their Own Cash for 'Kid Stuff'

By Don Blincoe Sr., Jacksonville, Florida

THE YEARS of 1938 through 1940 were tough ones for many American families who had survived the Depression by changing their lifestyles.

Many households were like ours, where father, mother, children, aunts, uncles and grandma lived together in one large house. More jobs were available then, and everyone worked, but the jobs paid little, and there was no extra money for "kid stuff." And in our house, there were four kids.

My younger brother, Bobby, and I could cadge a nickel or two now and then, and we could redeem pop bottles at the grocery store for candy money.

But money for the movies was out of the question—admission was a dime each. I was 9 and Bobby was 7, so we were too young to get jobs.

We thought our problem was solved when a neighbor's son, who was about 14, suggested we sell newspapers for him. Leo was a "corner captain," a position developed by the newspapers to organize crews of newsboys and supervise sales on downtown street corners. Papers sold for 3¢ each, and the newsboys kept a penny for each paper they sold.

The only hitch in our plan was Mom, who advanced every possible argument against it. We were too young, downtown was too far from home, we could get run over...you know, "Mom stuff"!

Leo went to bat for us and assured her he'd look out for us. And Leo was the kind of guy your mother would trust. Mom finally agreed, on one condition: that Bobby and I would turn our earnings over to her every night to be saved in a piggy bank. We'd get a dime on Saturday to go to the movies.

We started selling papers, and we looked forward to going to work every afternoon after school. I'm still not sure what Bobby had going for him, but he could sell three papers for every one I sold. Maybe it was because he was

"We gave our earnings to Mom every night..."

smaller, maybe he was more persistent, or maybe he just yelled louder. If you wanted to make any money, you had to hustle. Every passerby and store employee was a prospect.

My corner was the site of a huge Sears store, and traffic was heavy. It wasn't too hard to sell my allotment of papers (although it took me longer than Bobby), and I often had to go back to Leo's corner for more.

Weekdays were the best. On Saturdays, the evening papers came out earlier and we had to work longer to sell the same number of papers we sold on weekdays. Later, when we were older, we earned good money selling Sunday morning papers, which came off the presses at 11 p.m. Saturday. It's wonderful to remember how marvelously busy those downtown streets were on a Saturday night.

"Extra" editions brought us our best sales, and we'd come home with our pockets full of change. The day after the attack on Pearl Harbor, the circulation manager called in all the newsboys to sell extras. Every newsboy was excused from school. On that day, we weren't restricted to our usual corners, but could sell anywhere in town. Almost everyone we saw bought a paper.

There were some good learning experiences to be had 50 years ago, and a few Huck Finn-style adventures, too.

Selling Fish and Berries Helped Make Ends Meet

I WAS 7 years old when the banks closed, too young to know we were in a Depression. I just thought we were poor, but that didn't seem unusual. Everyone we knew was in the same predicament.

My father, along with millions of others, was out of work. When we could no longer pay the rent and other bills, we moved in with my grandparents, and my father and uncle opened a fish market in a small cinder-block building they rented behind the house.

There was no refrigeration then, except for the blocks of ice delivered by the iceman in a horse-drawn wagon, so we had to eat any fish that was left over at the end of the day. At the time, I thought I never wanted to eat fish again! Now that I'm grown, of course, going to a nice seafood restaurant is a treat.

Sold Fruit Door-to-Door

We also picked wild blackberries and sold them door-to-door during those years. When the berries ripened, Mama, Daddy, my brother and sister and I would go out about 7:30 a.m. to a narrow old road about four blocks from our house where the berries were thick. We'd pick until noon, then go home for a lunch of hot biscuits with Karo syrup.

After lunch, my brother and I would

By Margaret Wells Kirby
Richmond, Virginia

go out to sell the berries for 10¢ to 15¢ a quart. We'd take whatever money we had made home to Mama, who would decide what groceries to purchase with it and then send us back out to the corner store to buy food for supper.

Ate Berries All Day

If we had any berries left over, we'd have them with sugar and cream for dessert. Mama thought this was a real treat for us, but it was the last thing we wanted—we always seemed to eat as many berries as we picked, and we ate them the whole time we were trying to sell them!

My brother and I walked the eight blocks to and from school every day, no matter how hot or cold it was. We were never let out of school because of the weather, as students are today. We'd walk home for lunch, which was usually a warmed can of pork and beans with biscuits.

If it was raining, we had to eat lunch at school, as our shoes had holes in the bottom that were covered with cardboard. On those days, our grandmother would give us a dime each so we could

buy a carton of milk and a bowl of soup.

I don't think we even knew when the Depression ended, as it seemed we were always poor, even after my dad got a job as a salesman. Yet the hard times didn't seem to hurt any of us. It's made us appreciate everything we have now.

In 1987 I wrote a book about my life as a child and gave a copy to each of my six grandsons. They all thought it was the best gift they ever received. Until then, I don't think they could imagine life without television, ice makers, fast food, pizzas and all the other things they take for granted. It was hard for them to understand that not everyone had a telephone then, and that I had no pictures of that time because we didn't own a camera. But there were always things to do that didn't cost any money.

In both good times and bad, our parents always had time for us. We never had much money, but we had all the love any parents could possibly give their children. 🖗

ROADSIDE MARKETS like the one above on the C.G. Adams farm in Lost Creek, West Virginia attracted buyers with a wide variety of high-quality produce, and provided growers with an additional source of income.

Every Able-Bodied Man Was Expected to Work

By Lois Ashe Brown
Worthington, Massachusetts

HARD TIMES come and go, and the Bible tells us that the poor are always with us. Those of us who were children in the 1930s remember how hard times could really be.

The Canadian Pacific Railway was the mainstay of Lyndon, Vermont, where I lived with my parents and three brothers. Nearly everyone in town depended on the railroad, directly or indirectly, to keep food on the table.

As the economy worsened, the railroad passed out 10% wage cuts, and there was no union or negotiating team to protest. There were temporary layoffs, which meant workers put in only 2 or 3 days a week. There were few telephones, so public notices of layoffs were posted on bulletin boards.

Workers had no Social Security, old-age pensions or unemployment compensation to fall back on. People were expected to work as long as they were physically able, and there was no such thing as early retirement. It was every man for himself.

Workers Were Creative

Every able-bodied man and woman, and plenty of children, too, worked at something to bring in a dollar here and there. In season, people picked berries to sell house-to-house. Some picked dagger ferns to sell to florists. Men turned out to shovel snow or work on town roads for a dollar a day. Women and girls were glad to work in the homes of others who could afford to pay $2 or $3 a week, plus board, for help in the house.

Folks living on farms had it a little easier. Those who had enough feed usually kept a cow, one pig, a bull calf and a flock of hens. That would be called subsistence farming today, but in those days it made for a pretty good living.

Bread, milk, pea soup, johnnycake and oatmeal were the staples of many diets. "When we were very poor, we ate better than many do today," my mother said later. And so we did. With

---

> ## "People would have preferred to starve than ask for help..."

---

our own meat and milk, homemade bread, butter and cheese, all the fresh fruits and vegetables and home-canned foods, we ate like kings!

Welfare budgets were slim and it was only out of sheer desperation that anyone applied to the overseer of the poor for help. Records were carefully kept, and the amounts charged against each person were posted in the annual town report for all to see.

Recipients were expected to pay back every cent as soon as they were able. Those people felt great relief as credits were posted next to their names.

Folks would have preferred to starve than ask for help from the town, though. Being "on the town" was viewed with more fear than death itself.

Folks Were Tough

Vermonters had always known about "using it up, wearing it out, making it do, and going without," so most of them weathered the hard times.

At least one family in our town was known to have their horse and cow living in the family quarters to keep from freezing to death. The children had to take turns going to school because there wasn't enough footwear or clothing to go around. Those same children grew up to be decent citizens and live honorable lives.

After Franklin Roosevelt became president, relief came through various reform programs. Many men found work in the Civilian Conservation Corps on nearby Burke Mountain and in other camps all over America.

The Work Progress Administration provided work on bridges, highways and buildings, and supported some writers' projects. None of these jobs paid more than a few dollars, but they did offer the dignity of work for pay, and proved to be the salvation of many.

LUNCH BREAK: This work crew took a welcome break from its labors on a Midwestern farm in the early 1930s. Those who were out of work would take almost any job that was offered, no matter what the pay.

Hobos Came from All Walks of Life

BY 1931, the highways of our nation were filled with men searching for jobs.

They weren't like the typical tramps of the years before the Depression. They were young men who had just graduated from high school or college and should have been looking forward to a bright future. They were older men who'd worked all their lives. And they were men who'd once had successful careers in business. Now all of them were searching for any job to be found.

My husband was one of the fortunate ones. He was a school superintendent, with a good salary and a 3-year contract. But my heart went out to those other men whose lives had suddenly been thrown into confusion and chaos through no fault of their own.

We lived in Falfurrias, Texas, which had a warm climate and plenty of seasonal jobs, so many of the wanderers passed our way. It was also a rest stop for many who were traveling onward to the Rio Grande Valley, and there was a large hobo camp under one of the railroad bridges.

During the winters of 1931 and '32,

By Roberta Ferguson
Houston, Texas

hardly a day passed that I didn't have one or more hobos at my door, asking for a cup of coffee and a bite to eat or a small job they could perform for a quarter or 50¢. If my husband was home, we often

---

*"They were searching
for any job
to be found..."*

---

invited the man in to eat at our table and visit a bit. If he wasn't home, I didn't invite the men in, but I always had something to give them.

I recall one older man who'd been promised a job pouring concrete at a filling station that was being built. That job wouldn't start for a week, so he went to the valley to look for work in the interim.

When he returned, he found the concrete-pouring job had started earlier than expected, and the job had gone to another man. We made a couple of

small jobs for him, and invited him in for a meal and a visit. He was so intelligent and told such interesting stories that we really hated to see him leave.

Another one I recall was a handsome, fair-haired youth about 18 years old who asked for neither food nor work, but for a 5-gal. can. He'd spent the night in the hobo camp and stayed behind when the others left in the morning. He wanted to take a bath, but needed a good-sized can to heat the water. The worst thing about being on the road, he said, was the lack of privacy and the difficulty in keeping clean.

When Franklin Roosevelt was elected president, he began to put programs into effect that would provide jobs and fair wages and take the wanderers off the roads. It took time, of course, but by 1935 we were at least on the way to recovery.

**RIDING THE RAILS wasn't easy;
railroad detectives kept a sharp
eye for hobos trying to hop a freight.
The transients shown in the photo
above were taken off a freight
train in Los Angeles in 1936.**

Days of Riding the Rails Remembered

By Raphael P. Magelky
Eugene, Oregon

THE 1930s were tough years. There were no jobs to be had—even the farmers weren't hiring. Thousands of us rode boxcars from place to place in hopes of earning a few pennies. Sometimes, when there weren't any boxcars, we rode *on top of the* trains, no matter what the weather was like.

Anyone who remembers those days can vouch for the "yard bulls" who worked in the railway terminals.

We'd keep out of sight and wait for the "highball," which signaled the train was about to leave. That was the time to climb aboard. If the "bull" caught you, you were herded into a special housing area at the railyard and then put on a "work train" and sent out to repair the tracks. The railroad still owes me a few

HOPPING A FREIGHT was dangerous, as this hobo's precarious perch shows; but for those with no money, it was an inexpensive way to travel in search of work.

cents for some of the work I did!

On one occasion, about 300 of us climbed aboard an eastbound freight train in Laurel, Montana. Those riding with us through the dark night included a man and his wife and their young daughter, who was perhaps 10 years old. On that trip, I found a few days' work somewhere in the Bitterroot Valley of Montana, bleaching celery. (Yes, celery was bleached in those days!)

A Tough Way to Travel

Riding inside a boxcar or on top of the train was a dangerous way to travel. All of us were looking for work, but some were more desperate than others. If you had any money, you had to be careful; there was always the chance that other hobos might team up and overpower you so they could take it. A hobo also had to guard against the theft of his "bindle", a bedroll consisting of a piece of canvas wrapped around some blankets.

When there was no work to be found, we had no money for food. We sometimes went to the back doors of

cafés and restaurants (no one ever went to the front door for a handout) to watch for the floor-sweeper. Getting a word to him could help us get a sandwich, which was usually just a bit of leftover meat and two thin slices of bread, but it was usually enough to tide us over for a few hours.

We never went through garbage cans for food. The cans usually contained only ashes and a few empty tin cans. It was better to try a home in an outlying area of town and ask the lady of the house for a few sandwiches.

I remember one very generous lady who had just served a meal but hadn't cleared the table yet. She asked me to come in and wash up, and then served me chicken, potatoes and homemade gravy. It reminded me of the days when I was living at home and my own mother cooked food like that. When you were riding the rails, such meals were few and far apart.

Still, thanks to the generosity of those who shared their food with us, I can honestly say I never went hungry.

Grandma Kept Table Set for Travelers

I WAS FAR luckier than most during the Depression. I was being raised by my grandparents in a small Alabama town on Route 80, then the only coast-to-coast highway in the nation.

Granddaddy was the depot agent for the Southern Railway, and Grandma (who we called Nannie) ran a gas station and general store on the highway. For a long time, the worst thing that happened was when the railroad cut Granddaddy's pay.

Others weren't as fortunate. We'd see whole families walking on Highway 80 past Nannie's store, their few possessions on their backs, with pieces of old automobile tires tied onto their feet in place of shoes.

Nannie had a warm, loving heart, and she couldn't bear to see hardship; she had to do something to help. Whenever she spotted those wanderers, she'd send them to our house 2 blocks away for a hot meal. She and Priscilla, our cook and housekeeper, kept a big table set up in the backyard, and there was always a big pot of beans on the stove and hot corn bread in the oven.

Nannie also told Bailo, our hired man, to find something for the men to do, even if it was just cutting wood for the fireplaces, so they could feel they'd worked for the food and weren't getting a handout. Nannie was a wise woman; she knew those people had needs that went beyond hunger. Their spirits needed to be fed, too.

There was somebody eating at that table almost every day. When the weather was bad, Priscilla fed our guests on the long screened porch that ran alongside the house.

Thankfully, food was no problem for us. We kept chickens, raised a couple of litters of pigs each year and kept several milk cows. Pear, cherry and peach trees provided us with jams, jellies and preserves, and we could easily find persimmons, wild plums, dewberries and blackberries in the woods near the house.

Granddaddy and Bailo produced a bumper crop of vegetables each year, which Nannie and Priscilla preserved in shelf after shelf of fat mason jars. Much of that food was shared with others who were less fortunate.

Nannie's generosity eventually cost her the store. She let many of her customers charge their purchases, and continued extending their credit even when she knew they couldn't repay her. She just couldn't bear to see those people do without.

I don't know if Nannie ever collected the debts that were owed her, but I do know that she and Granddaddy paid off every penny *they* had owed, bankrupt or not. They were both fiercely honest people.

My grandparents taught me a lot about life. They taught me not to judge a book by its cover, and that money means nothing compared to decency and character.

—*Evelyn K. Martin, Lakeland, Florida*

Hobos Thankful for Food And Conversation

ALTHOUGH I was a young housewife home alone with my babies, I was never afraid of the men they called hobos. They were just down on their luck, looking for work, and hungry.

My husband kept a sawhorse where the hobos could see it, with a railroad tie ready to be cut into lengths to fit into the stove.

On most occasions, while I was fixing my guest a big beef sandwich, he'd go to work sawing the railroad tie. Afterward, I'd bring a basin of warm water, some soap and a towel. The men seemed to appreciate having a chance to wash their hands and face.

Sometimes I'd send the men off with an extra sandwich and cookies. Sometimes they'd just sit on the steps and visit for a while. Most of them were family men trying to make a few bucks to send home.

I had no money, as those were hard times even with my husband working, but I could share what food we had. God bless those dear souls for carrying on. —*Pauline Clark, Helena, Montana*

Hobo Doctor Cured Child's Illness

WHEN I WAS 3 years old, my whole body was covered with bandages be-

cause of a rash I'd had for my entire short life. In our small town of 500 people, everyone knew about my condition, and the word spread to the local hobo camp as well.

One day a hobo came to my father's store, said he was a doctor and asked if he could see me for a few minutes. My father was desperate to find a cure for me, so he agreed.

The hobo looked me over, then he asked for permission to use the town druggist's lab. Fifteen minutes later he gave my father a small jar of ointment. The hobo told my father to put the ointment on my rash, and to take me off cow's milk.

A week later, the rash was gone, and it never returned—and I'm now 84 plus! I think about that hobo often, and I will always be grateful to him for the help he gave me.

—*Earl E. Haight, Seattle, Washington*

Girl Learned Much from Wanderers

By Jean L. Jones
Carterville, Illinois

WHEN THE Depression began, many men found themselves wandering, without a job or a place to live. One summer those wanderers not only touched my life, but taught me some important lessons.

I was a child who loved the outdoors, especially the little stream that passed under a bridge near our country house. One day I slipped down the bank to explore under the bridge and saw a man kneeling beside the water. I scrambled back up the bank and headed for home, but I carried with me a mental picture. The man held a small piece of a broken mirror in his left hand, and a safety razor in his right. He had been shaving.

Back at home, Mother explained that he must have been out of a job. Maybe he was looking for work, maybe he was returning home, but whatever his circumstances, he wanted to keep up his appearance. He still had his pride. Hard times hadn't taken that away from him.

The second wanderer knocked on our door late one morning and asked if we could share some food with him, perhaps a sandwich. Mother had not yet fixed lunch and had no meat ready, but said she could give him a bread-and-butter sandwich if that would help. He accepted it gratefully.

My third encounter that summer was with not just a person, but a whole family. They had driven their Model A Ford into the woods and were camping there, cooking over an open fire and using tree branches and twigs around them to make baskets.

The baskets were square and sturdy, made of 8-in. lengths of wood, with bent branches for handles. Whenever they finished enough baskets, the children would sell them door-to-door for 20¢ each.

I was only 9 years old, but I learned several lessons from those wanderers that have stayed with me all my life: keep your pride, be grateful for gifts, and use your initiative and skills to provide for your family.

'Hobo Code' Directed Hungry Men to Meals and Caring Strangers

DURING THE early years of the Depression, I was living with my grandparents in the heart of San Francisco. The hobos would always come directly to our house, skipping every other house on the block. We'd see them coming up the street, looking at each house before stopping at ours.

My grandmother was a kind and caring person, and she never turned anyone away. She'd say, in her sweet way, "Just sit down on the stairs; I'll bring you something to eat."

Grandma always had a pot of homemade soup on the stove, so the menu was a bowl of soup, a sandwich, a cup of hot coffee and something sweet. Our guest was given a bell to ring when he was finished, and Grandma would take in the dishes, wash them and put them on the top shelf in the pantry, ready for the next visitor.

Even though the men were strangers and we never made conversation, somehow we weren't ever afraid. The hobos were soft-spoken and polite, and they appeared grateful for a simple meal.

My aunt and I would watch them through the curtains as they sat on the porch in the damp San Francisco fog, cradling a hot cup of coffee in their hands. As they walked away into the mist, we often wondered where they were going and where they'd get their next meal.

We also wondered why these men singled out our house for their stops. One day we found out. A friend had been to the train station downtown and had stopped to make a phone call. There, clearly printed on the wall of the phone booth, was our address—another form of the "hobo code."

—*Barbara Allen, Novato, California*

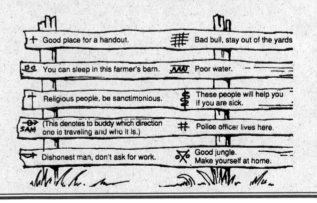

+ Good place for a handout.		‡ Bad bull, stay out of the yards.	
₀₀ You can sleep in this farmer's barn.		∧∧∧ Poor water.	
† Religious people, be sanctimonious.		$ These people will help you if you are sick.	
SAM (This denotes to buddy which direction one is traveling and who it is.)		# Police officer lives here.	
⊗ Dishonest man, don't ask for work.		⊗ Good jungle. Make yourself at home.	

His Words Gave Lonely Mother Hope

By Chester Skow
Eugene, Oregon

WHEN our slow freight to nowhere pulled into a small Iowa town, my traveling buddy and I were more than happy to jump off of it. It was just past dawn and we were both very weary from the long cold night on the noisy freight. We also were terribly hungry.

Although there was a cafe near the freight yard, we both knew that they wouldn't be putting out any free food. After all, times were tough in 1931.

Like thousands of other young men of our generation, John and I had decided to "ride the freights" to look for work. It was a rough life, and meals weren't easy to come by.

The two of us split up to try knocking on back doors for handouts. We knew that if we went as a pair we would intimidate people, and that was just another way to go hungry.

At first, I had no luck at all. Either no one was home or it was made clear that I was not welcome. To make matters worse, the sun was well up and I was becoming very thirsty.

I decided to try one last house before moving on to another neighborhood. Walking around to the back of the house, I knocked on the door frame of a screened-in porch.

Finally—Somebody Home

Just as I turned to leave, a voice from behind the screen said, "Yes?" Looking back, I saw a matronly woman in an apron awaiting my answer.

Quickly, I explained that I was hungry and thirsty and that I would be happy to mow her lawn, wash her windows or do just about any task for a sandwich and a cool drink. She opened the door and gave me a long look before inviting me in.

I followed her into the kitchen, where she again gave me a studied look before asking, "How long since you had a bath?" The question startled me, but I answered, "About 2 weeks ago."

She asked me to follow her upstairs to the bathroom. As we climbed the stairs, I began to wonder what in the world was going on.

"Here is your soap," she said. "There are the towels, and when you have taken off your outer clothes, place them outside the door and I will brush them off." I was so overwhelmed by this motherly lady that I was unable to speak—all I could do was simply nod.

Bathed, dressed and feeling like a new man, I went downstairs to the kitchen. It wasn't hard to find—all I had to do was follow the wonderful aroma to her stove.

The lady motioned me to sit down and then placed a heaping plate of food before me. On it were cottage-fried potatoes, eggs sunny-side up, toast and

---

> ### "I decided to try one last house before moving on..."

---

jam. While I was putting away the delicious king-sized breakfast, this quiet and enigmatic lady stared at me with unconcealed interest.

"I have a son who looks very much like you. How old are you?" she asked. "Twenty," I replied.

"My son will be 20 soon," she offered. Then, after a pause, she added, "He went 'on the bum' last spring. He was going to California to look for work."

After another long pause, she continued, "He sent me a card from Salt Lake City about 2 months ago and since then I haven't heard from him."

I thought she was going to cry, but she remained dry-eyed.

"I'm sure he's okay," I said in a fumbling attempt to reassure her. "If any-thing had happened, I'm sure you would have heard." It didn't seem like she heard my last comment at all—her thoughts were obviously elsewhere. Her silence was making me uncomfortable, so I asked what sort of work she would like me to do in exchange for the meal.

"No, you don't need to work," she replied. "I want you to go home to your folks and stay there. That will be your pay to me for your breakfast."

There didn't seem to be anything left to say, so I thanked her and walked to the door. As I opened it she softly asked, "Can we hope that someone has fed my son this morning?" I stopped and turned to answer, "Yes, we can."

With that simple assurance, I left, thanking her one last time for her kindness. When I reached the front sidewalk, I looked back. She was still standing at the screen door. I waved, but, through the screen, I couldn't be sure whether she waved back or not.

The sun was now high in a cloudless sky, predicting a very hot afternoon. As I made my way back to the freight yard, I thought about the calm and quiet lady who'd been so kind to me.

Walking along the streets of that somnolent Iowa town, I slowly began to realize that she really hadn't seen me as an unkempt stranger hoping for a handout. Instead, she'd seen a son who needed a bath, fresh clothes and a meal.

I only hope that, someday, she got the chance to welcome him home for real—and for good.

How Mom Managed to Postpone the Depression

THE GREAT Depression came to Harlowton, Montana at a very inopportune time, according to my mother. She and her friend Mrs. Lay were in the midst of preparations for their annual "payback" dinner and bridge parties, which meant entertaining 12 different ladies each day for 3 consecutive days.

Mom's theory was that once the house was cleaned, food could be prepared for 36 women as easily as for 12, and she and her friend would repay all their social obligations in one fell swoop.

These parties always followed a spring-cleaning frenzy. The living rooms and dining rooms had been freshly wallpapered for that year's parties, the rugs were beaten, the windows were washed until they sparkled, and all the furniture was polished.

Then Mom and Mrs. Lay started preparing the food while my friend and I set the tables with linen cloths and napkins, newly polished silverware, crystal goblets, the "company china" and a green springtime centerpiece of freshly gathered sweet peas.

By Alma Wheaton
Seattle, Washington

The final touch was hand-painted place cards made by Mrs. Lay's daughter, an art student.

Everything was going well until Dad came home unexpectedly from his drug

● ─────────────── ●

"The bank had closed, and all our money was gone."

● ─────────────── ●

store. Something must have been wrong; you could set your clock by his timetable. Yet here he was, home at 2 o'clock in the afternoon.

We started firing questions at him. When we stopped to catch our breath, he told us. The bank had closed, and all our money was gone.

We'd heard about the stock market crash the previous October, but that was New York. In Montana we didn't deal in stocks and bonds. We dealt in sheep and cattle and dryland farms. What hap-

pened in New York couldn't affect our bank! But it had.

After much discussion, Mom, Dad and Mrs. Lay decided to go ahead with the parties. The food had been bought and most of it was already prepared. Besides, the guests would be in the same spot we were. Their money would be gone, too, but for the next 3 days we'd enjoy the last of the good old days.

The parties went on as scheduled, and for a brief time, the bank closure and its ensuing problems were shoved aside.

Reality settled in soon enough. Instead of cash transactions, my father bartered medicine for eggs, pills for produce, and tonics for meat.

I guess I was too young to realize how my folks struggled to survive that period, but they did, and I never felt deprived. Thanks to them, I still look back on my childhood as a happy, carefree time. There may have been a shortage of money, but there was never a shortage of love and caring, and for that I'll always be grateful.

Years Were Filled with Warmth and Love

DOES THE Depression bring back bad memories for you? Not me!

My childhood was a warm and busy time. Mama, Daddy and my four older brothers were the center of my world. Aunts and uncles lived with us briefly as they began their lives in the city, enlarging the circle of love.

Daddy was an electrician for the railroad in Birmingham, Alabama. We lived in a middle-class neighborhood made up of railroad employees, executives and laborers. I don't remember when Daddy was laid off. My only bad memory is a time when I saw Mama crying and heard the word "foreclosure." I knew it must be a bad word.

My memory album is filled with happier times, like the days I followed my dad about. He was a jack-of-all-trades and did electrical repairs, painting and carpentry to supplement his commissary privileges from the railroad. Sometimes there was no pay for odd jobs, but Dad was happy to take care of the neighbors' "fix-it" problems anyway. His payment often was a

By Miriam R. Long
Selma, Alabama

bushel of sweet potatoes, a box of peaches, grapes or strawberries, or hand-me-down garments.

I also enjoyed following Daddy to his garden plot several blocks away. He'd gotten a permit from the city to cultivate an unimproved street. I tagged along while he cleared the stumps and vines, spaded the soil, and planted corn, pole beans, butter beans, squash, okra and tomatoes. The loamy smell of newly turned earth surrounded me like a snug blanket.

Fragrances to Remember

Aromas of that time occupy a special chapter in my memory album. Whiffs of Mama's rolls and buttery tea cakes always summoned the neighborhood kids. Velvet beans cooking in an iron wash pot in the backyard to feed our milk cow smelled good enough to dip into. (City zoning didn't prohibit farm animals then, and the neighbors didn't complain, because they shared in our

cow "Dotsy's" fresh milk and butter.) From time to time, our larder was blessed with a "care package" from my grandmother. Then we'd have smoked sausage, ham and fried chicken. And there was sugarcane syrup so thick it had to be pried out of the can!

We went to church regularly with all our neighbors. Church wasn't my favorite place—I hated having to be so still and quiet!—but I can't remem- ber a time when I didn't believe that God answered prayers and took care of us. A tithe was set aside from whatever income we received, whether it was from Daddy's odd jobs or my brothers' Western Union and newspaper deliveries.

I'll never forget those years: Neighbors helping neighbors, sharing whatever good fortune came their way; doctors rendering services regardless of patients' finances; and worship with friends whose faith far outdistanced their troubles. These are the memories that have kept my feet on a secure path throughout the years.

Lean Times Didn't Defeat Newlyweds

By Josephine Mortl
South Minneapolis, Minnesota

FRANK AND I were married in June 1929, and lived with his parents for the first year of our marriage so we could save money to build a house. The Depression started that October, but we both kept our jobs.

With our savings, and a loan from the local German Club, we built a small house the following year. The month we moved in, Frank's employer went out of business. I still had my job, but it was difficult to live on just my salary, because my hours had been cut.

Frank was a machinist, and he looked everywhere for a job. He finally found one after several weeks, but had to walk miles to and from work each day, since we had no car. After about a year, that company failed, too. When our first child was born in 1932, I quit my job. Mothers didn't work in those days.

Meanwhile, the Depression deepened. Frank went out every morning looking for a job—any kind of job. Once he scrubbed the floor of a restaurant and peeled potatoes. He also made deliveries for a liquor store. Some days he'd make a few dollars; some days, nothing.

We couldn't keep up the payments on our house, but the German Club kindly agreed not to foreclose if we could keep up the interest payments. To save money, we turned our whole backyard into a garden. I canned vegetables and fruit, and we buried carrots from the garden in sand in a small, cool spot under our porch.

We refused to go on welfare, and so did many others. Men were selling apples on street corners and standing in long soup lines. Families were moving back in with their folks.

Many houses were empty in those years. One house on our block sat vacant for a year and finally sold for $4,500. In 1990, 60 years later, that same house sold for $80,000.

In 1935, our son was born. Since we had no money for a hospital delivery, he was born at home. The doctor charged us $25.

After odd jobs, Frank found a job driving a delivery truck—a steady job, finally, with $25 coming in every week. We were in seventh heaven! We hadn't had that much income in years!

We were young, healthy and resolute. We were determined the Depression wouldn't defeat us. And it didn't.

Neighbors Organized Parties to Help Others

By Harry O. Jacobson
Orleans, Massachusetts

WHEN I was growing up, most of our neighbors were of Swedish descent. They were involved in many activities —meetings, dances, church gatherings, coffee parties and sewing circles. They all loved to get together to talk about current events and reminisce about their childhood days.

When the Depression came along, my father lost his job as a cabinetmaker. My two married sisters and their husbands moved in with us. My brother and I were still in school. The only person in the household who was working was one of my sisters, who had a job as a saleswoman in a Boston department store. That one salary bought food for all eight of us.

After the Depression had gone on for several months, many of our Swedish neighbors wanted to do something to help those who were having a difficult time making ends meet. They began organizing one or two "surprise parties" every month.

One Saturday night about 8 o'clock we heard a knock at the door. It was a surprise party for us!

There must have been 125 of our friends there, bringing all kinds of preserves, vegetables, bread, baked goods and other necessities. My mother was so happy she burst into tears.

After we'd all enjoyed the traditional treat of coffee and coffee bread, one member of the group presented my mother and father with an envelope containing $157 in bills and coins. In those days, that was a *lot* of money!

These gifts kept our family going for quite a long time. It was one of the nicest things that ever happened to us.

A HELPING HAND: Children looked on as unemployed men waited in line for clothing at a "relief depot" in Salem, Virginia.

His Quiet Confidence Shaped Son's Life

IT WAS early 1933. I came home from school in the afternoon and saw my father and mother in the kitchen, holding hands over the table. My father was crying, something I had never seen before.

I said, "What's wrong, Daddy?" He immediately straightened up, wiped his eyes and took hold of my shoulders. "Son," he said, "I lost my job today, but we have nothing to worry about. We will get through this together until I find another job."

Dad didn't get another job until sometime in 1935. Yet he never complained or worried, and because of that, I never worried about it at the time either. The quiet confidence my father instilled in our family got us all through the bad times, and it stays with me even today.

Dad went on to become a successful salesman, and had many happy years after his retirement. Now I'm retired myself, and I still attribute my good life to my father, who never doubted himself.

—Donald E. Gaul, Burlington, Wisconsin

Parents Made Sure Debt Was Repaid

ALTHOUGH I wasn't born until 1936, the Depression taught me a valuable lesson.

One of my earliest memories is of delivering an envelope to a woman named Mrs. Combs every Friday night. When I was old enough to ask what the envelope contained, I learned Mrs. Combs had been my parents' landlord during the years when my father had only odd jobs and couldn't pay the rent. Those envelopes contained the back

rent payments, even though we no longer lived in Mrs. Combs' house.

—Martha Lasure
West Palm Beach, Florida

She Knew How To Count Her Pennies!

DAD LOST his job early in the Depression, and we turned our backyard into a garden and sold the produce from house to house. My most vivid memory is the day my mother sold a 3¢ stamp so we could buy bread! She only had 2¢, so she sold the stamp to our neighbor. Then she was able to send me to the bakery for a nickel loaf of bread.

—Jane Hutchins, Yakima, Washington

Dad Did Whatever He Could to Help Others

MY FATHER took good care of us, and of many others, during the Depression. He and my mother ran a store, and they worked hard.

We moved from Alabama to Texas about 1927, and when the Depression began, families all along the route we had followed came to my dad for help. Some of the families were living in their cars and going without food.

One couple arrived at the store with their two little boys. They were tired, hungry and discouraged. Dad couldn't give them any money, since he had five children at home, but he gave them food and a place to sleep in exchange for work. The family moved on as soon as the father found a paying job.

Relatives who needed shelter came to us, too. One of my teenage cousins who couldn't find work came to live with us for a while, then moved on to

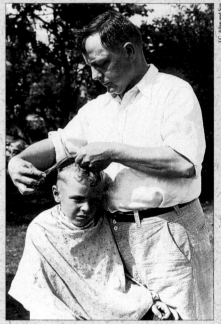

"JUST A TRIM, PLEASE": Many parent's cut their children's hair at home to keep expenses down. This anxious-looking youngster got his trim in the backyard in 1934.

stay with other kinfolks who took him in.

We saw a steady stream of families from Alabama. The grapevine had told them my dad would help when he could. And that's exactly what he did.

—Mary Heinlein, Hot Springs, Arkansas

Mom's Sacrifice Gave Him Lasting Memory

MY MOTHER made quilts and sold them to bring in a little bit of extra money. Her enterprise was so much a part of our family life that I grew accustomed to walking under quilting frames in the small living room of our home in southern Illinois.

As my high school graduation drew near, I wanted a class ring terribly, but there was no money to pay for one. My mother was determined to get me one, though. She began piecing together a double wedding ring quilt, and spent long hours finishing it with machine-like stitches. She sold that prized quilt for $9—the price of my ring!

Although my mother attended my graduation from college and later watched me receive my master's degree, neither meant as much to me as wearing the high school ring that had cost her so much time and work. I still have that ring. It will always be a prized possession.

—George Foster
Tucson, Arizona

Despite Hardships, Her Love Never Wavered

WE WERE living in Jackson, South Dakota when the Depression started. I was 8 years old, the youngest of eight children. Our father had died 5 years earlier, so our mother raised us alone.

It was very hot and dry during those years, and the older boys farmed as best they could. Many fires swept the prairies during those drought years, and often my mother and the boys went out to help fight the blazes.

Mama used our well to store the milk from our cows and our home-churned butter. She cooked our meals on a wood stove and baked eight loaves of bread every other day. We didn't have a car and lived 5 miles from town, so Mama laid in all her grocery supplies in the fall, like 100 lbs. of sugar, 10 to 12 bags of flour and a case of coffee. She butchered her own meat, and cured it in salt or canned it.

Come fall, Mama would sew all our clothes for school. The schoolhouse—a 2-1/2-mile walk from our house—was an old log building, and every year Mama gathered Badlands dirt and mixed it with water to paint the walls. Sometimes the color came out pink, sometimes gray, other times off-white, but it always looked clean.

When Mama thought we needed

MEMORIES OF MOM: Sun spills over Leora Collinge as she relaxes with a favorite radio program in 1938. Her son, Walter Steward Collinge of Stoughton, Wisconsin, says the family was living in Daly City, California when this photo was taken.

some entertainment during the winter, she'd hitch up a team and heat a big soapstone, which she'd put in the wagon with some hay and a couple of quilts. All of us kids would get under the covers to stay warm and go visit neighbors to work picture puzzles.

Our mother never lost her temper, and she loved each of us and praised us for whatever we could do to help out. Even after we were grown and married, she was always proud of us. She loved us right up until God took her home.

—*Frances Jensen*
Kimball, South Dakota

Teen's Enterprise Paid Off—Twice!

I WANTED desperately to go to college, but during the Depression years there were no funds available. So at age 16, I decided to earn some money during the summer.

My parents suggested baking. The local grocer allowed me to have a couple of shelves in his store, and I placed a sign there that said "Merilyn's Home Baking." I got up each morning at 4, had all my baking done by 10 and delivered it to the grocer, who received 10% of the sales. My parents furnished the milk, flour and butter, and I paid for the rest of my supplies. By the end of the summer, I had netted $150!

One evening our family was invited to dinner at my aunt and uncle's house. When I opened my napkin, I found a check for $100! My uncle said since I was willing to work so hard to reach my goal, maybe he could help in a small way. *Small?* It was the nicest thing anyone had ever done for me!

—*Merilyn Pafford, Dos Palos, California*

Children Helped Parents Earn Extra Income

WHEN MY dad's salary was cut from $19 a week to only $14, Mom answered an ad to do piecework at home. She brought home pounds of sparkling beads to string, which were used to adorn the pretty dresses that were in style then.

Every evening after supper, Mom, my sister and I would sit at the kitchen table and string those beads. Although my sister and I were just kids, we felt so proud to help our parents!

I was luckier than my best friend, Rosie. Her father had no job, so he sold

apples on a street corner, and Rosie would shine them for him. During those years in New York City, almost every street corner had a jobless man selling apples, in all kinds of weather.

I'm a grandmother now and still have to count my pennies, but I count my blessings as well!

—*Gladys W. Mitchell, Portland, Oregon*

Tough Times Couldn't Break Mom's Spirit

EVERYONE HAD problems during the Depression, and my parents were no different. They lost most of their money when the building and loan closed. My father's company fell on hard times, too. Some weeks he had only 1 day of work; other weeks, he had none.

We fell further and further behind in our taxes, although my parents paid as much as they could. One day my mother gathered $5 and walked to the City Hall to put it toward the past-due bill.

As she stood in line waiting to make her payment, she looked around the room and saw men and women who looked completely defeated and ready to give up. Some of them feared losing their homes, and did not know which way to turn.

Then and there, my mother decided she would not be broken by the Depression. When she reached the payment window, she said, "I want to pay $4.90 toward my back taxes!"

She left with her dime in change, walked across the street to Woolworth's, sat down at the lunch counter and ordered a 10¢ ice cream soda!

My mother was not defeated by the Depression. She held her head high throughout her long life, to the age of 91.

—*Marion Roberts, Oaklyn, New Jersey*

ROLE MODELS were important to Depression-era children, and schoolteachers were especially respected. The pupils in the rural Kansas school shown at left only had eyes for teacher.

those items to assist the family as well. During the next several weeks, the man continued to look for work. He carried in water for the school, and cut and hauled wood from the hillside for the stove. The grandmother took the two children outside whenever weather permitted.

Meanwhile, classes continued as usual in the front of the room. The husband, wife and grandmother listened intently as the students recited their lessons. At recess, they asked the teacher questions about history, arithmetic and

> ### "The family listened as students recited their lessons."

stories she had discussed with her pupils.

One day the grandmother said, "My son-in-law will find work soon, but I'm hearing things I never heard before, and I'm going to hate to leave!"

One morning Mrs. Eikleberry arrived for school and saw that the grandmother was preparing to deliver her daughter's baby. The teacher quickly ran back up the trail to meet the students before they reached the school. She told the oldest child to keep the others there until she heard the school bell. Then she went back to the school to help deliver the baby.

Mrs. Eikleberry had assisted at "birthings" many times in the remote Arkansas hills, but this was the first time she'd turned her school into a maternity ward! The delivery went well, and mother and baby were both fine.

By the time the mother was able to travel, her husband had found a job at a sawmill in another community. The family of six piled into their old car to move on. We pupils hated to see "our baby" leave, and a few tears were shed as we waved good-bye.

The Depression days were like no other time in the history of our nation. The dedicated teacher who walked those mountain trails met and overcame problems that might have defeated someone with less courage and determination. How do I know? She was my mother.🖋

How One Teacher's Love Helped Troubled Family Start a New Life

By Catherine E. Rogers, Danville, Arkansas

A COMBINATION of courage, pride, bravery, determination and hard work helped build rural America, and one of my schoolteachers had every one of those qualities.

Her name was Mrs. J.A. Eikleberry, and she'd taught in many one-room schools. During the Depression, she lived on Huckleberry Mountain in Logan County, Arkansas and hiked down a steep 2-1/2-mile trail each day to her little school.

One Monday morning as she came down the rugged trail, Mrs. Eikleberry saw smoke coming from the school's chimney.

"Now, who can that be?" she asked herself.

She opened the schoolhouse door and was greeted by a shy, embarrassed family—a man, his pregnant wife, two small children and a grandmother. The family members had moved everything they owned into the schoolhouse. Their possessions consisted of an iron bedstead, a cot, a few pots, pans and dishes, and several pasteboard boxes, all neatly arranged in the back of the room.

The man explained that he was out of work and looking for a job. When his family reached the schoolhouse, they couldn't pass up a chance to have a roof over their heads, a floor under their feet, and some warmth from the wood-burning stove.

He added that his wife was due to deliver a child soon, and he didn't want her sleeping in the cold, stripped-down car that they had converted into a pickup truck.

Could They Stay?

Mrs. Eikleberry was a compassionate person, and assured the man his family would not be turned out into the cold. She did advise him, though, that classes would have to go on. The family promised to cooperate as long as they could stay in the building.

The teacher noticed the family had only a meager supply of food, so she brought turnips, greens, and dry beans and peas from her farm to share with them. She also had some spare bedding and clothing at home, so she brought

Timing for Sunday Trip Was Eggs-actly Right!

ONE SUNDAY we wanted to take our new baby to see her grandma, but we didn't have the 25¢ needed to buy a gallon of gas.

We did have hens, though, and 11 eggs. At that time, eggs sold for 25¢ a dozen. So we all got dressed up, and then we sat and waited for one of the hens to lay an egg! Finally one of them cackled, my husband put that egg with the 11 others, we took them to the store and exchanged them for a gallon of gas. Off we went to see Grandma!

—Cora M. Johns
St. Charles, Missouri

'Depression Taught Us A Better Way to Live'

UNTIL THE Depression, my life was like a fairy tale: beautiful parents, beautiful homes, beautiful friends. We lived in a world that satisfied our every whim.

I had just enrolled in college and was packing my trunks to leave home for the first time when we received a telegram saying my father's business had collapsed. That moment was a turning point in my life.

My mother became ill, and I took care of her and our new, much smaller home. I had a lot to learn. I didn't know how to cook, or that dust was an enemy, or how quickly dollar bills could disappear. I learned that I could wear the same dress more than once or twice, and that my shoes didn't have to match anything.

I found myself beginning to enjoy this new way of life. I not only learned to cook and clean, but found myself with more time to read and sew. Now that I didn't have everything I wanted at the snap of a finger, I appreciated what

TRUSTY BOBSLED provided transportation when this family from Lafayette, Indiana made a trip to town to sell eggs from their farm.

I had, and even learned to save money.

Folks were always coming to the back door to sell their wares. Once a man selling shoes came by, and Mother realized he was someone she'd known in the "old days." He came in for a visit, stayed for dinner and spent the night on our couch. After breakfast the next day, he made himself at home on a cot in the basement.

The man who had been our chauffeur was staying in the basement, too, and the two men became fast friends. Both stayed with us for a long time.

The Depression was terrible in some ways, but it taught many Americans a better way to live. We began to not only think more about others, but to help them. The Depression helped me grow up.

—Juni Dunklin
Sandersville, Georgia

Girls' Secret Club Gave Aid to Needy Families

WHEN I WAS 12 years old, there were several needy families in our town of Leonardo, New Jersey. My friends and I wanted to do something to help. So seven of us started a club called "The Secret Helpers," with one girl's mother,

Mrs. Budd, overseeing our projects.

We met once a week and paid 10¢ in dues to buy food for the six or seven families we decided to help on a regular basis. Mrs. Budd got soup from a local restaurant and bread from a bakery. When we had a box filled with food, we'd put it on the porch, ring the doorbell, and then dash out to the car so our identities would remain a secret.

Two of the families had five or more children, so we helped them the most. We heard one of the boys needed shoes, so we found out what size he wore and added those to the box.

Mrs. Budd also got permission to use our school's auditorium for a variety program to raise additional money for the food boxes. We sold tickets for 50¢, and many people donated baked goods for a bake sale we conducted at the same time. We raised between $30 and $40—which was a great amount of money for that time!

At Christmas and Thanksgiving, the boxes included an envelope that contained money so the families could buy turkey or other meat. At Christmas we put gifts in the food boxes, too, usually items like mittens and scarves.

The recipients never knew who we were; we identified ourselves only as "The Secret Helpers." It was so much fun, and so rewarding. Children *can* help!

—Toni Johnson
West Sullivan, Maine

A SMALL CROWD turned out for a children's public health clinic in the rural town of Lake, Wisconsin. The project was sponsored by the WPA.

He Kept Town from Running Out of Gas!

THE DAY the bank closed in Spencerport, New York is one that I will never forget.

Word travels fast in a small town, and my husband heard the news early in the day. We had just ordered $200 worth of gasoline for our little service station the night before, and we wouldn't be able to write a check to pay for it. We had only $60 in the cash drawer, and the gas tanks were empty. We were out of business.

Customers pulled in for gas, but Harold had to turn them away. Neighbors stopped by to offer their sympathy.

We thought we had hit bottom. But that's when fate sent us a miracle.

A man who owned a successful insurance business in town pulled up to one of the empty pumps.

"How did it get you, Harold?" he asked sympathetically.

"About the same as it did everyone else, I guess," my husband replied. "I've got $60 on hand and $200 worth of gas ordered. I don't know what to do."

To Harold's amazement, the man reached into his pocket and handed him $200!

"Here, young fellow," he said. "Take it. Pay me back whenever you can."

The gas was delivered, Harold paid for it and we were back in business!

In fact, we were the only station in town that had any gas. Cars lined up all the way down the street for a turn at the pumps. Harold was so busy that I had to come in to help out!

We were forever grateful to the good Samaritan who'd helped us. After we repaid and thanked him, he just laughed.

"I pulled my money out of the bank just in time," he said. "Otherwise *all of us* would have run out of gas!"
—*Ilma Wright Wiesen, Tavares, Florida*

Keepsakes Saved Thanks To One Man's Generosity

THE BANKS in Stanley, Kansas closed on March 5, 1933. It was a blow for all the adults, of course, but it was also devastating to our senior class. That same day, our class pins and rings arrived at the post office, C.O.D.—and all the money to pay for them was in the bank!

Many people in the community were concerned about our plight, but since they didn't know how long the banks would be closed, they were hesitant to help. The situation was so uncertain that even taking up a collection was out of the question.

With the encouragement of our class sponsor, G.W. Lindberg, we decided to wait. We knew our postmaster would hold the package as long as postal regulations would allow. Maybe the banks would reopen in time.

One morning we arrived at school and were surprised to find our pins and rings were waiting for us! We were delighted, but since the banks were still closed, we wondered how they'd got-

THIRTIES FUEL PRICES seem low today, but many families scrimped to buy gasoline. Walter Linge of Storm Lake, Iowa posed with price sign (above) in 1936. Heating fuel was costly, too; the men at right cut their own firewood in 1937.

ten there. Much later, we learned Mr. Lindberg had cashed in his insurance policy to pay for them!

Some of us may have forgotten the whereabouts of those pins and rings today, but we will never forget Mr. Lindberg.
—*Floriene Boehm Fontana, Kansas*

MILK LINE: The Salvation Army provided milk for needy children, who lined up with their own containers (below). This photo was taken in 1932.

Depression Years Filled with Courage and Sharing

By Mrs. R. E. Quinn
Ivyland, Pennsylvania

MY MEMORIES from the Great Depression are of unbelievable love, courage and sharing.

I was too young to work—you had to be 16 to get a work card—but old enough to know what was going on. My daddy lost his job, what little he had saved in the bank was gone, and our home was scheduled for a sheriff's sale.

We moved out at night, after the sheriff's sale sign went on the front door. Daddy said that if we stayed until the day of the sale, we'd lose everything we had left in the house.

My parents went into the city on a trolley car and found us a little house to rent for $20 a month. I was enrolled in the National Youth Administration program, which provided job training for youths and part-time jobs for needy students.

I stayed after school and worked in the building, doing whatever needed to be done, and once a month I received a small check from Washington. This was intended to pay for books and other school expenses and to encourage our parents to keep us in school.

I worked on the NYA through all 4 years of high school. I must have marked thousands of test papers for teachers! I also cleaned rooms, cleaned blackboards, emptied the trash, did fil-ing in the office—you name it, I did it.

A neighbor of ours who was a widow fed us one night a week during the worst years. Her only daughter had steady work and they got by fairly well. The menu was always the same: stewed tomatoes over macaroni and cheese, bread, tea and coffee. No meal ever tasted as great to me as that one!

Accepted Neighbor's Kindness

Another neighbor cut down every tree on his property to provide firewood for us, and for others, during winter. There was precious little money to buy coal for our furnace.

Any coal we did have for the furnace was picked up along the railroad tracks. On Sundays, young and old alike would take a bucket and walk the tracks, looking for pieces that had fallen off the coal cars. I was so proud and happy when-ever I filled my own bucket with coal!

And let's not forget the little corner grocery stores where everything people needed to survive was "chalked on the ice." Most owners kept a little book listing the families to whom they had given food. They gave it freely, not knowing whether they'd ever be repaid.

We sometimes had no money to pay for our food, either. Once the store owner's wife told me, "Honey, if you're on your way to school and your mother needs bread and you have no money, just go on the landing to the store box and get some." The store box was where the deliverymen put their goods early in the morning, before the store opened.

The wonderful folks who lived through those times were so brave. They've made our country what it is today.

Bus Owner Footed Bill for Class Trip

IN 1932 I was treasurer of our senior class in Conshohocken, Pennsylvania. I had put our class funds in a bank that later closed.

Our class of 55 had worked hard for 4 long years to save that money, because we intended to visit Washington, D.C. for our class trip. When the bank closed, we were heartbroken.

Then along came a businessman everyone admired. He owned the local bus company and offered to take the whole class on the trip, and pay all our expenses! I signed over the bank account to him, and we had a marvelous trip. And he did get his money back—10 years later.

—*George W. Reinert*
Oceanside, New York

'I Like the Depression!'

Editor's Note: After Sally Wall's father died, she found this account, written in the early 1930s, of how his family got through the Depression in Texas. "I don't remember much of this, but it must have been a delightful period in his life," says Sally of Dallas, Oregon. "He was always jovial, as his story shows."

I LIKE the Depression. No more prosperity for me. I have had more fun since the Depression started than I ever had in my life. I had forgotten how to live, and what it meant to have real friends, and what it was like to eat common, everyday food. Fact is, I was getting a little too high-hat.

It's great to drop into a store and feel that you can spend an hour, or 2, or 3, or even half a day just visiting and not feel that you are wasting valuable time.

I like the Depression. I am getting acquainted with my neighbors and following the Biblical admonition to love them. Some of them had been living next door to me for 3 years; now we butcher hogs together.

I like the Depression. I haven't been out to a party in 18 months. My wife has dropped all her clubs, and I believe we are falling in love all over again. I'm pretty well satisfied with my wife and I think I will keep her.

I am feeling better since the Depression. I get more exercise because I walk to town, and a lot of folks who used to drive Cadillacs are walking with me.

I like the Depression. I am getting real honest-to-goodness food now. Three years ago we had filet of sole, crab Louie, and Swiss steak with flour gravy. We had guinea hen and things called "gourmet" and "Oriental." Now we eat sow bosom with the buttons still on it!

I like the Depression. Three years ago I never had time to go to church. I played checkers or baseball all day Sunday. Besides, there wasn't a preacher in Texas that could tell me anything. Now I'm going to church regularly and never miss a Sunday. If this Depression keeps on, I will be going to prayer meetings before too long.

Oh, yes! I like the Depression!

Memories Bring More Laughter Than Tears

SOME THINGS in life must be experienced for one to truly grasp their meaning—like the Great Depression. Although I was very young at the time, my memories of those years bring more laughter than tears. I remember...

● It was rare to be able to afford a meal in a restaurant in those days, but when you did go, you always looked for a seat by the window. The proprietor always gave larger portions to the diners with window seats so passersby would think it was a good place to eat!

● Our father would sometimes take us to the Bronx Zoo, but never on Mondays. That was the only day the zoo charged admission, which was a nickel. Charging admission kept attendance low so the zoo employees could do the cleaning.

● An Italian family lived downstairs from us, and on Fridays the family's three boys went across the street to the pizza shop, where they could buy a very large pizza for 25¢. Think about how remarkable that was—feeding three boys for a quarter!

● For adults, most socializing consisted of people visiting one another. Whenever a woman became engaged, for instance, a steady stream of women would visit her house. My mother always baked a cake for such occasions, putting a ring from the dime store inside it. The girl who got the ring was supposed to be the next one to get married.

● And finally, I'll never forget a toast my uncle used to make while holding up a glass of my mother's home brew:

"May you all live to be 150 years old—and may the last voice you hear be mine!"

—John Ford
Wellesley Hills, Massachusetts

CHAPTER TWO

Braving
The Dirty
'30s

Braving the Dirty '30s

THE DUST BOWL years ravaged thousands of square miles in the Great Plains during the 1930s. With the Depression already well under way, the massive drought made it even harder for poverty-stricken farm families to get by. But many did. These are their stories.

L et me set the stage: before you can understand the great droughts of the '30s, you need to understand what things were like. There were still hundreds of thousands of homes without running water, indoor plumbing or electricity. Homes were not insulated. Poorly crafted windows had chinks and cracks through which wind, dust and snow came inside.

There was no air conditioning. Farming still was done mostly with horses. The social programs we take for granted today were either not yet in place, or in their infancy. A common expression was, "Root, hog—or die."

The Great Depression was at its worst when the great droughts hit. Banks had failed. There was no credit to be had. Tens of thousands of people had already lost their homes, businesses or farms.

Now superimpose upon this world a string of years unlike anything any living humans had ever seen. Most of today's records for low temperatures, high temperatures and lack of rainfall were set in those years. The hardships were unimaginable as crops died, wells went dry and grasshoppers ravaged the land. In these extreme conditions, the aged and unwell perished.

Kansas Flew By

I remember a day at noontime, standing with my dad in what seemed like a dim twilight or an eclipse of the sun. The sky was choked with dust, driven toward the east by a howling wind. "There goes Kansas," Dad said.

Yes, the soil in Kansas and Oklahoma and parts of Texas, Nebraska and the Dakotas had been reduced to dry powder. Every time the wind blew, another layer of topsoil took to the air.

During the summers, people slept on their lawns or in the parks because houses were too hot to be livable. And the moment the morning sun crept over the horizon, you pulled down your blinds, trying to retain whatever coolness had crept into your home during the night. Electric fans ran 24 hours a day—where electricity was available.

The sky played cruel tricks, too. At night, "heat lightning" would flicker in the sky, holding out false hope that perhaps, at last, a little rain was on the way. But it never came.

Lawns turned brown and crunched underfoot. Crops withered in the fields. Trees died from thirst. After a while even optimistic people began to entertain the idea that perhaps it *would never rain again!* Perhaps America was destined to become a desert.

Swarms of Insects Invaded

As if all this wasn't enough, great insect plagues swept the land. Grasshoppers marched across the wheat lands, leaving bare stubble behind.

And a BB-sized insect called a "chinch bug" came to destroy the corn. We opened a furrow around the perimeter of our cornfields and poured in creosote. It killed the chinch bugs—but *millions* more simply marched across the bodies of the fallen in the trench and reduced our fields to leafless stalks that weren't even fit for animal fodder.

Then in the winter, things swung to the opposite extreme. Subzero temperatures froze snowdrifts so solid you could drive your car or pull a sleigh over them without breaking through. There were no snowplows to clear country roads, and this I well remember, because as an 11-year-old I worked beside my dad shoveling roads for the $1 a day paid by the township.

In the pages that follow, the survivors of the Dust Bowl years share their memories. Many use the word "indescribable" as they tell their stories. And that's exactly the right word. —*Clancy Strock*

AGAINST THE WIND: Art Coble and his sons leaned into the wind as they passed an outbuilding on their rented farm near Felt, Oklahoma in 1936 in photo at right. This picture has come to be regarded as the definitive image of the Dust Bowl.

Storm Lashed Ranch Hand With Balls of Mud

WHEN I WAS 17 years old, I worked for room and board on a ranch in the Sandhills of northwest Nebraska. One pretty, sunshiny morning, I was planting corn with six head of horses. About 10:30, one of the horses signaled me to look over my shoulder. To my surprise, a huge dust storm was moving in from the southwest.

I stopped, but before I could even unhitch the horses, that blinding cloud had moved in on top of us. Having worked with horses before, I knew they would take me home, so I turned them in the direction of the ranch and let them lead the way.

There was little I could do—I couldn't see beyond the horses' heads—so I draped the lines around my neck. I soaked a bandanna with the perspiration from one of the horses and covered my face with it.

The horses made it to the corral just as the storm began to pick up speed. By the time I'd unharnessed the team, the wind was so fierce that it ripped off part of the barn roof, and hail, rain and mud balls poured down on me. I managed to make it to the well house, where I sat out the rest of the storm.

—*John Ross, Georgetown, Georgia*

MULE TEAMS were a common sight on many farms during the 1930s. Tom Clark of New London, Iowa posed with this pair of mule colts he was raising in 1937.

Keeping a home clean was almost impossible.

Heaven, for My Mother, Was a Place Without Dust!

MY PARENTS married in 1930 and raised their five daughters on a rocky farm near Sylvan Grove, Kansas. Our only running water came from a small hand pump in a galvanized sink in a small anteroom off the kitchen. The pump brought up water from a cistern, a concrete storage tank for rainwater that had been filtered through charcoal.

Unfortunately for us, the 1930s provided very little rain. The dust storms didn't help, either. They were most frequent in spring and fall, when there was less vegetation in the fields.

One storm in particular is seared in my memory. I was 4 years old on that evening in March, and we were at a great-uncle's home for a birthday party. The air was so heavy with fine dust that all of us had covered our mouths with wet cloths so we could breathe.

That was memorable enough in itself, but my parents had reason to remember that night with even more distress. When we came home, we found one of our four outside doors had blown open, and a 2-in. layer of dust covered everything in the house!

I can still see my parents using scoops, shovels and bushel baskets to haul out the dust by kerosene light just so we could sleep. My mother's comment, that her idea of heaven was "a place without dust," was perfectly understandable.

The combination of the Depression and the drought forced farmers to come up with some innovative ways to survive. There was a weed called Russian thistle (also called "tumbleweed"), which in good times was raked and burned for the noxious plant it is. But during the drought, it continued to grow when other plants would not, so it was cut and stacked as feed in hopes it would keep the cattle from starving.

In 1936 Kansas had a plague of grasshoppers. Our family has a picture of one of my sisters and me in sundresses. standing against a backdrop of two trees that are absolutely bare of leaves. The grasshoppers ate everything in sight, but wouldn't touch Russian thistles! The cattle became quite thin that year. I still can see them, their rib bones visible through their skin.

The grasshopper plague made that year especially difficult for my mother. She was pregnant with her third child and gave birth at home in July, on a day when the temperature was 117°. Despite the heat, we had to light the kerosene lamps in the house to be able to see, because grasshoppers had covered all the windows!

—*Juanita Merz Burke*
Minneapolis, Minnesota

'Hot, Dirty Times' Are Seared in Her Memory

THE 1930s are still vivid in my memory. When I was in school, I remember dating my papers when I practiced penmanship and thinking, "I'll never forget these hot, dirty times." And I haven't.

During the Dust Bowl days, we dipped sheets in water and hung them at the two doors of our farmhouse. Just before lunch, we mopped the linoleum floors and rinsed the sheets so the men could eat in some comfort and get a short nap. Everything was gritty.

The smell of some nail polishes still reminds me of the banana oil and tobacco dust farmers used to try to control the grasshoppers.

And I remember my dad taking cattle to the market in Kansas City. He came home and told Mother the price he received, and how much he *still* owed the bank because prices were so low. Then, and when my mother died. were the only times I heard my father sob. Other times he just dug in his heels like all the other farmers.

—*Arlone Soderstrom*
Emporia, Kansas

Ewing Galloway/Classicstock.com

'We Were There When the Dust Bowl Days Started'

SOME MAGAZINES claim the Dust Bowl days started in 1937. They're wrong. We know, because we were there!

It was the first of April 1935. We were with some friends and decided to take a drive in the country. It was a beautiful day.

As we were driving, we saw the storm approach. It darkened the sky in front of us. We could see every kind of bird in the sky, staying just ahead of the storm. It was like a rolling cloud at a 45-degree angle. We drove back to Durham, Oklahoma and hid in a concrete cellar. The wind hit Durham at 4 p.m., and we waited half the night for it to stop.

No one was hurt, but people were scared. They were trying to figure out what was behind it. Some saw the end

By Bill and Ocie Christian
Chowchilla, California

of the world, some the judgment of God in the storm.

When it stopped, we could see the humus in the soil was gone, and a thick layer of dust had formed on the cars and houses. Farming would be a horrendous gamble, and many moved on immediately. People had breathing problems. Our daughter contracted dust pneumonia, as did others.

A lot of people were broken by the conditions and left, but we stayed, raising cattle, vegetables and turkeys. The times weren't as bad as the magazines and books say.

But we were always fighting the dust. When the winds blew, we'd have to put sheets on the windows and doors to keep

the dust out. We'd always be wiping layers of dust off things. In the mornings we'd wake up and see our silhouettes on the bed, with dust all around us.

One time the wind blew for 9 days and took away 4 in. of soil. In the fields, we could see the plow points where the steel had reached into the ground.

We were poor, all right, but we didn't know it. We had enough to eat and we were happy. We didn't resent our poverty. Some people say they hated those times, but we're thankful for them. Being poor didn't hurt us. It made us better people.

ROAD CLOSED: After a dust storm blew through, it covered everything in its path with a blanket of bone-dry soil. High winds in a drought-ravaged area of Colorado left the rural road pictured above impassable.

'Rollers' Defeated Many Who'd Vowed to Stay

MY HOME in the southwest corner of Kansas was often referred to as the spawning grounds of the terrible dust storms of the 1930s. After several years of extremely light rainfall, the farmland was easy prey for the devastating winds. They came from the southwest, the north and the northwest about 9 a.m. almost every day, lifting a cloud that would blot out the sun by 10 a.m.

Sometimes the morning would be quiet and we'd call the neighbors on the party line and rejoice with them. We'd plan a day of washing, cleaning and shopping and confidently get out the "jitney" for a trip to town.

The men would gather around the big stove at the pool hall and swap stories about the last big storm, while others shot pool or played checkers. Sometimes they'd talk about the latest sale held by some farmer who was giving up and seeking a place where the grass was green.

There always were those who vowed they would never give up. They were staying! Surely it would rain again and the plains would bloom with wheat, corn and maize, and the grass would provide food for the cattle.

Then about 4 o'clock, someone would report a "black roller" was coming in. Each man would scurry out, gather his wife and kids, pick up the groceries, collect a check for the cream

By Eleanor M. Wellborn
Topeka, Kansas

and eggs, and start home. Those who lived nearby made it easily, but those who had to travel 6 or 7 miles in a horse-drawn wagon could be in for trouble.

They'd mask themselves with bandannas to protect their faces from the driving sand. Sometimes they'd tie a mask over the horses' eyes, too.

A "roller" was a dense cloud of topsoil, some of it carried along for hundreds of miles. Sometimes it came

---

"Some vowed they'd never give up..."

---

in deadly quiet until it had enveloped everything; then the wind became vicious, gusty with little whirlwinds all along the leading edge of the cloud. There'd be lightning, thunder and maybe a few drops of "black rain." Sometimes the dust blocked out the sun completely, and wagon drivers would hang out a lantern so they didn't collide with anyone on the road.

Some storms lasted several days. Sunsets became curtains of flaming clouds interspersed with small whirlwinds of various colors. We were filled with awe at the intensity and

immensity of the agonies of nature.

When it got so dark that people literally couldn't see their hands in front of their faces, they'd head for the "fraidy hole" to pray for comfort and an end to the winds. Chickens went to roost, and cattle gathered on the lee side of the outbuildings, trying to protect their eyes from the blowing sand and dust.

If a roller came from the north, we could recognize the rich black topsoil from Nebraska and Colorado; if it was from the south, we'd get the red dust of Oklahoma and Texas. Our topsoil would be exchanged in a day or so as it blew away to a neighboring state.

The dust began to pile up in drifts along the barbed wire fences. At last there were no more barriers, and the people and animals who remained simply walked over the fencerows.

Grazers Were Goners

Farmers thinned their herds down to a few milk cows and a horse or two. They sold anything that grazed because all the grazing land was gone. Cows were fed for their milk, and chickens for their eggs and meat. My dad tried to keep a calf or two and a couple of pigs for our table in winter.

Every week some family had an auction. Those who were staying went to every sale, knowing the farmer who was moving had to raise a few dollars

"ROLLERS" swept through the Dust Bowl with a vengeance. In photo at left, a roller sweeps through Oklahoma. After a storm, farmers like the Colorado man below often found dust piled as high as their fencerows. The drought forced many off the land, resulting in farm auctions like the one at right near Fowler, Indiana.

to be able to leave. Finally it was my dad's turn to give up.

In 1937 my family ran out of both money and food. From the sections of land Dad had farmed, he was down to just a few acres. The rest had been transferred to foreclosing banks. He could borrow no more.

Sold Family Heirlooms

Dad lined up the necessities we'd take, and the auctioneer sold the rest. We all still weep when we read his journal listing every item sold, from livestock and furniture to the beautiful wedding presents he and my mother had treasured. Dresser and bed, $3. Oil heater, $2. Tiffany lamp, 25¢...

The buyers at the auction averted their eyes when some articles were mentioned. They knew how many years of hard work and sacrifice those items represented.

Those who stayed believed that one day the rains would come and the desert would bloom again. In the 1940s and 1950s, it did. The determination of those farmers helped turn the economy around. As oil and gas fields were developed later on, some of those farmers became millionaires.

Driving through that country now, we can pick out not only the land that once belonged to Mom and Dad, but also that of our neighbors and friends. Today those old farms are punctuated by oil derricks. But we're not envious. We're just glad for the good fortune of those who waited it out.

One Downpour That Wasn't Welcome

AFTER 4 or 5 years of drought in the 1930s, Dad let the bank have our farm in Missouri and we left to make a new start in New Mexico.

Twelve of us—Mom and Dad, my four siblings and me, and my aunt and uncle and their three children—piled into a 2-ton truck covered with a tarp.

It was so hot and dry that every now and then we'd see a cow that had died from the heat. Feed was scarce; in the Texas Panhandle, farmers were stacking tumbleweeds, in hopes the cows would eat them.

We were way out on the prairie late one day and stopped at an old country store, where Dad asked if we could pull off the road and camp for the night. The storekeeper was agreeable and gave us his blessing.

Then Dad asked, "What if it rains and our truck gets stuck?"

Years of drought had ripped away the topsoil, leaving only bone-dry dirt behind. Rain would turn everything that wasn't paved to mud.

The storekeeper just smiled. It hadn't rained there for 3 or 4 years!

"If it rains," he told Dad, "I'll pull you out and it won't cost you a cent."

We were eating our supper beside the truck when big clouds started rolling in. Next thing we knew, it was pouring! We sat up in the truck all night, listening to the rain.

The next morning it was *still* raining, and, of course, we were stuck! The storekeeper brought out a big rope and tied one end to our truck's front bumper and the other to his little Model A roadster on the pavement.

The storekeeper pulled and pulled—his tires were smoking. Eventually he did get us out. And, just as promised, he didn't charge us a penny for his trouble.

—*Virgil Cleveland, Weir, Kansas*

Dirty Thirties Filled with Joys and Woes

THE DUST STORMS of the 1930s provided some unique experiences for me as a child on a South Dakota farm.

Two or three of us kids often watched the storms approach from the west window of our house. We could see the characteristic huge, rapidly moving cloud when a storm was miles away. We watched it roll across the fields, envelop the school building a half-mile down the road and blot out our view of the neighbor's house.

"Here it comes!" we'd say, then we'd run to the east side of the house to see if the strong wind would blow down our outhouse. Sometimes it did.

A favorite chore during those years

By Sister Margaret Peter
Jefferson, Wisconsin

was collecting Russian thistles. Dad considered it necessary work to be done each fall, but the three kids who helped considered it a special celebration. We walked through the fields with pitchforks, collecting hundreds of these tumbleweeds, most of them wind-driven into barbed wire fences.

Loved a Thistle Chase

It was fun to race a blowing thistle across a field on a windy day. The strong wind tore up the dried thistle by its shallow roots and sent it flying across the dusty field. I could run like the wind for a short distance, but often a thistle would outdistance me. So then I'd have to trail behind and catch up when the thistle was snagged by a fence or a tall weed.

I know that gathering those prickly thistles and packing them firmly into a tight stack must have been hard, sweaty work, but I remember only the

joy of it. The more thistles we gathered, the larger the bonfire we would enjoy that evening, the flames shooting high and the heat waves forcing us back. We felt close to nature and each other as we watched in silence, wanting the bonfire to last forever.

During the late '30s we moved to a farm that had two apple trees just outside the bedroom my sister Dorothy and I shared. We'd lie across the bed and gaze at the trees' delicate pink and white blossoms, breathing deeply of their fragrance.

I tried to live the moment so fully I would never forget it. We watched as the blossoms magically turned to tiny apples. I eagerly awaited the day when the apples would be ripe. Mom had been promising us apple pie, apple dumplings, applesauce... and apples for school lunches—a rare treat.

Then one fateful day, a dark cloud moved toward our farm. An ominous whirring sound emanated from the cloud's ever-changing shape as it settled on our field of grain. Millions of grasshoppers devoured our entire crop.

We watched helplessly, listening to the enemy ravage our once-promising field of wheat. They outnumbered us 10 million to one.

The grasshoppers weren't satisfied

LACK OF RAIN left behind barren farmyards and fields throughout the nation's midsection (top photo), making it virtually impossible to raise crops. The Colorado farmer at left had piles of dust that were as tall as 9 ft. on his land.

with just destroying our fields. They descended on our beloved apple trees, too. My sister and I climbed the trees and tried to kill off the hoppers one by one, but they escaped us easily.

I had another idea. I grabbed a large washtub from the porch and placed it under one tree. Dorothy and I filled the tub with water from the stock tank, then climbed the tree and tried to knock the grasshoppers into the tub so they would drown.

Fought Losing Battle

Our mother came out of the kitchen and told us, "You can't fight grasshoppers. There's nothing you can do to stop them." She smiled as we continued our desperate efforts. "I know you want to help," she said, "but there's nothing you can do."

Although I didn't want to give up, I knew Mom was right. You can't fight grasshoppers. I watched as they ate all the leaves from our trees and then attacked the tiny apples. Soon the tree was bare except for the apple cores clinging to the stripped branches. I cried then, just as I do now, writing this nearly 60 years later. It was my only experience of total defeat.

Despite yet another complete crop loss, my parents accepted the situation and continued to trust in the goodness of God. The memory of that faith has influenced my whole life. It probably had a lot to do with my becoming a Franciscan nun.

Letters Relate Trials of Life in Dust Bowl

THESE LETTERS were written in the 1930s by a Dust Bowl survivor from Mc-Cracken, Kansas. Wanda Childers of Alvin, Wisconsin says the writer was one of her husband's relatives.

March 24, 1935

Dear Family,

Did some of you think that you had a dust storm? I'll tell you what it was. It was us shaking our bedding, carpets, etc.

For over a week we have been having troublesome times. The dust is something fierce. Sometimes it lets up enough so we can see around; even the sun may shine for a little time, then we have a frenzied time of cleaning, anticipating the comfort of a clean feeling once more.

We keep the doors and windows all shut tight, with wet papers on the sills. The tiny particles of dirt sift right through the walls. Two different times it has been an inch thick on my kitchen floor.

Our faces look like coal miners', our hair is gray and stiff with dirt and we grind dirt in our teeth. We have to wash everything just before we eat it and make it as snappy as possible. Sometimes there is a fog all through the house and all we can do about it is sit on our dusty chairs and see that fog settle slowly and silently over everything.

When we open the door, swirling whirlwinds of soil beat against us unmercifully, and we are glad to go back inside and sit choking in the dirt. We couldn't see the streetlight just in front of the house.

One morning, early, I went out during a lull, and when I started to return I couldn't see the house. I knew the direction, so I kept on coming, and was quite close before I could even see the outline. It sure made me feel funny.

There has not been much school this week. It let up a little yesterday and Fred went with the janitor and they carried dirt out of the church by the scoopful. Four of them worked all afternoon. We were able to have church this morning, but I think many stayed home to clean.

A lot of dirt is blowing now, but it's not dangerous to be out in it. This dirt is all loose, any little wind will stir it, and there will be no relief until we get rain. If it doesn't come soon there will be lots of suffering. If we spit or blow our noses we get mud. We have quite a little trouble with our chests. I understand a good many have pneumonia.

As for gardens, we had ours plowed, but now we do not know whether we have more or less soil. It's useless to plant anything.　　—Grace

April 30, 1935

Dear Family,

Here it is the last day of April and a wild day at that. I did not think when I wrote on the 24th of March that we would still be having storms. Part of the time today we can see a block. Then it will lift till we can see two blocks.

O.E. thought I took the prize before for the best dust story. Well, I have had much experience since then. It's almost useless to tell you for you can hardly conceive how it would be. We are very, very weary fighting dirt.

Yesterday was a lovely day, the first whole day we have had that there was no dust in the air. Today is making up for it. There are some days when it is not nearly so bad; then we get out and do everything we can.

One day I went with Fred over to Brownell. The horizon seemed to be about a quarter of a mile all around us. It sort of seemed we were set out in a little world by ourselves.

Sunday afternoon it was not very bad. I went with some other people to see about some sick folks who lived 8 or 9 miles southwest. Along the road I saw piles of powdery dust 5 and 6 ft. deep. There have been several auto accidents caused by dust. This sand and dust is awful hard on car engines. We have had two small local showers, which would clear the air for half a day, but soon it would be coming again from the dry regions. I think Brownell has not had a drop of rain yet. Cows look pitiful. Many people are not able to buy feed. Around town here we have some grass, which our little rains started, but out there, where there was no rain, there is nothing.

When the storms came within miles, there was so much electricity in the air, it interfered much with our radio. One fellow was telling us that he had his turned off, but still it seemed to make noise.　　—Grace

'I Was a Child of the Dust Bowl'

THE YEARS OF 1933-35 brought Dust Bowl days to the Texas Panhandle. It was a bleak time, and memories of it are painful. The Weather Bureau in Amarillo reported 192 dust storms in that 3-year period. I believe there were more.

I was a young girl then, and looking back, those years are like a dream, unreal and unbelievable. It was eerie to look across the countryside and see curtains of thick sand blowing, with thousands of tumbling weeds rolling ahead of the dust, spinning on and on until they were caught by the fencerows. A dust storm was like a monster devouring the topsoil as it moved along, leaving high drifts of sand against buildings and anything else that stood in its path.

There were times it became dark as night in the afternoon, and chickens went to roost.

Often we'd awaken to a bright clear morning, and as my sisters and I walked the 1-1/2 miles to school, we'd be hit by a dust storm. We didn't turn back; we plowed on. A dust storm was no excuse for missing school. Walking into the dust was difficult because bits of gravel would hit us in the face. We walked with our backs to the storm to help move us along. One of my fond memories is of an older boy taking off his coat and holding it in front of my

By Lee Nelson
Waco, Texas

face to protect me from the cruel wind.

Visibility was only a few feet. If we walked in the middle of the road, we could not even see the telephone poles across the ditch.

Keeping the house clean and doing laundry was a never-ending job. There were times we could write our names in the sand on our table. A slow lick of the lips would give us a taste of mud. Eating sometimes came to a halt be-

---

> **"A dust storm was like a monster devouring the soil."**

---

cause dust had fallen in our food, giving it a gritty taste.

Breathing was difficult for those with respiratory problems. My sister Midge often covered her face with a wet cloth so she could breathe.

The most memorable storm of all was on April 14, 1935—"Black Sunday." I remember that terrible day.

We had retired early, like most farm people, and were in bed by 9 p.m. A gorgeous bright moon illuminated the countryside, almost like daylight. My brothers Otis and Winfred came from church and told us they'd heard a report on the radio that the blackest dust storm

we'd ever experienced was moving in.

At 10 o'clock it arrived like an ocean of dust, engulfing us. The moon was instantly diminished by the blackness, and did not reappear all night.

The next morning was bright and clear; the storm had left as quietly as it came, but it left gallons of black dust behind. Farmers said it was topsoil from Kansas.

Rainfall during those years was scant, and harvests almost nil. There was little pasture, so the cows gave only small amounts of milk. When describing the Dust Bowl in later years, Mama said the coyotes' howls pierced the stillness of the night like never before. They were hungry, too.

A popular song during that time was *Rain, When You Gonna Rain Again?* Otis said it was written in New York City for us Dust Bowlers.

For us, the Dust Bowl and the Great Depression were one and the same. Our harvests were not only small; they brought low prices, too. President Roosevelt's New Deal was put in place to provide government help.

One program was the WPA, which offered relief to those who were out of work. In our town of Turkey, Texas, many people worked for the WPA by repairing roads. But Papa's pride wouldn't let him accept relief. He believed a person should work for what he

HOMEMADE MACHINERY like the six-row cultivator at left helped many farmers make it through the Depression years.

got, and he thought the WPA men spent a lot of time leaning on their shovels.

The New Deal also had a program to help agriculture recover. Farmers had never before been paid not to grow crops, but it was believed that if production went down, prices would go up. So we received parity checks.

In 1934 the supply of cows was greater than the demand. To help farmers and raise prices, the government bought cows and shot them. On a clear summer day, with no dust in sight, the government men came to our farm. Papa told us four girls to stay in the house with Mama, and took the three boys with him and the government men to the barn. We heard the guns go off. Mama cried.

"The Bible says it is a sin to destroy," she said.

We were paid $15 for each cow, $8 for each yearling and $2 for each calf, but this was only subsistence money.

Despite the hardships, life went on. We attended school during the week and church on Sunday. Children adapt to circumstances, and I accepted this as a way of life. Didn't everyone have dust blowing in his face? Though we had few material possessions, the love of our family was free.

Memories of the Dust Bowl are painful, but they are a part of me. I would not trade them. I believe the hardships of those years shaped me into a stronger person.

Farm Life a Learning Experience for 'City Girl'

WHEN THE stock market crashed, my husband and I weren't affected immediately. Claud's place of employment was so busy that the workers often had to put in overtime.

By the middle of 1932, though, Claud was working only 3 days a week and we could no longer make the payments on our washing machine. When things got so bad we could no longer make our house payments, something had to be done. We didn't want to stand in soup lines or accept welfare, so we decided to try our luck at farming.

We decided to move in with Claud's parents, although he'd keep his city job as long as possible. I remembered a time when I had sworn I'd never marry a farmer, but I agreed to try, and we took our two small sons to live in the country.

For a year we lived upstairs from my in-laws, leaving all our city conveniences behind. I managed to feed our family of four on $1 to $1.25 a week. Claud had no watch, so whenever he was working within sight of the house at dinnertime, I'd tie a clean white diaper on the end of a broomstick and attach it to the porch railing!

To start farming, we needed horses. We found a pair, but had no money to pay for them. The dealer said he'd accept a note if we could come up with a down payment. We didn't have that either, but we did have a vacuum cleaner we couldn't use anymore, since my in-laws' house had no electricity. The dealer agreed to take it as a down payment.

Found Their Own Place

After a year, we had another baby on the way, so we started looking for a place of our own. We heard a nearby farm was for rent, but were told the buildings weren't much. What an understatement! The house looked like a shack, the barn had a lean-to but no basement, and all the outbuildings had seen better days.

I stepped to the kitchen window and saw ceiling paper hanging almost to the floor. I told Claud I couldn't ever live in such a place, but he reminded me there was nothing else available, and, after all, we could fix it up. So we moved in. The landlord offered to plaster the worst walls and ceilings and buy paper to cover the rest, so that took care of that problem. There was no well on the place, but there was a spring bubbling some distance from the house. We didn't need to pump the water, but we did have to carry it, which was a job not to be taken lightly. We learned to be careful how we used it!

After our third son was born, Claud bought a cow for $31 at an auction. Of course, we didn't have the money, but his cousin was at the auction and co-signed the note for him, and we were in the dairy business.

At another auction Claud and his brother bid $10 for four tables. One of ours became a washstand, and the other occupied a spot in the living room with a doily hiding the crack in the top.

We spent very little for clothes; we wore everything until it wore out, then patched them and wore them some more. The boys' clothes were made almost entirely from castoffs, but with many hours at the old Singer, I managed to keep the little shavers covered!

They Bought the Farm

Improbable as it may seem, less than 2 years after moving into our little shack, we bought it. The bank had foreclosed on our landlord's mortgage and put the place up for sale. For an incredibly small down payment, which we borrowed from a relative, we were able to deal with the bank. All thoughts of returning to the city evaporated.

After that, we concentrated on paying off our mortgage and improving our living conditions. In 1936 a well was driven and we had water just a few feet from our back door. Such luxury! The following year we bought a windmill, and then we didn't even have to pump the water as long as the wind was blowing.

Those few years were very trying, but we survived and learned from them, and we're not sorry we experienced them. As Claud once said, "We aren't poor, just a little hard up."

—Jean Bergman, Sand Lake, Michigan

Poor Prices Changed Corn from Feed to Fuel

I WAS in my early teens when the Depression hit. We lived on a farm in Iowa, so even with a family of six, there was never a shortage of food. We all pitched in to can pork and beef, and we had chicken, eggs, milk and vegetables from a large garden.

Though we didn't go hungry, we did have a problem finding enough money to buy the things we could not produce ourselves.

When the price of corn dropped to 10¢ a bushel, it was not economically practical to sell it so that we could go out and buy expensive coal. There were always plenty of corncobs to fire the cookstove in the kitchen, but the furnace needed something else. Wood wasn't all that plentiful on the Iowa prairie.

My parents decided the sensible thing to do was to burn whole ears of corn in the furnace, much as they hated the thought.

I'll never forget the day my father backed up to the basement window and dumped a wagonload of corn into the furnace room. It turned out to be good fuel, as it held a fire well and got us through a long winter.

Still, shoveling those big, beautiful ears of corn into the furnace may have been the hardest thing my father ever had to do. It was that winter that his hair started to turn gray!

—*Marjorie Paneitz*
Berryville, Arkansas

Sparks on Fence Led Teen Through Storm

IN 1935 I had a birthday I'll never forget. I belonged to a boys' club in the little town of Catherine, Kansas and had gone to the club's big old hall to play a few games of basketball.

Suddenly, toward evening, the wind came up with a big *whoosh*, sifting everyone in the hall with a grayish-brown powder. Four 50-watt light bulbs were strung through the center of the building with pull strings for switches. They all went out. We could barely see where the bulbs were to turn them off, but we didn't need to.

The whole town was blacked out. The dust storm had blown down the electrical poles.

Our home was about half a mile from town as the crow flies, so I decided to take the shortcut. I managed to find my bearings, but I also got the biggest scare of my life. I walked right into our neighbor's fence, which was charged with static electricity with sparks jumping from the three wires. So I followed the sparks home!

—*Gilbert J. Karlin, Victoria, Kansas*

Sense of Humor Was Weapon Against Dust

I WAS only 10 years old in the spring of 1935, but I well remember the red dust that blew in from Oklahoma. We lived on a farm in Reno County, Kansas.

I'll never forget my mother's instructions for setting the dinner table: lay all the plates upside down, place the water glasses and coffee cups bottom side up, and place the napkin over the silverware. When we gathered at the table, everyone turned their place settings over and there was a nice clean circle on the checked tablecloth where the dishes had been. The rest of the table was covered with fine red sand.

My father would make jokes about not having to pepper the potatoes and gravy. The milk was always dusty, even after being strained through a cloth, and

DARK DAYS were common during the Dust Bowl. The billowing clouds that descended on Guymon, Oklahoma (top photo) and other communities were so dense they blocked out the sun. Travel was risky if not impossible; even a short walk to the mailbox had to be put off until the storm passed.

my father would kid us children about drinking "chocolate" milk. I think my parents' good sense of humor helped us get through those days!

—*Lila M. Williams*
Leavenworth, Kansas

'We Moved from Dust Bowl to...Heaven!'

I ATTENDED a one-room schoolhouse in Kansas, and sometimes when the dust storms came, the whole world seemed darkened. We'd either stay in the schoolhouse, sometimes spending the whole night there, or cover our faces with wet rags and follow the fence lines home.

In 1936 my family lost the farm and moved to Colorado. My uncle owned a sawmill camp high in the Rocky Mountains and offered work to my father and two brothers. When I awoke my first morning there, I saw a light covering of snow on the ground, with the red ripeness of wild strawberries peeking through. I thought I had died and gone to heaven!

—*Zada L. Johnson*
Boulder, Colorado

CHAPTER THREE

Looking For Work

JOBLESS MEN lined up three deep outside the employment office in downtown Milwaukee, Wisconsin in the mid-1930s. For many men, the wait in line was a daily ritual.

Looking for Work

My Uncle Bill and Aunt Grace moved in with us sometime in 1934 or 1935. I'm not sure just when, because during the Depression years we also were a hostel for Aunt Martha, Uncle Wadsworth and assorted other relatives. Not all at once, but when one bunch moved out, another moved in on their heels.

They were all with us for one simple reason: no work. And if you didn't have work, you couldn't pay the rent. And if you couldn't pay the rent, you looked for relatives who could take you in.

Uncle Bill had come to the United States from Germany some time after World War I. He had sporadically attended art school in Chicago before marrying my mother's sister Grace.

Even in the best of times, employment as an artist can be a dicey thing. During the Depression years, it was hopeless. So finally they moved in with us.

The major employer in our little northern-Illinois town was a steel mill —certainly an oddity for what was mostly a farming community. If there was work to be found, the best bet was at "the mill." So for more than a year, Uncle Bill got up early every morning, walked 3 miles into town, and joined a near-endless line of men, all hoping for employment.

Unemployment Was Rampant

Now repeat this picture in every town and city of any size all across America, and you have some idea of what the Great Depression was all about. Day after day you stood in line, hoping someone would open the door and announce that two or three jobs were available. The lucky ones at the front would rush inside, and the hundreds of others, heads down and shoulders bent, would start the slow walk home again.

There were no unemployment benefits, no unemployment offices. "Going on welfare" was dreaded more than going hungry, and it was a large step below working for the WPA.

(Just in case you weren't there, the WPA was the Works Progress Administration, one of the "alphabet-soup agencies" created by the Roosevelt Administration to provide jobs. Like most such programs, the WPA came in for much scornful criticism. WPA workers were called "shovel-leaners" and the agency's initials were said to mean "We Putter Around." But at least the needy did useful things in return for some subsistence money.)

There was another problem. When you have lots of people competing for very few jobs, the employer is in the driver's seat as far as hours, wages and working conditions are concerned. So those fortunate enough to have jobs worked long hours for low wages, often under miserable conditions.

Assembly lines were sped up, and then accelerated again and again. On-the-job accident rates soared. An acquaintance tells of complaining about the speedups to his foreman in the auto plant where he worked. The foreman led him over to a window, pointed down to 2,000 men standing in line waiting for a job and said, "If you don't want to work, any one of those men will gladly take your place."

Idleness Equaled Indignity

In case you ever wondered about what fueled the union movement with its strikes and sit-ins and violence, there's as good an answer as any.

Yes, it was a different time. People didn't want handouts, *they wanted to work!* To be unable to support your family was the ultimate indignity. We've been through "recessions" and "economic downturns" many times since.

But there's been a difference. These days we turn for help to the government. There were no safety nets during the Great Depression, so we turned to our families.

And, mostly, the door was always open.

—Clancy Strock

Search for Work Kept Family on the Move

By Edna Brown
Fresno, California

CAN YOU IMAGINE wanting to relive a time when a pan of fried potatoes with a crust of bread was a delicacy? It might sound a little crazy, but I'd love to go back to those days!

It was 1931, I was 13 years old, and we were living in California's San Joaquin Valley. There was no work to be had, but we were told there might be work in Oregon. Our family and my uncle's family decided to head there.

My uncle's family had an old touring car for the trip, but our family didn't have a car. We raised a small amount of cash by selling our meager belongings. When that was added to a little money scraped together by my sister and her husband, we had enough to buy an old square-backed Essex.

Dad and my sister's husband built a cupboard with a drop-leaf table on the back of the car for dishes and food. We stacked mattresses, boxes and our shabby suitcases on top of the car. Gunnysacks filled with clothes were stored on the running boards. What a sight we must have been as we "shambled" down the highway!

We started our trip on April 1. At night, we camped in an old square tent. I'll never forget the night we set up camp alongside the McCloud River. What a beautiful place it was, with the smell of pines filling the fresh, crisp air. I can still smell the coffee boiling in the early morning. It has never tasted as good since.

Our first misfortune was the loss of a gunnysack over a steep mountainside. The clothing in that sack included my best shoes and Dad's long johns. The rest of the trip was fairly uneventful, and we enjoyed the indescribable beauty of the forests along the way.

Rebuilt Run-Down Cabins

We finally arrived in North Bend, Oregon, but could find no work. Some people who learned of our plight invited us to live on their land, which once had been a logging camp. The property had a well and two run-down cabins.

There was much to do to make the cabins livable. They needed new shake roofs, so new ones were hand-hewn. The cabins had no stoves, either, but luck was with us. We learned of a deserted hunting lodge that had a wood-burning stove with an oven, and received permission to take it. However, the lodge was some distance away, across a small lake, and the site was not accessible by car. But that wasn't about to stop us!

The men walked to the lodge and decided to place the stove on some planks and wade across the lake with it. They thought the lake was shallow. Unfortunately, they were wrong—but that *still* didn't stop them!

They somehow got that stove across the lake, and then had to figure out how to move it back to our cabins.

Finally someone came up with the idea of sliding the stove on planks down the railroad tracks, which would bring them close to home.

When the stove finally arrived, we were so excited—this meant hot biscuits and homemade bread! We couldn't have felt richer if we'd just been handed all the money in the U.S. Mint!

ROADSIDE REST: Families who moved on to seek jobs picnicked alongside the roads they traveled (left). Travelers could rarely afford the luxury of a restaurant meal, so they packed their own provisions and bought staples along the way.

AFFORDABLE HOUSING was hard to come by during the worst years of the Depression. Some families, unable to keep up with mortgage or rent payments, had to move into run-down houses like those at right.

With a few odd jobs and the garden we planted, we fared well, but one day our family of eight decided it was time to head for home. My uncle's family decided to stay behind.

On the way back, our tires started to go, but we had no money to replace them. Eventually, as we drove through the peaceful countryside, we found ourselves riding on the rims. What a racket! But my dad was wonderful, and kept our spirits up with his humor. He even made up poems about how noisy the car was: "We scared the cattle and frightened the sheep, and woke the farmers out of their sleep."

Noisy Trip Back Home

After we hocked a few belongings to replace the tires, loud noises began coming from the engine. The bearings had started to go out. Precious shoe leather was used to repair them.

We kept limping along and were heading up a hill along the Oregon coast when the Essex—and our trip home—came to a screeching halt. A connecting rod had gone through the engine.

It was summer, so we pitched our tent on a hill, which was within walking distance of the nearest town. We would remain there for some time, and eventually became known to the townspeople as "the folks on the hill." We all found something to do in that town—I did housework and cared for children in others' homes.

Before we knew it, winter was upon us, and we moved into an old two-story house in town. When Dad became ill, an aunt in California came to our rescue, and we soon found ourselves back where we'd started. We'd been gone 9 months.

It was a trip I'll never forget. Even with all our misfortunes, I'll always be grateful for our experiences and the closeness of our family. When we all get together today, that Depression-era trip is always a topic of conversation!

Pay Cuts Forced Family to Relocate

WHEN THE stock market crashed, we didn't know it was the beginning of a long, hard depression. Jobs were lost and businesses were closing, but it was all happening to someone else.

I was working at the St. Louis *Star Times* newspaper, and in early 1931 my pay was raised to $107 a week—all take-home, no deductions. Six months later, everybody on the staff took a pay cut. More would come over the next 2 years.

We had always had to economize, but now we couldn't buy clothes, so my wife, Helen, maintained what we had by mending, I began cashing in insurance policies, and we refinanced our mortgage twice. When our fifth child was born in 1933, I borrowed $300 to pay the doctor and hospital.

By 1934, my pay was down to $50 a week. I'd stopped making payments on the house, and the mortgage company was hounding me; it was in trouble, too. I cashed the rest of my insurance policies and took out a single policy for $5,000. It was the only protection my family had.

When I found a new job at a newspaper in Philadelphia, we offered our house for sale at $6,200—half of what we'd paid for it in 1924. No one even came to look at it. Finally, I told a friend I'd give him the deed for $100.

On a Monday morning in 1935, all seven of us packed into the car for the trip to Philadelphia, our few pieces of clothing in paper bags in the trunk. The moving van went on ahead with our furniture. I had in my wallet a certified check for $170 to pay the van driver, $200 in cash, and the $100 check we received for our house.

The trip took 4 days. We spent the first night at a "tourist home," the next in a log cabin next to a noisy garage, and the third in a mountain hotel whose rooms were separated by boards instead of walls.

On Thursday morning, a billboard directed us to a hotel in Philadelphia, where we booked three adjoining rooms for $25 a night. We found a real estate agent in the phone book, and he took us to a repossessed house we could move into immediately. We paid the first month's rent of $55 and notified the driver of the moving van where to deliver our belongings.

On Saturday, we moved in, put a down payment on a refrigerator and bought groceries to last us through the weekend. We had much to be thankful for, and we knew God had been with us. When I started my new job Monday, I had $20 left.
—*Stanley Cryor, Lansdale, Pennsylvania*

Young Family Started New Life in California

By Madonna Wyckoff
Chico, California

MY PARENTS were just kids of 18 and 16 when they married in 1927. They moved to an Iowa farm, where Dad made $55 a month—a very good start.

But within a year, my young dad found himself supporting a household of five—my grandmother had moved in with them, and shortly afterward, my twin sister and I were born.

Then the Depression hit. Mom had relatives in California who urged us to come West, and they decided to go. It was a "burning your bridges" decision; they knew once we arrived, we wouldn't have the means to come back. We left Iowa in 1931 with $85 cash and all our possessions packed in and on our 1925 Model T.

Like pioneers of old, we set up roadside camps each night, where we prepared the evening meal and the next morning's breakfast. Lunch was never elaborate; we simply pulled off the road and ate wherever we happened to be at noon. Travel was much different then; traffic was light, and towns and accommodations were few and far between.

Discovered the Desert

It was a dirty, dusty trip, and when we reached clear water near the Nevada-California line, we laid over an extra day so everyone could bathe and shampoo their hair. The laundry was done on a washboard and spread out on bushes to dry.

To eyes accustomed to Iowa's cornfields, soft green timber and rolling hills, the desert plains, antelope, prairie

MOVING ON: Families who went in search of greener pastures would load their car with as many of their belongings as it could hold. Lola Eagle of Albuquerque, New Mexico shared photo of herself, her mother and brothers.

dogs and mountains were marvelous curiosities. But California, we believed, would be lush and green. How wrong we were! The weather had been so dry that water was being rationed.

When we arrived at our destination of Paradise, California, my parents' $85 had dwindled to $8, they had no jobs, and the old Model T was worn out from the trip. We stayed with relatives for a couple of weeks. With a few odd jobs and an assist from the Salvation Army, Mom and Dad were able to rent a small cabin for us before winter set in.

Dad scoured the countryside for work, with no success. One day he heard about a rock-crushing job, hurried to check it out and was hired immediately. He commuted to work with a fel-

low employee, but one morning he overslept and had to take his own car to work. The boss saw Dad's Iowa license plates and fired him on the spot, saying the jobs were only for native Californians.

My parents' landlord then put Dad to work cutting firewood for the rest of the winter. When spring came, the landlord contacted a friend who worked for a lumber company and managed to get Dad on there for $2.42 a day—mighty good wages for those days! Mother stayed behind to clean cabins for our landlord to pay our back rent, and once that was paid we followed Dad to the lumber camp.

Dad was never without work after that. He was a good worker—responsible, handy and able to make do with little. We went wherever his work took him. Mom was a born homemaker, and it was never long before our new living quarters were clean, repaired and cozy, no matter how primitive they'd been when we moved in.

Those were hard times, but they were happy times, too, and we still reminisce about them. My sister and I even feel sorry for our younger sister and brother, who arrived in later years and missed all the fun!

WAGONS, HO! Some farm families moved cross-country in covered wagons. This caravan was photographed near Clovis, New Mexico in 1932.

Family Sailed Down Mississippi to Look for Work

By Faye Underwood
Washington, Illinois

MY DAD was a farmer, but when farm prices plummeted and a venture in a small-town restaurant failed, our finances grew increasingly worse. Like many others, we were faced with foreclosure, and Dad couldn't find work.

But Dad was never afraid to take risks. In 1934 he heard the Army Corps of Engineers was starting to build dams on the Mississippi River, and thought that project could provide work for him and my two older brothers. So Dad took what little money we had left and bought a houseboat to take us there!

The boat was 16 by 48 ft., powered by a Model A Ford engine. We thought it would be a great adventure to cruise down the mighty river, swimming and fishing whenever we chose. But we soon found the trip would be quite an undertaking for an inexperienced pilot and green deckhands!

From our starting point in Durand, Wisconsin, we had to navigate the treacherous Chippewa River to reach the Mississippi. Our first hurdle was getting stuck on a sandbar! Our drinking-water supply was limited, and even with two rowboats. we felt very much marooned. While fishing one day, we found a limestone spring at the river's edge, which provided us with cool, pure water. We spent most of our days hunting clams so we could sell the shells later at a button factory along our route.

After 2 weeks, a heavy rain raised the water level and floated us free. Several miles upstream, the Chippewa widened into a body of water known as Lake Pepin. We anchored in the backwaters before reaching the lake, and spent a month digging clams and catching fish to sell. We got only 9¢ a pound for catfish, but we made enough to buy groceries and gasoline.

When we finally reached the Mississippi, we discovered that houseboats

> *"It was quite a trip for an inexperienced pilot and green deckhands."*

were a novelty. Captains of steamboats eyed us with curiosity, then sounded a loud blast in greeting. People waved at us from shore. Dad said, "Guess I'll go light up that cigar I've been saving. Maybe they'll think I'm a celebrity!"

When we reached Guttenberg, Iowa, Dad and my brothers applied for work, only to find no one was being hired until the following spring. Discouraged, we backtracked to Prairie du Chien, Wisconsin to dry-dock the boat and prepare for the cold months ahead.

Dad found temporary work with a salvage operation at 35¢ an hour. We ate a lot of fish and wild game, although we all got a little tired of rabbit. Mother joked that she was afraid we were all going to sprout long ears!

We soon became acquainted with the residents of the shantytown along the riverbank. They were good people, always eager to lend a helping hand.

We played cards with them, and on Saturday nights we all pooled our quarters to buy refreshments for gatherings hosted by a lady known as "Aunt Cora." One man played the guitar and banjo, and someone else usually joined in with an accordion or fiddle. We all had an enjoyable time dancing or playing games. We learned that it wasn't what a man had in his pocket that counted, but what he had in his heart.

At last spring arrived, bright and beautiful. It was time to leave our friends and travel back to Iowa, where my father and brother did find work. We lived on the houseboat for another year, then sold it and moved to a small house near our former hometown.

Living on the river was an unforgettable experience. The hardships made our family closer, secure in the knowledge that whatever difficulties we faced, we'd solve them together. As we look back, it's the good times, not the bad, that linger in our memories.

FERRYBOATS, like the one above, and steamboats were often spotted on the Mississippi River in the 1930s, but houseboats were an unusual sight.

Grant Heilman

Friends Saw Each Other Through Hard Times

THE 1930s were tough times. There's no way I'd want to live through them again, but I still have some warm memories.

I lost my job in 1932, just a few weeks before our eldest daughter was born. For the next 6 years, I shoveled snow in winter, mowed grass in summer, and loaded coal for 35¢ to 50¢ a ton. My wife did piecework sewing at home and baked homemade bread, which I sold to about 30 customers.

Our income was supplemented by a state work program, through which I made $1.50 a day for 10 days each month. The pay came in vouchers that could be used for food, rent and other necessities. Then came the WPA, where I eventually was assigned to a writers' project at 75¢ an hour.

During planting season, I worked a large garden plot in river-bottom land mornings and evenings. By planting

By George T. Liedel
Palm Bay, Florida

early, I managed to get a jump on the market, and traded beans and other vegetables to a store for bread and meat. The garden also provided food for our own table, and for us to share with others.

Our recreation was listening to the radio and attending "Depression par-

---

"Those who had work helped those who didn't."

---

ties" with our great friends and neighbors. Each person furnished snacks, Kool-Aid or whatever else they could bring. We had big poker games (using kitchen matches for money), danced to music from the radio, and talked about our job prospects. Whenever one of the

group found employment, we weren't jealous; rather, we helped them celebrate their good fortune.

And those who had work helped those who didn't. In 1937, I had a part-time job and was laid off just before Thanksgiving. One of my friends was working at the same place, but he had more seniority and kept his job.

At Christmas, my friend took 2 weeks off without pay, with the provision that I replace him for that period. I am eternally grateful to him for enabling me to provide my children a bit of Christmas cheer.

I wonder if there are still such men, or women, who would do the same for a friend.

COMMUNITY SPIRIT helped many families weather the Depression. A group of neighbors (above) gathered for a summer watermelon feast.

Hitchhikers Found Rides, Food And Hard Work on the Road

By Del Rocheleau
Outing, Minnesota

IN THE SUMMER of 1930, I was 19 years old and jobs were scarce. So one Sunday, I kissed my girlfriend good-bye, and my buddy and I left Minneapolis with blanket rolls and knapsacks to look for work. We hitchhiked around northern Minnesota for a month or more, and then headed for the harvest fields in the Dakotas and Montana.

The first ride we got was with an older fellow in a Cadillac. He shared some hamburgers he had in a bag, and some cookies. But he was a horrible driver, so we decided to get out at the first town, where we told him we planned to look for work.

It was fairly easy to get rides then, and many good people helped us out. The best rides were on bread and meat trucks, where we could count on getting sweet rolls or sausage. Once we were given a ride by a woman traveling with her two nieces in exchange for changing the tires and helping with repairs. They even took us to lunch and supper.

Another time, a young fellow in a Model T Ford roadster stopped and asked if we could help with the gas. We couldn't; we only had $2 between us. He gave us a lift anyway, and later we came upon an abandoned car that had been stripped of everything but the gas in the tank. We took our driver's gas can and a hose and siphoned the fuel in-to his tank. The young man dropped us off in Montana, where we slept in a little park across from a café.

In the morning, a fellow from the café asked us if we wanted work. He fed us breakfast and charged it to the farmer we'd be working for, who lived about 20 miles away. It took us until noon to walk to the farm, where we had a good dinner and then were given a team of horses and sent to the field to do the threshing. We were paid 30¢ an hour.

Headed for Home

When that job was finished, we decided to go back to Minneapolis. We figured it'd be faster to take the train, so we went to the depot and hopped a fast mail train.

Seven hours later, we were in Minot, North Dakota, where a railroad detective caught us. He seemed to be 7 ft. tall and 3 ft. wide! We were thrown in jail for 2 days and fined $2 each. The judge told us to get out of town and stay away from the railroad.

We ignored the second part of his advice and hopped another freight about 1 p.m. We stayed on that train until about 2 o'clock in the morning, when a brakeman warned us there was a rough bunch on the train and suggested we get off in the small town where he lived. *That* advice we followed! We got a room for $1 a night and slept in the first bed we'd seen in months.

We didn't hop a train again after that. The next morning we were back on the highway, hitchhiking our way back to Minneapolis.

Tents Were Home for WPA Worker's Family

DURING the Depression my stepfather worked for the WPA, building roads in southern Missouri. Our family went along wherever he was working. Since we didn't have trailers or motor homes then, we lived in three tents with dirt floors. My mom swept the floors so much, they were as hard as concrete!

One tent was the "kitchen," and my uncle slept there, too. My two brothers and I slept in the second tent, which also was used to store all our clothes. The third tent served as our "living room" and our parents' sleeping quarters. We were lucky; some people traveling this way had only one tent for the whole family.

I was so pleased in later years when my parents were able to enjoy a nice electric home and a camping trailer! —*Ruby Matlock, Mount City, Kansas*

THE CCC

In 1933, President Roosevelt launched the Civilian Conservation Corps, a work relief program whose enrollees restored public lands, provided disaster relief and built flood-control projects. By the time World War II erupted, 2.5 million unemployed young men had served in the CCC's ranks.

CCC a Learning Experience For Young Nebraska Man

I JOINED the Civilian Conservation Corps in July 1934 and was sent to Company 756 in the heart of South Dakota's Black Hills.

The camp was composed of small tents, each with room for five cots and a stove that looked like an upside-down funnel. There was one gravel street, about 10 ft. wide, for walking to the mess hall and other offices.

This was my first time away from home, and it was quite an experience. There were over 100 new recruits, most of whom were young men from Nebraska, just like me.

It took about a week to get every-one assigned to a work unit. Mine was assigned to build fire trails high in the mountains. It was hard work, and sometimes meant blasting out rocks with dynamite.

In August our work got even harder. We were sent to fight a forest fire in Custer, and worked several days with little sleep. We were very glad to get back to camp!

In October, we were sent to a new camp in Nelson, Nebraska. Barracks had been built, but the grounds hadn't been leveled yet, so that was our first assignment. After that, we started building brush and earthen dams.

The following year, the Republican River flooded, and about 50 of us were sent to clean up damage to farm build-

WOOD SPLITTERS created jobs for themselves when other work couldn't be found. These men (above) pulled driftwood from a river, split it and sold it for use as firewood.

ings and basements. It was a messy job; at the end of each day we'd wade into the river, fully clothed, to rinse off the dirt.

I spent a total of 27 months in the CCC, and while the work was sometimes demanding, I learned more in that time than in any other 2-year period of my life. —*Lawrence S. Callander Elk Grove, California*

Six Months in CCC Provided Lifetime of Pride in Work

THE CCC offered unemployed men and boys not only a source of income, but jobs and training. All my friends and two of my brothers had signed up, and in the winter of 1937, I did too.

The CCC was run like a military camp, but we had warm clothes, clean bedding and plenty to eat. (Some of us even got fat!)

In true military style, anyone who misbehaved was assigned to kitchen duty. Speaking from experience, that was no easy task! Breakfast consisted of 25 dozen eggs and 25 loaves of bread, and cocoa was made in brand-new 30-gal. garbage cans.

For 6 months, I worked on projects throughout West Virginia. Whenever we traveled one of those roads or saw one of those dams, I was proud to be able to tell my children and grandchildren, "I helped build that."

—*Basil McGuire, Ocala, Florida*

TAKING A BREAK: A few of the 200 men from CCC Company 1279 took a break before Saturday inspection at their camp (above) in Bassett, Virginia. Helen Fern of Reseda, California shared the photo; her husband, Joe, was a member of the company.

He Helped Build Road Through the Grand Canyon

SOON AFTER I graduated from high school in 1937, I realized there were few jobs in Kansas City, Missouri. Since none of my brothers could find work either, I decided to do whatever I could to ease the burden at home. Within a month, I had enrolled in the CCC.

After a brief train ride—my first—to north-central Missouri, we received an orientation assignment: clearing brush and tree stumps from a riverbed. After a couple of weeks, we were ready for permanent assignments out West.

Seeing mountains out the train window was quite exciting for a 17-year-old who'd never traveled more than 25 miles from home!

After several days, we arrived in Pocatello, Idaho, then took a truck to Alpine, Wyoming and CCC Camp 730, which would be my home for the next 2 years. Our assignment was to build a road from Alpine to Jackson, Wyoming through the Grand Canyon. Today

By Theodore L. Latta
St. Clair, Michigan

that well-traveled road is paved and designated as U.S. Highway 89.

We also learned how to fight forest fires. If a lookout in one of the fire tow-

> ## "Seeing mountains for the first time was so exciting..."

ers spotted smoke, he'd phone our camp and someone would pound on an empty oxygen tank with an iron pipe to sound the alarm.

Trucks took us to the road closest to the fire, and we'd use shovels and brush hooks to dig ditches that would contain the blaze. Those assigned to the water crew carried water from the nearest stream in tanks strapped on their backs to put out the "hot spots."

In our off-hours, we could walk to Alpine—population 7—to take in the sights at the filling station. On some Saturdays we were trucked to Afton, a town of 2,000, to enjoy the skating rink and a movie.

The cold Wyoming winters interrupted our road project, so we cut trees in a nearby national forest for telephone poles, fence posts and fuel to heat our barracks. In spring, we set up and wired the telephone poles to provide phone service for ranchers.

After 2 years, I was discharged so another disadvantaged man could fill my spot. When I enlisted in the Army Air Corps a short time later, my CCC experience made it much easier to adapt to the Army routine.

ROAD WORK projects were undertaken across the country after the WPA was formed. Crew in photo above was building a road in Lincoln Park in Milwaukee, Wisconsin in 1935.

CCC Made Men Out of Many Young Enrollees

I WAS an instructor in a Civilian Conservation Corps camp in Iowa for 2-1/2 years and saw enrollees from all walks of life. The one bond that held them together was their need for work —and they got plenty of that!

The CCC provided a warm bed, clean clothes, hot meals and meaningful work to nearly 3 million unemployed men. An enrollee received $30 a month, $25 of which was sent back to his family. With room, board, clothes, medical care and vocational training provided, some men found camp life so pleasant that they stayed for as long as 6 years. Many found the experience changed their lives forever.

Take Hank, a man from upstate New York. He was broke, unemployed, hungry and had holes in his shoes when he joined up. He was sent to Company

By M. Chester Nolte
Denver, Colorado

1208 near Speculator, New York, where he helped build a beautiful campground still in use today. He also worked in a quarry, mining stone for fireplaces, riprap and fences.

After a year in the CCC, Hank left in search of work, but found none, so he re-enrolled. At a camp in Gallagher,

> *"The CCC provided
> a warm bed, clean clothes,
> hot meals and work..."*

Idaho, he split logs for fence posts, helped build wilderness roads and a ranger station, and fought forest fires. He said it was the happiest time of his

life, and an experience that served him well when he joined the Army later.

"I owe the CCC a lot. I went in as a boy and came out a man," he told me.

Many men felt the same way. They came out of the Corps healthier, more confident and better able to earn a living. Illiterates learned to read; others finished their high school educations. And many learned a trade that enabled them to earn a living the rest of their lives.

But what they remember most is that the government believed in them enough to help start them on a new and productive life.

WORKING AGAIN! Civilian Conservation Corps crew (above) cleared brush and felled trees in the state of Washington. Corps members also built dams and worked on projects to stop soil erosion.

The Corps Turned Millions Into Responsible Citizens

ABOUT 60 years ago, I hitchhiked 40 miles to the county courthouse and enlisted in the Civilian Conservation Corps. My older brother had served in the Corps before me, and now it was my turn as the breadwinner for my widowed mother and two younger siblings.

Like many other kids in the rural South, I had to quit school at an early age to work in the corn and cotton fields and do whatever odd jobs came along. Joining the CCC helped us get a start in life, and I'll always be grateful for the experience we gained and for the monetary aid. The CCC turned millions of young people into responsible citizens, and sustained many families that otherwise would have been on welfare.

Provided Stone for Roads

My first camp was near Chatsworth, Georgia, alongside a mountain stream with water so cold and pure that we were able to drink it. Our job was to furnish stone for roads in the county, which we provided with dynamite and 16-lb. sledgehammers. We used wheelbarrows to haul the stone to the crusher.

Lunchtime was the only break unless you smoked; the smokers got to stop and roll their cigarettes. I nearly took up smoking just to get a rest!

We felt almost elated when the fire gong sounded; it meant we'd be sent to put out a forest fire. Although we were only trading our hammers and wheelbarrows for brush hooks, axes and saws, we at least got to ride through the mountains for a while in one of the canvastopped trucks.

The discipline and self-respect that I gained in the CCC was invaluable. It smoothed the way for my Navy service in World War II, and it helped me appreciate life in general. I wouldn't trade my experiences for anything.

—*Joseph Lee, Porter, Indiana*

Army-Style Camps Taught Discipline and Work Ethic

I WAS in the CCC at Wilton, Minnesota from April 1939 through April 1941, and have never regretted the time I spent there. The CCC planted trees, built dams, roads and bridges, surveyed lakes, improved timber stands, and a lot more. Much of our work is still visible throughout the nation.

It was strictly a volunteer organization, but when you joined, you were sworn in and took an oath much like those administered in the armed services. Each camp's commander was an Army officer, who was responsible for housing, dressing, feeding and disciplining the enrollees.

The 200 to 300 men in our camp were housed in long, narrow barracks and slept in Army-type cots stacked two high. Our cots were always made with military precision, with the corners carefully tucked in and the top blanket stretched so tight you could bounce a coin on it.

The barracks were heated with a single wood-burning stove near the center of the building. On the long, cold winter nights, we took turns working 2- or 3-hour shifts to keep the fire roaring.

The camp also had a recreation hall with pool and card tables and reading materials. Those who wanted to improve themselves could take classes in

BARRACKS LIFE awaited young men who signed up for the CCC. Ernest J. Sweigert of Lyndhurst, Ohio (lower left, above) served at Camp Snowline (below) near Placerville, California. He and fellow enrollees built roads and stone bridges, maintained parks, fought forest fires and planted trees.

a separate education building. These courses not only taught us more about the work we were doing, but enabled us to try for promotions. Assistant leaders were paid $36 a month rather than $30, and leaders made $45. Any increase in salary was not sent home; it was the enrollee's to keep.

The CCC gave us discipline and a work ethic, taught us how to get along with others, and enabled us to help our families back home. It was an experience that enriched my life.

—*Emil M. Hallin*
Rapid City, South Dakota

'Green Kids' Transformed Themselves into Greengrocers

THE GREAT Depression was tightening its grip. Our local banks were closing. Family members and friends were coming home from work to say they wouldn't be going back tomorrow. This was no mere recession. It was a disaster.

I was fresh out of college, and job-hunting was futile. "No Help Wanted" signs hung in employment offices. My friend Jerry Edlund had been laid off, so we decided our best bet would be to make our own jobs—but doing what? Companies were failing everywhere. What could a couple of green kids do?

Jerry's father had a suggestion. He was a financial reporter who'd been laid off himself, and his territory had included Chicago's great South Water Street Wholesale Produce Market.

"Why don't you boys try selling fruits and vegetables?" Pa asked.

"I've been doing credit reports on the big wholesalers for years and I know them pretty well. I can introduce you, and I'm sure they'll give you some

By Ford Charlton
Gulfport, Florida

tips. They're always looking for new customers."

Over the next 2 weeks, we acquired an old Model T Ford truck, painted our names on the door, and scraped up enough money to buy a load of produce.

First Day on the Job

Our first day in business was quite an adventure. About 3:30 on a freezing November morning, I cranked up the truck, joined Jerry and Pa in the cab, and headed for the bustling market.

The open stalls displayed more fruits and vegetables than we had ever seen. Trucks of all descriptions were parked down the middle of the broad street as the drivers went from stall to stall, checking the produce and haggling over prices.

Pa made introductions for us, and we made our purchases. Back home, we washed and trimmed everything to

make it as attractive as possible. Then we spruced ourselves up and set out to visit the housewives of the community.

It had been a long time since our neighborhood had an old-fashioned peddler. The novelty, convenience and high-quality produce combined for a surprisingly favorable reaction.

On subsequent buying trips, we scoured the market with Pa for the best produce we could find. We started checking supermarket prices and set ours slightly lower. It was quite some time before we realized we were selling deluxe produce, which ordinarily went to the finest hotels and restaurants, at chain-store prices!

Our customers were enthusiastic—

GREENGROCERS and huckster wagons provided fresh produce, staples and, as photo above shows, sometimes even chickens to rural and urban families alike. A few enterprising young men started their own grocery wagons when other jobs fell through.

none had ever heard of broccoli, and few knew about avocados, Michigan hearts of celery or Temple oranges. Profits were slim, but our business was thriving.

Our schedule was rigorous. We rose at 3:30, shivering as we cranked up the truck. Then we drove to the market for the usual session of bargaining. We returned home as the sun began chasing the morning mists. Our wives, Ginny and Peg, helped us trim and sort what we'd bought.

By 9 a.m. we were back on the street, knocking on doors, smiling, displaying our baskets and making sales. By 4 p.m., we rolled down the truck's canvas sides and headed for home. We'd climbed a thousand apartment-build-

> ### "Our best bet was to make our own jobs..."

ing steps, trudged through hundreds of backyards, and lugged a quarter-ton of food into the townspeople's larders.

One evening our wives told us they wanted to go along with us to the market the next morning. "No way," Jerry and I replied. "The market is no place for girls." Our wives argued that they were part of the business, too, but Jerry and I didn't budge. The market was a very rough place.

The next morning, we were about halfway to the market when we heard muffled giggles from the back of the truck. We pulled over to investigate, and out popped our wives. "Surprise!" they shouted triumphantly. We *were* surprised, and at that point we had no choice but to take them along.

We were even *more* surprised when we discovered the effect that two attractive young women had on the gruff workers at the market! Ginny and Peg were greeted warmly, shown around, given little gifts of special fruit and generally treated like visiting royalty. When we headed back home. Jerry and I took a lot of teasing about how "tough" the market was!

The little Charlton-Edlund Company became an unforgettable chapter in our lives. Although it didn't develop into an empire, it brought in a few precious dollars, put food on the table for two families, and gave us all a little more confidence. We knew we could cope with whatever life brought us in the years to come.

Family Admired Dignity of 'Thread Man'

"THE THREAD MAN" came to our neighborhood four times a year during the early 1930s. He stopped at each house on our street, rang the bell, knelt to display his wares to the housewife who answered the door, and waited for a decision. The visits on our short street alone took an hour out of his day, and he made few sales.

His black case contained sewing notions, each held neatly in place with an elastic band: boxes of thread, pins, needles, cards of shirt buttons, safety pins for diapers, silver hooks and eyes, black snaps on blue cards, shoelaces.

He handled those simple wares as though they were fine jewels. When a customer closed her door, he carefully returned each item to its proper place and moved on to the next house.

Our mother admired the thread man. Whenever we called "Thread man's coming!", she'd drop whatever she was doing and make a quick inventory of her sewing supplies. She always bought something whether she needed it or not. "He has dignity," she said. "He's neat and clean, and he tries."

Mother thought he must have held a fine position before the stock market crashed. "I can tell from his clothes—the good white shirt, that blue serge suit, the coat with the velvet collar. They're old, but good quality."

Neat from Head to Toe

It was true the thread man was much neater than other peddlers who came to our door. He wore a black derby in winter, and black galoshes over polished shoes when it was damp. In summer, he tipped his neat straw hat to all the females, slightly inclining his graying head.

Mother also was impressed by the regularity of his schedule. "He walks the rounds like it's a good job," she said. "He gets dressed in his best clothes and goes to work. I like him."

At each visit, Mother continued to increase her supply of notions, scanning the case's contents with her hand on her cheek and then taking the required coin from her apron pocket. The thread man graciously thanked her.

One day during the spring thaw, the thread man spotted my little sister stuck in the mud in the vacant lot at the end of the block. After carefully placing his black case on the sidewalk, he waded into the muck, dirtying his boots and trousers, then waded back out with a crying child under one arm.

Mother was surprised to find them at the back door, and invited him in to clean up. After a little brushing and scraping, a shoe shine and a cup of tea, the thread man went on his way. "Such a gentleman," Mother said.

That summer, the thread man visited us once more. Mother offered him a glass of iced tea and bought another spool of white thread. As he left, my little sister rode her tricycle on the sidewalk alongside him. "Good-bye, you old stick-in-the-mud," he teased her gently, patting her curls. "Good-bye, thread man," she called after him. It was the last time we ever saw him.

—Helen Ueberbacher, Stamford, Connecticut

Family Got a Fresh Start by Opening Tourist Home

By Mary Joe Beyeors
Orange, California

DURING the Depression many people couldn't even pay the taxes on their homes, let alone pay the mortgage. That's what happened to my parents. We had a big, rambling house in town, and there were four children, with twins on the way.

Although we were losing our house, my mother was determined not to give in. "I have an idea," she told us. "If I can get it working we'll have a house again." She went to a neighbor who owned several pieces of property and asked him about a big brick house on the main

thoroughfare. He asked how we expected to pay the rent. Mom said she had no money, but if he would trust her, she'd have it by the end of the month. She intended to open a tourist home!

"I know it will work, with all the salesmen that pass through here," Mother told him. "And it's just down the street from the train station."

The owner was impressed with the idea, and we had a new home! My fa-

ther made a wooden sign with lights on either side and hung it on the veranda. The rest of us scrubbed and cleaned to get the house ready for visitors. Mom charged 50¢ a night for rooms and $7 a week for room and board, with laundry included.

There were some hard times when no one came, but Mom would always say, "The Lord will send someone." Sure enough, there soon would be a knock at the door and someone would want a room!

One night a man came to the door and asked if Mom could put up his telephone crew of 10. You should have seen her face. Room and board for 10 men—it was a miracle!

We saw some interesting characters, but most of our guests were people just like my parents. Some had lost everything and didn't want to give up, and were on the road trying to make a few cents to send home to their families.

It was hard work and everyone in the family had chores to do, but we were happy. In later years. Mom bought that house, and then another. That's what determination gets you. "Never say die," Mom would say. "Hard work never hurt anybody."

ROOMS FOR RENT: Providing room and board to travelers looking for work helped some families make it through the Depression.

Warehouse Owner Started Over as Auctioneer

WHEN THE banks closed, my father lost his savings overnight. In another 8 months, he had to close what had been a prosperous furniture and antique storage warehouse. But he was young and strong, with plenty of imagination. He decided to become an auctioneer!

Dad would buy stocks of merchandise from failing businesses, hold an auction, pay the owner his share of the profits, and then move whatever was left over to a store he rented for $15 a month on South Broadway in Yonkers, New York. He called the store "The Broadway Bazaar," where a shopper could buy anything from a lace-up corset to a spool of thread.

Although those were lean years, Dad's business provided many items our family could use. We didn't have store-bought shoes for years; we just waited until Dad bought out a shoe store's stock and hoped there would be some to fit us. Most were usually too big for me, but I could wear them with a little paper tucked into the toes.

Whenever Dad bought out a toy store, my doll collection grew. I discovered bonbons when he bought a candy store. A bookstore purchase gave me my own set of poetry volumes bound in blue leather. One year my aunts, cousins and I got silk pajamas with Chinese lettering embroidered on the jackets.

My mother was feeding us on a dollar a day then, so we were all pleased when my father bought a grocery store that had sustained a fire. He brought home boxes of canned goods whose labels had been washed off by the firemen's hoses.

Every night at dinner, we'd gather around the table and try to guess what was in the cans, watching with great anticipation as the contents were revealed. It was usually beans, fruit cocktail or soup, but that didn't matter; it was *food*. Somehow, those same foods don't taste nearly as good now as they did then!

—*Carol Greenberg*
Philadelphia, Pennsylvania

Bottle Business Paid Him 'Pretty Good Dividends'

I WAS practicing recycling a half century before it was fashionable—and making money at it, too! As a young boy in a small village in central Michigan, I collected many different types of bottles and sold them.

For instance, early on in the Depression when Prohibition was still the law of the land, I looked for empty whiskey bottles that clandestine nippers would leave behind the old dance hall. I'd go at daybreak every Sunday, and would sell the bottles to the local bootlegger for 5¢ each.

He paid me a premium of 10¢ for one special bottle with deep, intricate etchings. This bottle undoubtedly came from the days when whiskey had been legal, and I retrieved and resold it week after week!

Most of the Saturday-night "nippers" always drank in the same hidden locations, so I knew where to find the empties. Some were more brazen and left their bottles in plain view on the dance hall's outside window ledges. It was like plucking nickels off the sills as I walked by!

This part of my bottle business took no more than 20 minutes and brought in about $1.50 a week—not bad when $2 was the going rate for a day's labor.

Medicine bottles from trash piles and the village dump provided ready cash, too. I washed the reclaimed bottles in boiling water and then delivered them to the veterinarian. My heart would pound as he divided the bottles into three groups. The very small bottles brought a penny; medium-sized ones, 3¢; and large ones, a nickel.

By Carl W. Gregory
Higgins Lake, Michigan

I also liked doing business with the old horse doctor because he usually gave me a little something extra for my trouble. One day, though, I was disappointed when his "tip" turned out to be a shot for my dog, who had tagged along. I didn't even know dogs needed shots. I would have much preferred the extra dime!

While I searched for medicine bottles, I also put aside small pickle and olive jars for a special, once-a-year venture: selling horseradish. I'd come upon a horseradish patch on an abandoned farm north of town, and knew that once a year, my father splurged and bought a jar of the stuff. I reasoned there must be others who could part with a dime for a jar of fresh-grated horseradish, too, and I was right.

My bottle business taught me at a very early age that imagination, hustle and hard work paid pretty good dividends.

Home Bakery Became Family Affair

THE DEPRESSION was at its peak. My husband, a building supply salesman, had just lost his third job as yet *another* company folded. Our thoughts for the future were not hopeful.

One day I was baking a pan of chocolate tarts, and when I pulled them from the oven my mother remarked, "I'll just bet there are many people who'd like one of those." Although I'm not a naturally impulsive person, I said, "Well, I think I'll find out!"

I filled a basket with the tarts and went over to a house in the next block. Fortunately, it was the home of a "chocoholic," and she bought all my tarts! I was so overcome by the sale that when I got home I made out a shopping list and went to the grocery so I could bake again the next day.

I soon worked up quite a little business, making cupcakes, tarts, cookies, doughnuts and pies to order.

My husband was unsuccessful in finding another job, so he became my deliveryman. Our 5-year-old daughter went along with her own little basket of goodies.

We were able to survive on this income for some time, but we just couldn't pay our rent. We put everything into storage and found a two-room apartment in a private home. My husband found three part-time jobs after that, and the good times finally came again.

—*Irene Skelton Baldwin, Arlington, Virginia*

and did more sewing. Dress materials were 17¢ a yard; I was paid 25¢ for making a woman's dress, and twice that for a two-piece garment.

Landlord Provided Work

Our rent was $10 a month, and even with the extra work I was doing, there were some months we just couldn't pay all of it. Our fine landlord told us to just pay a quarter at a time as we got it. He always seemed to find something I could do, such as cleaning one of his buildings, to earn the additional amount needed to pay the rent.

Food prices were high, too, compared to our wages. Milk was 8¢ a quart, bread 10¢ a loaf and eggs 7¢ a dozen. Many mothers learned not to be hungry. My little ones never did understand why Mama didn't like the bread they thought was so wonderful.

One day as I was sewing, I heard a vehicle stop by the garage. When no

> ## "I knew the delivery wasn't mine...it must have been a mistake."

one came to the house, I laid my sewing aside and opened the door. There on the porch sat a big box of groceries, with the name of the store printed on the side of the box.

I knew the delivery wasn't mine; it must have been left at our house by mistake, and someone else would be waiting for it. How I longed to be able to provide such abundance for my own family! With a heavy heart, I loaded the box into our little homemade wagon and pulled it to the grocery.

When I told the owner what had happened, he said, "Did you look in the bags?"

"Of course I didn't!" I exclaimed. "I had no right to do that."

He reached into one of the bags, pulled out a note, and handed it to me. I'll never forget those words.

"I admire your quiet willingness to do anything that is decent and honest to care for your family without complaint," the note said. "Please accept this small gift from a friend and well-wisher."

"She asked me to deliver it to you and keep her identity secret," the grocer told me. The groceries were worth $5—nearly half a week's wages at the print shop! It was one of the most wonderful things anyone ever did for me.

Anonymous Well-Wisher Rewarded Her Efforts to Support Her Family

By Cecile Cowdery
Long Prairie, Minnesota

IN 1933 we were still in the throes of the Depression. I had three small children, and my husband, a printer, was developing arthritis in his fingers. When he was able to work, he made $12 a week.

I'd always done whatever I could to add to the family income, mostly sewing or painting, but now it became necessary for me to do more, so I put in longer hours. When I could, I left the children with my husband and painted murals in the houses of those who could afford the cost, which was $3 to $5. (Some of those paintings are still on the walls today!)

I also made fancy cakes and pies,

CHAPTER FOUR

'Beans
Bacon &
Gravy

Beans, Bacon & Gravy

FOOD WAS a precious commodity during the Depression, and many families produced much of it themselves. No matter how humble the meal, they savored whatever they had.

ne of my daughters had just finished buying the week's groceries for a family of four. The bill was considerably more than a hundred dollars.

"How in the world did people eat during the Depression when there was no money?" she asked.

Truth to tell, we ate pretty well. Just read the memories in this chapter. "We ate like kings," recalls Juanita Urbach of Brush, Colorado.

Not everyone did, to be sure. Years after the Depression some people would confess that they were driven to such desperation that they actually stole food—and had a guilty conscience for the rest of their lives.

Others, like hobos, resorted to begging. Usually it was a simple request for a sandwich, or a few potatoes and carrots that would be added to the big community pot that was always cooking at the "hobo jungle" down near the railroad tracks. To eat, you had to contribute, no matter how little.

Those were also the days when you could charge your groceries. Chances are that the owner of the corner grocery was your neighbor, not someone working for a giant corporation in a big-city skyscraper a thousand miles away. So you ran a tab, and paid what you could, when you could. He understood.

Food was simpler in those days and therefore cheaper. What we buy today is food that's already been peeled or shucked or chopped up and then seasoned and cooked and boxed or canned or frozen. In short, we pay others to do most of the hard work that once was done in the home.

Sunday night supper often was bread and milk. Or crackers and milk. Or leftover popcorn and milk. Not fancy, but tasty, cheap and filling.

Tricks Kept Food Bills Down

Parents learned tricks that cut the food bill. You parked outside the grocery until 10 minutes before closing time on Saturday night and then hurried in to snap up bargains on fresh produce. It was priced for quick sale because it wouldn't keep over Sunday in those unrefrigerated times. I remember Dad buying an entire grocery sack full of bananas for 10¢. We feasted on them for nearly a week.

During the summer I was dispatched at dawn on my bicycle to scout country roads for wild asparagus. After a while you knew where it grew, so in a half hour you could collect enough for a couple of meals.

In the fall the whole family went with gunnysacks to a heavily wooded county park that had dozens of walnut and hickory trees. In a few hours we had enough nuts to last us until the next autumn.

Most people had gardens. *Big* gardens. They not only provided vegetables and berries and rhubarb for the summer months, but also the raw material for canning—which Ron Stauder of Belleville, Illinois describes so well in this chapter. The measure of a dedicated homemaker was how many hundreds of jars of vegetables, fruit and jelly she "put up" for the winter. No social visit was complete without a trip to the basement to admire shelf after shelf of mason jars filled with string beans and corn, red beets and tomatoes.

There were other tricks. In our family we still make "Depression syrup." The process is a simple matter of cooking down a mixture of white or brown sugar plus water, and perhaps some maple flavoring. It's not Karo syrup, of course, but tasty, warm and cheap.

People who lived on farms had a big advantage, and in the '30s, 20% of all Americans *did* live on farms. You had cows that gave milk and chickens that laid eggs (or else were the featured attraction at Sunday dinner). Your orchard produced apples and cherries and plums and pears.

You planted long rows of sweet corn out in the fields.

Every farmer in our area knew that the man who tested milk for butterfat at the milk depot didn't work on Sunday. So on Sunday mornings before the milkman drove in to pick up your milk cans, you skimmed off the cream. Once you've tasted ice cream made from pure cream, you're spoiled for life!

Now turn the page and enjoy some warm memories of how America ate pretty well even though money was scarce. You'll even discover some wonderful recipes from that era, delicious and still costing just pennies to prepare.

And you'll never find them precooked in your supermarket's freezer case.

—*Clancy Strock*

HOME CANNING was a means of survival for many families during the Depression. Fruits and vegetables canned in late summer and fall provided enough wholesome food to last until a new garden was planted the following spring.

'We May Have Been Poor, But We Had Plenty of Food

By Floyd Hedge
Mountain Home, Arkansas

IN 1934, when I was boy of 12, my mom and dad and I moved in with my grandma in the southern-Illinois town of Albion.

The Depression was in full swing in that little town, and jobs were as scarce as diamonds in a coal mine. Dad was between jobs and we had to go on government relief until we got back on our feet.

We never had any luxuries like electricity, a furnace, air-conditioning or even an electric fan. I did my homework at night by the light of a kerosene lamp. Dad used to joke that we were so poor, the flies had to carry a lunch when they came to our house!

But we had a big potbellied stove to keep us warm, plenty of homemade quilts to snuggle under at night, and lots of good, wholesome food to eat.

My step-grandfather raised tobacco and had a big garden and several fruit trees. It was my job to pick the fruit and vegetables, and Mom and Grandma slaved over a hot stove all summer to can them and make jams and jellies for the coming winter.

I especially remember the huge platters of fried bread that Grandma made for supper every night, along with the ever-present pot of great northern beans, and a No. 10 cast-iron skillet filled with fried potatoes.

I always finished off my meal with

"We were so poor, the flies had to carry lunches when they came to our house..."

---

peanut butter mixed with either a half-pint of blackberry jam, peach preserves or sorghum molasses.

We ate a lot of inexpensive meat then: a steak probably would have made us sick! We had a lot of jowl meat, salt pork and liver—cuts of meat that "better offs" didn't want. And we were glad to get it.

On rare occasions, we had what Dad called "Hoover ham" (baloney) along with cheddar cheese and crackers.

When President Roosevelt started the WPA, Dad was lucky enough to get a job for a dollar a day running the wooden end of a long-handled shovel used to grade ditch banks.

After that, we were able to rent a house of our own, but those earlier recollections will have a special place in my mind forever.

Neighbors Shared Produce Through Vegetable Exchange

OH YES, I recall the Great Depression. I was a teenager then, and the way I remember it, it was more a challenge than a depression.

Mom dug up our front yard to plant a garden, and it really thrived. Some of our neighbors did the same thing, so vegetable swapping was a common occurrence. Sometimes we'd get a nice surprise through the neighborhood exchange, like corn on the cob.

One afternoon I asked Mom what we were having for dinner that evening. She grinned and said, "I don't know. Let's wait and see what the neighbors bring in."

People helped each other then, just as they still do when the chips are down. That's the American way.

—Michelle Beffa
Carpinteria, California

Pancakes Required Only Flour and Some Creativity

WHEN MY sisters and I think of the Depression and how we got through it, I'm sure all three of us immediately think of pancakes!

Pancakes could be made even when it seemed we had no food in the house. All we really needed was flour—the rest of the ingredients are subject to alteration, as we quickly learned!

For instance, I learned that a tablespoon of cornstarch could be substituted for one egg in any recipe that called for more than one egg. (You still need that first egg, though.) I also learned how to make an acceptable maple syrup substitute with a small bottle of maple flavoring, sugar and a little water.
—*Jenese L. Nelson*
Redwood City, California

Bean Soup a Reminder Of Simpler Times

WHENEVER I'm in my kitchen, smelling the aroma of beans slowly cooking for our evening meal, my mind goes back to my childhood, when this food was vital to our survival. We may not have had many material things, but we never went hungry, thanks to beans and corn bread.

This simple meal reminds me that the essentials of life need not be ex-

PEAS, PLEASE: This young girl helped with the family's gardening chores by shelling peas.

travagant. We often think that to be happy, we need bigger and better things. And yet, when I was growing up, there was so much love in our family that we just didn't think about needing anything more.

I've never forgotten that period of my life, or that Depression-era meal. It remains one of my favorites, and I still enjoy cooking up a "potful of the past."
—*Oneta M. Whitlock, Altus, Oklahoma*

'Lunch Truck' Delivered Meals to WPA Workers

LONG BEFORE street vendors or lunch wagons started making the rounds at offices and construction sites, my mother invented and operated her own "lunch truck"!

We were living in a rural area near Pittsburgh, Pennsylvania. When a WPA project began on our road, she seized the opportunity by providing sandwiches, hot coffee and cold lemonade to the crew, right on the work site.

My brothers and I were Mom's "crew." We'd go to the site in the morning and collect the workers' orders, then take them back home to Mom. When the orders were filled, we'd deliver them in a little truck we'd made with wheels from a red wagon.

The prices were 10¢ for a spiced ham sandwich, 5¢ for a fried egg sandwich, 10¢ for a pint jar of coffee, and 5¢ for a pint jar of lemonade. We kept a charge book and collected our money when the men were paid on Fridays. —*Jean Conboy McFeeley*
Merion Station, Pennsylvania

Ice Cream, Snow Candy Were Wintertime Treats

ONE OF MY favorite winter memories is of making ice cream. (Yes, I did say winter!) We'd scoop some of the rich cream from the top of Grandpa's milk cans to make our chilly treat. When it was done, we would open the oven door on the old Home Comfort stove, prop our feet on it to keep warm, and enjoy that homemade ice cream!

For another wintertime treat, we'd scoop up clean snow and pack it in pie tins while Grandma boiled down a pint of maple syrup to the point where it would pour in a sticky, thread-thin stream. We'd slowly trickle this sweet topping over the tins of snow. Boy, did that make great candy!

OFF TO MARKET: Many families raised chickens for meat and eggs. The eggs were sold to supplement the family income or bartered for other supplies during trips to town.

During summer we'd carry a quart of home-canned beef, a loaf of homemade bread, and a basketful of onions, tomatoes and cucumbers from the garden down to the creek. Grandma would pile stones in a circle and build a fire.

While we kids stripped down to our "underduddies" for a swim, Grandma would cook the beef and onions in her old black cast-iron frying pan. How wonderful they smelled as they simmered over the fire! The whole meal was delicious, especially after a refreshing swim.

Maybe it was because I was so young, but the Depression era seemed to me to be a loving, beautiful time. Everyone needed and respected each other. It might not be such a tragic thing to have to go back to some of that way of life! —*Lela M. Moll*
Allegan, Michigan

'Depression Soup' Still One of Her Favorites

WE OFTEN made a meal of sliced raw potatoes, onion and, on occasion, a few strips of bacon. We added some water and cooked everything together in a covered pot. It was really good. In fact, we still make "Depression soup" today!
—*Grace MacAdam*
Whitehall, Pennsylvania

Bean Sandwiches, Stew Standard Fare for Hobos

IN MY HOBO days during the late 1930s, I ate an awful lot of bean sandwiches. You first had to acquire, by some honest method, a loaf of bread and a can of pork and beans. (In those days, either cost about 10¢.)

Then you took out your trusty pocketknife, cut the bread in half, hollowed out part of the inside of the loaf, and filled the hole with beans. This sandwich was eaten from the outside in, and no utensils were required.

Hobo stew was another favorite. The list of ingredients could be endless, because anything that was edible went into the pot. Hobos commonly congregated in camps or "jungles" at the edge of town. Each man in the camp contributed something to the stew pot—whatever could be scrounged from a store, garden or farmer's field across the tracks was fair game.

Meat was the toughest ingredient to come by. The best we could usually contribute was fish, crawdad tails, squirrels and rabbits. Once in a while a hapless chicken would be hit by a train or a flying rock, and it would find its way into the stew pot too.

Finding water for the soup was never a problem, as most hobo jungles were on creek banks under a bridge or trestle. No one worried that cows and other livestock were wading and drinking in the same stream. We hadn't heard much about pollution then, and wouldn't have cared even if we had.

Biscuits and bread, after a fashion, could be made with a little flour, salt and water. The dough was twisted on a stick and baked over the fire. It didn't taste like much, but it was filling.

It's been 55 years since I ate those meals, and I've suffered no ill effects!
—*James D. Moore III*
Olympia, Washington

Leg of Lamb Lasted Until Bank Reopened

MY PARENTS had just adopted me when the banks closed, so my father was caught with about $2 in his pocket. His brother owed him $10, which he collected right away. My parents then went to the store and bought a leg of lamb.

We had lamb for a couple of meals, and then Mama made a lamb stew out of the leftovers, and we ate that…and ate that…and ate that. At each meal, Mama would throw in more potatoes and carrots and serve it one more time!

Of course, each time the dish had less and less lamb in it, but it lasted until the bank reopened.

After that, my father swore he would never eat lamb stew again. And he never did!
—*Marie Shull*
Strasburg, Virginia

Food from Government Helped Needy Families

THERE WERE six children in our family, and during the Depression our father worked at whatever job he could find. In 1938 he got a job building roads with the WPA in Maine. He was paid a dollar a day, but that wasn't enough for a family of eight to live on.

My mother helped where she could, cutting potato seed for a local farmer, hanging wallpaper for those who were more fortunate, and taking in a little ironing.

When the towns began distributing government food for needy families, we received split peas, dry beans, canned milk, rolled oats, flour, lard, butter and sometimes oranges and smoked ham. When we got ham, we carefully rationed it out at one slice per person to make it last as long as possible.

Our breakfasts usually consisted of oatmeal or pancakes with molasses. For other meals, we ate pea soup, baked or stewed beans, corn chowder, tomato bisque, macaroni with stewed tomatoes, fried salt pork with brown gravy and potatoes, and "poor man's soup"—salt pork with potatoes, onions and milk. We ate biscuits with every meal.

We got by on just the bare necessities back then, but we had each other and lots of love. Those days made a survivor out of me.
—*Lorraine Neal Lane*
Brookfield, Massachusetts

Menus Show How Woman Fed Family on a Dollar a Day

I FOUND this account in a book of how one woman fed her family of eight for $1 a day in 1934. I wonder how many folks today would be satisfied with such a menu!

Day 1—Macaroni with tomato sauce; apples.

Day 2—Mutton stew with potatoes; cookies.

Day 3—Broiled fish with cream sauce; bread; orange.

Day 4—Warmed-over fish on toast; baked sweet potatoes; prunes.

Day 5—Hard-boiled eggs scalloped with rice; cabbage; gingerbread.

Day 6—Beef hash; string beans; apple pie.

Day 7—Thick soup; biscuits; mixed fruit.

Day 8—Vegetable salad: baked potatoes; apricots.

Day 9—Codfish cakes; cauliflower; watermelon.

Day 10—Spanish rice with liver sauce; brown muffins; gelatin.

Day 11—Potatoes Suzette; lettuce; baked pears.

Day 12—Beef pie; squash; plums.

Day 13—Hot boiled potatoes with butter and milk; jam; crackers.

Day 14—Baked beans; brown bread; bananas.

Day 15—Tomatoes; eggs; potato salad; corn bread hotcakes.
—*Ethelyn Nelson*
Canaan, Maine

Seasons Determined Many Families' Menus

OUR EATING HABITS in the 1930s were regulated by the seasons. The grocery bill always had to be kept to a minimum because our only reliable source of income came from selling eggs and cream.

We welcomed spring each year. It was a time of hope. We searched the fence corners for lamb's-quarters, added winter onions to our scrambled eggs, and pulled tender rhubarb shoots for pies.

Soon there would be leaf lettuce, radishes and green onions from the garden. Topped with a sweet-and-sour cream dressing, they would become tasty salads.

The meat supply would be running low as spring approached, so whatever we had left was alternated with stewing hens.

In summertime, since we had no refrigeration, we cooked only enough food for one meal. Excess vegetables were preserved in a variety of ways. Green beans and tomatoes were canned. Sweet corn was cut from the cob and spread on a white sheet to dry. Cabbage was shredded and put into stone jars with salt for sauerkraut.

When fall came, we bought a few bushels of peaches and pears for canning. Baskets of grapes were bought for jelly. Potatoes, carrots and onions

By Juanita Killough Urbach
Brush, Colorado

were dug up and stored in the cellar.

Winter was soup season. A meaty bone boiled with vegetables made a tasty appetizer. Thicker, meatier stews were meals in themselves. Chicken noodle soup was a favorite, as were potato soup, and navy bean soup with bits of ham or bacon.

Tomato soup was a Depression specialty. Home-canned tomatoes and milk were heated separately, and a little soda was added to the tomatoes to keep the milk from curdling when the two were combined. It had a unique flavor unmatched by any other tomato soup.

Food preparation required more work then, but the cooks were creative. If they were out of one ingredient, they substituted another: Flour replaced cornstarch, honey or syrup took the place of sugar, and soda and baking powder were used interchangeably. The changes were rarely detected. and the food was just as delicious and filling.

We might have felt poor during the Depression, but we ate like kings!

GROUP GARDENS were popular in many communities, with several neighbors pitching in to tend one large plot. And, as the photo above indicates, everyone in the family had his or her own row to hoe!

Dandelion Dish Was Free for the Asking

AT AGE 10, I didn't know we were poor. It seemed we had just as much as everybody else. We didn't eat much meat in those days. What we did eat was fried potatoes—and lots of them.

One day my mother decided we needed something a little different. She handed me a small knife and a paper sack.

"Go up to the telephone company and ask if you can pick the dandelions from their lawn," she told me.

I came back with a whole sackful. Mother cooked the dandelions in bacon fat, and they were *delicious*. I was so proud to have made a contribution to our meal!

—*Gracie Thomas*
Flagstaff, Arizona

'Newsboy for a Night' Put Food on Our Table

By Julie Probst, Bronx, New York

THE YEAR was 1930, the Depression was rampant, and we were having pea soup for supper again—for the fourth day in a row. I wondered where my mother had found a steel pot that big!

All of us kids were grumbling and griping, and Mother replied that the soup improved with each passing day. I sneezed in disbelief. "It's the truth," my mother said firmly.

Some Slang Terms for Food Started During Depression

IN THEIR fight to cut costs during the Depression, restaurants, hash houses and lunch counters asked customers to use less sugar, and often stretched the coffee by watering it down and adding chicory. Some businesses displayed signs that said: "Don't complain about the coffee. You may be old and weak yourself someday!"

Those businesses also contributed a few picturesque and even bizarre terms for food and beverages. The menus of the time often referred to eggs as "cacklers," doughnuts as "sinkers," seltzer as "belch water" and milk as "moo juice." If you heard a waitress talk about "wrecking a pair," she was ordering scrambled eggs.

—*Marvin Dodson, Hendersonville, North Carolina*

My oldest brother, then 14, was the breadwinner of the family, and he seemed just as dejected with this meal as the rest of us. He seemed deep in thought, as though he was searching for a solution to our food problem. On days when we didn't have pea soup, it was boiled rice with sugar and milk.

Suddenly he produced the 50¢ he had earned shining shoes that day and asked if he could withhold it. He had a plan, he said, that would more than triple that amount. My mother was skeptical; how could she part with 50¢?

Although my brother didn't explain his scheme, he eased her fears, for she allowed him to pocket the five dimes.

What Was His Plan?

When my brother left the house later that evening, I sneaked out and followed him. He headed for the candy store and bought 25 copies of the next morning's newspaper at 2¢ each. Then he scrounged around for a large apple box and headed for the theater a short distance away. So he planned to sell newspapers. But what was he going to do with that huge box?

I hid near the theater and watched as the audience slowly began filing out. Just then my brother stood up on his box, waved his arms and said in a loud, clear voice, "Step right up, ladies and gentlemen, for the greatest show you will see tonight!"

The large group of theater-goers approached him, looking quite jolly. My eyes widened as I saw my brother leap into a tap-dance routine he'd taught himself. I thought he was every bit as good as Fred Astaire!

My brother's audience was very receptive, and everyone applauded. Before they began to walk away, however, he jumped from the box, grappled with the newspapers he had hidden behind it and shouted enthusiastically, "Buy a paper? Buy a paper?"

The happy throng couldn't resist, and in a few moments he'd sold every paper—not for 2¢ each, but 10¢. A few generous patrons even rewarded him with a quarter!

The next night, it was clear his plan had worked. Mother fixed us a juicy leg of lamb with all the trimmings. We ate with zest, thankful for our brother's ingenuity—and thankful that the pea soup would be saved for another day!

ENTERPRISING FARM WIVES opened the Women's Farm Market in Stillwater, Oklahoma in 1930. To ease the Depression's effects on their families, they sold foods fresh from their farms, including: baked beans, 10¢ per pound; 12-egg angel food cake, 50¢; hens, 18¢; pressed chicken, 30¢; and eggs, 18¢ per dozen.

Spaghetti Got Family Through Jobless Year

TODAY, nutritionists say we should choose low-fat, high-fiber diets. Sixty years ago, my family had no choice. That's how we survived.

My father could not find work the entire year of 1932, and he was too proud to go on relief. He borrowed against his insurance policy to keep us from losing our house, and he used his savings to buy us flour, spaghetti and dry beans. The spaghetti came in wooden boxes containing 25 lbs. and the flour in 25-lb. cloth sacks.

My father planted several hundred tomato plants in our garden and in the empty lot next door. My mother canned more than 100 quarts of tomato sauce, and we had spaghetti with meatless sauce as our main dish at least four times a week. On the other days, we had spaghetti with garlic and oil or spaghetti with beans.

But my father and I didn't mind. Spaghetti was our favorite, and we'd gladly pass up a steak for it. When I served in the Navy during World War II, the dish I missed most was my mother's spaghetti!

—*Michael Lacivita*
Youngstown, Ohio

Family Relied on Old-World Recipes

By Anthony F. Cordone, South Weymouth, Massachusetts

MY PARENTS came to America from Foggia, Italy, and after the Depression began, they had the biggest garden in Quincy, Massachusetts! Almost everything we ate or drank was homemade.

My mother was always busy canning fruits and vegetables for winter, and she made her own dough for crusty Italian bread. We also made our own Italian pork sausage with fennel seed.

Dad Made Pasta Machine

Mother made her own pasta, using a machine my father had made that looked like a square guitar. Thin strips of dough were laid on top of copper wires, and then flattened out with a rolling pin so they dropped onto the waxed paper below. They were the greatest strands of golden spaghetti you ever tasted!

Another special treat was when my father and his friends went to nearby Wollaston Beach to dig clams. They'd bring back enough to feed us for a whole week! We'd feast on mussels, quahogs, razor clams and periwinkles (small snails). We had baked, stuffed clams on the half-shell, chowders, stews, and plenty of clam juice for linguini.

For school lunches, my mother would make my favorite: dandelion sandwiches on fresh-baked bread. After the dandelions had been cleaned and boiled, she'd squeeze out the juice and fry the greens in olive oil, seasonings, salt and hot red pepper. We saved the juice, too, and drank it like a hot soup with a dash of olive oil and salt.

Tomatoes for Lunch

A favorite noon meal was crushed garden tomatoes mixed with a little olive oil, water, Italian herbs, salt and pepper, and spread over bread. When we'd finished, we'd soak up the rest of the juices with more bread until there was nothing left on the plate!

My father loved a dish made of spinach, seasonings and boiled potatoes, with stale bread dipped in the juices. That was a meal fit for a king!

Polenta fed many hungry families during the Depression, too. It's Italian-style cornmeal, which we ate either plain or covered with tomato sauce.

Our parents showed us the meaning of life and the importance of family during those tough times, and we've been on track ever since. I wouldn't have traded places with anyone.

My wife and I are now blessed with four daughters, and they and their husbands and children have given us more good reasons for living and loving than they will ever know. Looking back, I wouldn't change a thing. After all, how lucky can you get?

Depression-Era Recipes You Can Try!

THESE satisfying dishes helped today's readers of *Reminisce* magazine get through the tough times of yesterday. Just for fun, why not give them a try?

POTATO BREAD

2 medium potatoes, cooked, mashed with
    a little water (1-1/3 cups mashed potatoes)
2 tablespoons butter, softened
2 tablespoons sugar
2 tablespoons salt
3 cups warm water combined with
    2 cups warm milk
1 package (2 ounces) cake yeast, dissolved in
    1/2 cup warm (80°-90°) water
16 to 17 cups all-purpose flour (about 4 pounds)

In a large bowl, combine all ingredients except flour; stir well. Stir in 10 cups of flour, or enough to give mixture consistency of stiff cake dough. Cover and let rise 1 hour. Add enough remaining flour to make a moderately stiff dough; knead until smooth and elastic, about 10 minutes. Divide dough and shape into four loaves. Place loaves in greased 8-1/2-in. x 4-1/2-in. x 2-1/2-in. loaf pans. Cover and let rise until dough has almost doubled. Bake at 375° for about 45 minutes or until golden brown. **Yield:** 4 loaves.

THIS IS a recipe my great-grandmother brought with her from Scotland. —Lloyd G. Witt, San Diego, California

GRAHAM GEMS

1/4 cup sugar
1/4 teaspoon salt
1/2 cup all-purpose flour
2 teaspoons baking powder
1 cup whole wheat flour
1 cup milk
2 tablespoons sour cream
1 egg, beaten
Butter or margarine
Honey

In a mixing bowl, stir together first five ingredients; make a well in the center. In another bowl, combine milk, sour cream and egg; add to dry ingredients, stirring just until blended. Pour into greased muffin cups. Bake at 425° for 15 to 20 minutes or until lightly browned. Serve warm with butter and honey. **Yield:** 12 muffins.

THIS RECIPE was a staple of my mother's during the Depression. We had our own eggs, milk and cream, so with a bit of flour and leavening, these muffins were very economical. They could be served with any meal or as a snack, and they were standard fare in my lunch box! —Esther Bruning, Flagstaff, Arizona

DEPRESSION PUDDING

PUDDING:
    1-1/2 cups graham cracker crumbs (21 squares)
    4 teaspoons sugar
    1-1/2 teaspoons baking powder
    1 cup milk
    1 egg, beaten
SAUCE:
    1/2 cup packed brown sugar
    3 tablespoons all-purpose flour
    1/4 teaspoon salt
    1 cup boiling water
    1 teaspoon vanilla extract
    1 tablespoon butter *or* margarine

Combine all pudding ingredients in the top of a double boiler. Steam, covered, over simmering water for about 1 hour or until pudding tests done with a wooden pick. For sauce, combine brown sugar, flour, salt and water in a saucepan; mix until smooth. Cook, stirring, over medium-high heat until thickened and clear. Cook and stir 2 minutes longer; remove from heat. Stir in vanilla and butter. Serve over warm pudding. **Yield:** 6-8 servings.

BACK IN the 1930s, the Wear-Ever Aluminum Co. sponsored parties to sell its cookware. This dish was always served as dessert. —Edna M. Stout, Crawfordsville, Indiana

CHICKEN POTPIE

3 pounds chicken
9 cups water, *divided*
3 cups all-purpose flour
4 medium potatoes, peeled and diced
1 small onion, chopped
1 teaspoon salt
2 tablespoons snipped parsley

In a Dutch oven, combine chicken and 8 cups water. Bring to a boil; reduce heat and simmer, covered, about 2 hours or until chicken is tender. Meanwhile, mix flour and enough water (about 1 cup) to form a stiff dough. Roll very thin and cut into 1-in. squares; set aside. Remove chicken from water; set aside. Strain broth and set aside. When chicken is cool enough to handle, cut into small pieces. Return broth to Dutch oven and bring to a boil. Add dough, potatoes, onion, salt and parsley. Cook, uncovered, about 20 minutes or until vegetables and dough are tender, stirring occasionally. Season to taste with additional salt if desired. **Yield:** 10 cups.

MY great-grandmother was famous for her potpies. This is a Pennsylvania Dutch recipe that has been handed down for generations. —Joy Ryniak, Boswell, Pennsylvania

BUTTERMILK PIE

5 eggs
4 cups buttermilk, *divided*
2-3/4 cups sugar, *divided*
2/3 cup cornstarch
1/4 cup confectioners' sugar
1/8 teaspoon salt
2 pastry shells (9 inches each), baked

Separate eggs; let whites stand in a bowl at room temperature. In the top of a large double boiler, beat egg yolks with a small amount of buttermilk, 2-1/2 cups sugar, cornstarch, confectioners' sugar and salt. Add remaining buttermilk; mix well. Cook, stirring, for 20 to 25 minutes, or until thickened. Pour into pastry shells. For meringue, beat egg whites until fluffy, gradually adding remaining sugar. Spread meringue over filling, sealing to edges, and bake at 350° for 10 to 15 minutes or until lightly browned. **Yield:** 2 pies (about 16 servings).

ONE OF my favorite foods from the Great Depression was buttermilk pie. My mom had passed on the recipe verbally, which I copied down as "a handful of this and a pinch of that." With the help of my sister-in-law, I refined it, although it took at least a dozen attempts to fine-tune! —Glen H. Wallace, Pensacola, Florida

EGGLESS, MILKLESS, BUTTERLESS CAKE

2 cups packed brown sugar
2 cups water
4 tablespoons lard *or* shortening
2 cups raisins
3 cups all-purpose flour
2 teaspoons baking soda
1 teaspoon salt
2 teaspoons ground cinnamon
1 teaspoon ground cloves

In a saucepan, combine brown sugar, water, lard and raisins. Bring to a boil; reduce heat and simmer 5 minutes. Cool. Stir together flour, baking soda, salt, cinnamon and cloves. Stir into cooled raisin mixture; mix well. Pour into a greased 13-in. x 9-in x 2-in. baking pan. Bake at 350° for about 45 minutes or until cake tests done with a wooden pick. **Yield:** 16 servings.

MY GRANDMOTHER made this often during the lean years, and we loved it Now I make it for my mother. It always brings back memories. This is one cake that's good even without frosting. —Mrs. Eldon Lorenz, Cedar Falls, Iowa

Nature's Beverages Cost Nothing—Except Effort

*By Catherine Rogers
Danville, Arkansas*

IF YOU DON'T count the labor, many of us who lived in the rural South during the Depression enjoyed delicious beverages for free!

Most farmers had at least a few apple trees. After the apples were picked for pies, canning and winter storage, there were usually many culls—bruised, oddly shaped or slightly wormy apples. These weren't wasted, though; they were used to make cider. Anyone who owned a cider mill in a rural community was always popular at apple-harvesting time!

The apples were tossed into the mill, a slat-tub contraption that crushed the fruit. The juice was squeezed out into another tub, mixed with a little sugar and allowed to age a bit. That was all there was to it!

In spring, we'd watch for the sap to rise in the sassafras trees. Then it was time to dig up the roots, which were cleaned and boiled until the water turned a brilliant pink. Sweetened with a little sugar, sassafras tea was considered a tonic that helped "rebuild the

APPLE BUTTER filled the air with mouth-watering aromas as it cooked slowly over an outdoor fire. Excess apples were also saved for making tart cider.

blood" after the long, cold winters.

Later in the year, the fields and hillsides were filled with wild huckleberries and blackberries, which were gathered for pies and jellies as well as juices. In fall we'd search the hillsides for wild grapes, which were also used

to make tasty jellies and drinks.

Those with a little ingenuity could provide themselves with many beverages just by using nature's gifts. We never had to dip into the limited cash supply for these drinks, and they always lifted our spirits.

Fish, Potatoes and Milk Made Economical Meal

ONE OF my jobs as a child was to bring home "frost fish" (cod in about the 6-in. range). I often stopped on the way home from school at our fish trap in the river and brought home a bucket full of jumping frost fish. We'd have a really good meal with that fish, "pig potatoes" (the small ones that farmers left in the fields) and skim milk the dairy gave us after it removed the cream. I guess they'd call that health food today! —Arthur D. Bradford
Duxbury, Massachusetts

Home Bakery Kept Family Off Relief

WE WERE living in Milwaukee, Wisconsin during the Depression, and I did baking at home to supplement our income. I got 9¢ for a loaf of bread and 25¢ for an apple cake. I also made a "reducing bread," and had customers for that from way on the other side of town.

I cleared about $65 a month. At the time, my husband was making $1.25 a day at a friend's farm 125 miles away.

One day I heard a knock at the door. When I opened it, there stood a man who said he was a state inspector!

He said, "I understand you're baking and selling food, and as you know, there are restrictions on that." He proceeded to tell me the rules about square footage of floor space, cleanliness and so forth.

I finally told him, "Well, if you take

WORKING THE FIELDS, whether the crops were grown for food or feed, often required a little ingenuity. This young man weeded the family corn crop with a homemade cultivator.

this means of making a living away from me, we'll have to go on relief."

The inspector was very understanding, said everything was perfectly sanitary and promised not to turn me in unless the neighbors complained.

I had friendly neighbors, so I guess there were no complaints, because I kept baking for another 2-1/2 years!
—Edith Hartman Petersen
Burbank, California

Bacon Skins Seasoned Greens and Beans

HEARING the phrase "beans, bacon and gravy" reminds me of the butcher in our town, who would trim the skin from slabs of bacon and sell them in rolls for 10¢. Mother used those skins to season everything from greens to beans. Oh, how I remember those beans!

The first day we'd have beans. The second day Mother would add water and elbow macaroni to the leftovers. The next day she'd add a can of tomatoes. If there were any left after that, she'd add more water and drop dumplings into it. Seems like we ate beans all week, but they were filling and helped us survive the Depression!
—Freida E. Farrell, Suitland, Maryland

Quarter Bought Gunnysack Full of Bakers Goodies

I WOULDN'T want to live through those hard Depression years again, but I'm glad I experienced them. One treat, when we could afford it, was going to the bakery and buying a gunnysack full of baked goods for 25¢. We never knew what we had until we came home and spread it all out on a clean towel.

Each of us would pick out our favorites—bread heels, rolls or cookie pieces—and eat our goodies with a glass of milk from our cow. That quarter's worth of baked goods lasted us several days. —Eve Ernst
Milwaukie, Oregon

CHICKEN FEED: A healthy flock of chickens (left) provided plenty of eggs to sell or trade, as well as an occasional "fryer" for Sunday dinner.

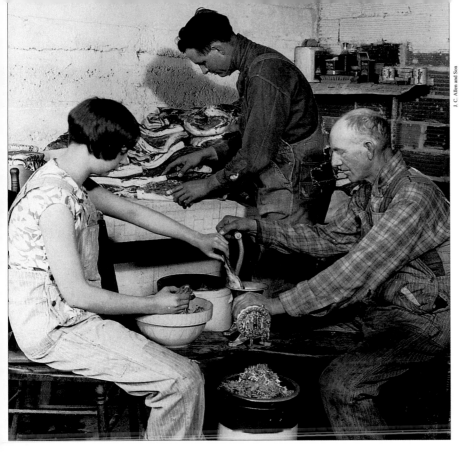

J. C. Allen and Son

The Good Earth Provided

By Ronalda H. Warren
Middlefield, Ohio

WE LIVED on what the good earth gave us during the Depression. We grew our own fruits and vegetables, and our cow provided milk, cream, sour cream, butter, buttermilk, cottage cheese and curds for my mother's cheese curd pie.

Mother was a very good cook, so we never went hungry even though the food wasn't fancy.

I recall many meals made of bread and milk, onion sandwiches or fried egg sandwiches. We'd have codfish gravy, too—when we could afford the quarter for the box of codfish. One of our favorite snacks was bread fried in bacon grease. Can you imagine what they would say today about all the cholesterol we consumed back then?

Another good dish was fried salt pork with milk gravy served over homemade bread, biscuits or mashed potatoes. My mother also made her own tomato soup from home-canned tomato juice. It wasn't very thick, but it sure was good.

One of my favorite foods from the Depression era was dried corn. Mother would cut the corn off the cob and leave it in a big pan on low heat overnight. The next day she'd put it in jars. When she wanted to use it later, she soaked it for a while, then cooked it with cream and butter.

We butchered two pigs every year, and rendered the lard for frying, preserving and baking. The press used to separate the lard from the hot fat left us with brown, crispy "cracklings," which were delicious.

The hams and bacon were smoked with bark from our hickory tree. Mother would preserve the ham in a big crock; she'd fry some ham, put it in the crock, then cover it with a layer of lard. Then she'd continue layering ham and lard until that crock was full. The crock then was stored in a cold basement for use later.

We may not have had anything fancy when we were kids, but what we did have was real and genuine. We knew we were loved, and everyone was there for each other. It was a feeling as warm as the feather ticks we slept on.◗

SAUSAGE-MAKING time (above) came each fall for farm families. After butchering, the meat was smoked, cured or ground for sausage, providing the family with enough meat to last through most of the winter.

Favorite Restaurant Served T-Bone for 75 Cents

WE HAD a large garden and raised our own chickens and rabbits during the Depression, but we did have a favorite spot for dining out when we could afford it—The Barrel in Pendleton, Oregon.

It was a drive-in restaurant with fountain service, and there was also "booth service" for an extra 10¢. The hours were 6:30 a.m. to 1 a.m. This is what part of the menu looked like in 1936:

BREAKFAST

Hamburger Steak	40¢
Ham or Bacon and Eggs, Toast, Potatoes and Coffee	50¢
Two Eggs any style, Toast, Potatoes and Coffee	35¢
Hotcakes and Coffee	20¢
Side of Ham or Bacon	15¢
Milk, Coffee, Buttermilk	5¢
Tea and Hot Chocolate	10¢

BARREL SPECIAL

T-Bone Steak, Salad, Potatoes, Toast and Coffee	75¢

SANDWICHES

Juicy Pig Barbecue	20¢
Hamburger	10¢
Hamburger Deluxe	15¢
Cheeseburger	15¢
Hot Dog	10¢
Hot Dinner Sandwich with Potatoes and Gravy	25¢
Cold Ham with Potato Salad	20¢
Fried Ham with Potato Salad	20¢
Cold Pork with Potato Salad	20¢
Tunafish	20¢
Bacon and Tomato	20¢
Ham and Egg	25¢
Cheese, Swiss or American	15¢
Lettuce and Tomato	15¢

SPECIALS

Fruit Salad	25¢
Pineapple and Cottage Cheese Salad	25¢
Shrimp Salad	35¢
Crab Salad	35¢
Potato Salad	15¢
Baked Bean Plate	25¢
Macaroni Plate	25¢
Cold Plate Lunch	35¢
Watermelon on Ice	15¢

—Dorothy Buresh
Chehalis, Washington

Tasty Reward Made Kids' Work Worthwhile

By Ron Stauder
Belleville, Illinois

AS CHILDREN during the 1930s, my sister and I enjoyed the rewards we earned. During summer, we picked fruits and vegetables from our garden and orchard, and from the neighbors' orchards for a small fee. Our mother would can what we picked, using recipes handed down from our grandparents.

My job was to retrieve last year's fruit jars from the cellar and wash them in a big tub outside before they were sterilized in the kitchen. Then I'd be sent to the store with my wagon to pick up supplies like sugar, vinegar and spices.

Since we lived some distance from the store, the trip took a while, but it was so rewarding to come home to those wonderful fragrances emanating from the kitchen! I could pick up the scent as far as a block away. I'd walk in with my mouth watering, and Mom always handed me a spoon or bowl to lick.

After everything was canned, it was carefully carried to the cellar. My sister and I always looked forward to the day when we were told to bring up the first home-canned goods of the year, usually a week after the first heavy frost. I can still taste those peaches, pears, pickles and tomatoes, and especially the jellies and preserves spooned onto a piece of warm bread.

Our father's trucking business fell off during the Depression, but he occasionally did some hauling for the WPA. We were told that whenever one of the Treasury Department checks arrived, Dad would buy us a quart of ice cream. Our mailbox was about 3 blocks away, but the promise of a treat like that gave us plenty of incentive to check the mail regularly! The taste of that vanilla ice cream covered with strawberry or raspberry preserves is something we've never forgotten.

We didn't have much, but we appreciated the small returns we received in reward for our labors.

WATER BATHS, mason jars and canning lids crowded the kitchens of many Depression-era families during late summer. It was a lot of work, but home canning preserved fruits, vegetables, juices and even meats for the long winter ahead.

'Our Parents Were Our Greatest Gifts'

WE DIDN'T have much during the Depression, but we learned how to get by. During the leanest years, we usually had oatmeal with diluted canned milk for breakfast. I can't remember ever having fresh milk; I guess the canned variety was cheaper.

For lunch or dinner, we ate a lot of what Mother called "poor man's dish," which consisted of macaroni, tomatoes and some ground beef.

Greens were there for the taking in the spring. We often went out to look for dandelions before they bloomed, then Mother would cook them like spinach, mixing them with a mayonnaise sauce and serving it over potatoes. If she had any bacon, she'd add bits of that, too.

Our parents never complained, nor did they expect anyone to give us anything. The government was giving food away then, but my dad was too proud to take it.

I'm happy I lived during that time; it taught me that material things aren't what's important in life. The greatest gifts we had were our parents and the example they set for us. They taught us that you can accomplish anything if you believe you can, and if you work hard enough.

—*Dorothy Rhoads Ness*
Annapolis, Maryland

CHAPTER FIVE

Make It Last, Wear It Out

Make It Last, Wear It Out

There are some things about the Depression days that you can explain to people who didn't live through them. You can talk about people being out of work, and they understand. You can talk about money being scarce, and they understand. You can talk about families having fun without spending a lot of money, and they, well, sort of understand. But start talking about clothing and you have a big problem. The problem is that people under 45 can't imagine a time before orlon and rayon and nylon and phony leather and permanent-press fabrics.

It's a little like trying to explain to a centipede what it's like to have just two legs.

I'm convinced that the one big thing we had going for us during the Depression was that none of these test-tube marvels had come along yet. There was cotton. And wool. And genuine leather. This was sturdy stuff that could be passed along through a whole generation, unlike most of today's clothing, which seems barely able to make it through a single season.

Didn't Cotton to Shrinkage

Of course there were drawbacks, too. Cotton tended to shrink, but in totally unpredictable amounts. Kids did not enjoy this, since the prudent mother always bought things at least one size larger than needed "because it will shrink some."

She also had her eye on saving money, so she bought at least one size larger than needed "because you will grow into it."

The upshot of these strategies was that when you saw a kid with new clothes, you saw a lot more clothes than kid. Things generally were dandy the second year, but then took a turn for the worse the third year when cuffs and shirtsleeves were 3 in. short of where they were meant to be.

The same thing happened with shoes, although at least they didn't shrink. I don't know about your family, but in ours, Dad was the boss when it came to shoe-buying. He followed the same plan Mom did—buy 'em a size too large "because you'll grow into them."

But all this is from a male perspective. Sometimes I think girls had it better. Every Depression mother knew how to sew. Most were very good at it, too. So they'd take daughters in hand, go to the local dry goods store and pore over the Butterick and Simplicity pattern books until they found the "perfect" pattern. Then they'd paw through bolt after bolt of yard goods until they found just the right color and design, pick out buttons at the button counter, buy a spool of J&P Coats thread and head home.

Stitched to Fit

Patterns were shuffled and rearranged to get the most efficient use of the material (leftovers went into the "ragbag" for future quilts). Pieces were pinned together and tried on, and then the Singer was fired up for a flurry of stitching until a custom-made, hand-tailored dress was finished.

That's why my sister's clothes always seemed to fit. None of this "you'll grow into it" stuff. Hems and even seams could be let out next year. Me, I just walked around with pant legs somewhere between my ankles and knees.

I ask you, how can a person of the Depression explain this to people of the Disposable Society, who buy their synthetic marvels at Wal-Mart or Kmart and hope they'll last until spring?

How do you explain it to kids who refuse to wear their perfectly good T-shirt on the grounds that last month's rock star is now old hat and no one at school would be caught dead wearing a shirt with his picture on it?

How do you explain it to the young parent who shells out $80 for a pair of sneakers that have the life expectancy of an ice cube in a frying pan?

You don't. Like they say, you had to be there…. —*Clancy Strock*

PRETTY PROJECT: When Bee Henisey of Glendale, California was 12 years old (far right), she made the dress she's wearing as a project for her seventh-grade sewing class. This photo appeared in her hometown newspaper, with a caption explaining that the only items purchased for the project were a zipper, a few inches of ruching (lace trim) and a 10¢ pattern. "I still have the dress," Bee reports. "My granddaughter can wear it."

Feed Sacks Helped Stretch the Family Budget

DURING the Depression, when I was growing up, we couldn't afford many "store-bought" things. I didn't mind that at all, because I knew there would always be plenty of clothing for Mom and me, made from those pretty sacks that our feed came in!

Mom sewed aprons, nightshirts, pajamas, dish towels, tablecloths, sheets and pillowcases from those feed sacks. If we were lucky enough to get quite a few sacks with the same color and pattern, Mom would make curtains and comforters, too. When there was material bearing any print Mom didn't like, it went into a special box for use later in weaving rugs.

Not all feed sacks were printed, though. When Mom got the plain ones that were light tan, she bleached them. The whitest, softest ones were made into warm petticoats and bloomers.

By Margie Landegard
St. Olaf, Iowa

Flour sacks were usually white with a simple plaid design. These had a softer weave and were very absorbent, so they were packed in the back of our kitchen drawer for use as special "Sunday dish towels."

Sugar sacks were smaller, plain white, and made of thinner fabric. They

---

*"Those feed sacks
were precious
to the farm wife..."*

---

were ideal for straining "crackling" from fresh-rendered lard. We also used them for straining milk, as drip bags for jelly and as bandages.

We made good use of seed bags,

too, in those days. Seed usually came in cloth bags printed with a bright company logo. Those labels were stubborn and wouldn't always bleach out, so Mom turned them into hand towels for the men. With repeated washings in strong soap, the print eventually faded. Factory-made bags were sewn together with sturdy cords that could be unraveled and saved.

So we even made secondary use of that string—we used it for mending, patching, tying sausages and even securing bandages.

Those sacks were precious to the farm wife, and if she had any she didn't need, she saved them. Even when she and her husband retired from farming and moved to town, any remaining feed sacks went along with her. You can still find them at estate sales, but the bidding is always brisk!

He Wanted a Shirt, But Got an Heirloom

I CAN STILL remember my dad bringing home chicken feed and flour in printed bags, and listening to my mother and sisters talk about what to make out of them.

When I was a young lad of about 8, Dad was going to town to pick up four sacks of flour. He said I could go along. Mother told me she needed two sacks printed with small blue flowers, and that I could pick out two other sacks in any pattern I liked, because she wanted to make a shirt for me.

At the store, I found the two sacks my mother wanted, but what really got my attention was two sacks covered with a print of big yellow daisies. I thought it was the prettiest material I'd ever seen!

When we got home, I asked my mother to make my shirt from those colorful sacks. But Mother told me that boys just didn't wear loud clothes, and *certainly not shirts with yellow daisies* on them. She made my sister a blouse from those sacks instead. I was disappointed, but eventually I forgot about it.

But Mother never forgot. Many years later, she gave me a patchwork quilt she'd made. When I opened the gift box, I immediately saw the quilt was made with several squares of that yellow daisy material that I had loved so much!

—*Royce Verges, Sikeston, Missouri*

Shirley Sutton

THE FIRST FEED SACKS, like those at left, were emblazoned with the feed companies' names in bold type. Thrifty homemakers transformed the sacks into household linens, and even bloomers like those above hanging out to dry. The patterned sacks used for dresses and other clothing arrived later.

From Single Sack to Special Dress

I GREW UP in a small, exclusive suburb. We were considered "different" in our neighborhood because we had a garden and raised chickens. Who can say how the other kids would have reacted if they had found out my sister and I wore dresses made out of feed sack cloth?

I never cared, because one of the most exciting things for me was to go to the feed store with my father on Saturday mornings. My sister and I would take turns choosing the bags with the designs we liked best. Whoever picked out the bag got something made out of it.

One Saturday it was my turn to choose the sack, and, since it was getting close to the new school year, I thought a new dress for my first day would be nice. I found a beautiful sack that had a sky-blue background with gorgeous mallard ducks on it.

The only trouble was, there was only one sack like this. I was getting a little big for a dress made out of just one sack.

My mother, being the sewing whiz she was, found a pretty dress pattern and managed to complete the dress out of that one sack by making the sleeves out of white pique.

It was the prettiest dress I had ever seen! I was very happy to wear it the first day of school—and many days after that.

—*Florence Davis*
Amesbury, Massachusetts

That Was No Hand Towel!

WE USED feed and flour sacks for bed sheets, pillowcases, curtains, towels and all our apparel, including underwear.

On one memorable occasion, our washing machine broke down and it was beyond repair. An enterprising young salesman brought a Maytag washer out to demonstrate its merits. My mother sorted the wash and asked him to start with the sheets and towels, which were all made of feed sacks.

At one point, the salesman wanted to wipe his hands. He reached down into the laundry pile and grabbed some white material he thought to be a towel.

Much to my mother's embarrassment, he was wiping his hands on her bloomers! They just happened to be made out of the same material as the towels and sheets. My sister and I laughed so hard our sides ached!

—*Dorothy Paterick, Shawano, Wisconsin*

Her Favorite Feed Sacks Are in the Smithsonian!

I WAS ONE of seven children, and the feed sack was the *only* fabric our mother had for making our clothes. I never realized how poor we were. I only knew how much fun it was to go into town on Saturday and look through the new sacks of feed to find a pattern Mother and I were fond of. It was such a treat to be able to pick out my very own design!

Many years later, my husband and I were visiting the Smithsonian Institution in Washington, D.C. I lingered over one of the exhibits while my husband went on ahead. Suddenly, he called back over his shoulder, "Guess what? There's a display up here of feed sack patterns with explanations of how they were made into dresses!"

Excited, I rushed to join him. To my amazement, hanging there in the exhibit were the two patterns Mother had used to make my very favorite dresses! We'd just seen a display of America's first flag, and that had given me goose bumps—but those were nothing compared with the goose bumps I got when I saw those feed sacks again. What memories!

—*Mrs. Dave Morton, Orlando, Florida*

These Pajamas Were The Cat's Meow

DURING THE Depression, most of us felt the challenge of "making do." One friend's husband was lucky enough to have a job during those years, but his salary was low, so he supplemented the family income by raising chickens.

He bought his chicken feed in large bags made of good cotton muslin, and

SEEING TRIPLE: When Muriel Church of Kingsley, Michigan set out to make new clothes for her three daughters, she didn't stop at just dresses. She made them matching feed sack bathing suits, too (see photo at lower left)! Daughters Neta, Eva and Loann apparently were proud of their mom's stitchery and enjoyed showing off her handiwork for the camera.

the back of each sack was printed with a lion's head.

My friend was happy whenever her husband emptied these sacks, for this couple had two small boys. To save money, she used the sacks to make their pajamas. The boys loved them because she cut the material so each pajama top had the lion's head on the back.

When some of the family's more affluent relatives brought their small son for a visit, the youngster was so taken with those feed sack pajamas that he began crying. He wanted a lion's head on *his* pajama top, too!

The problem was easily solved once my friend got a few more empty sacks. In a short time, the little cousin had lion's-head pajamas all his own.

—*Mrs. Harry R. McLaughlin
DeRidder, Louisiana*

Up, Up and Away!

WHEN I WAS a girl of 9, my favorite feed sack dress had a yellow background and a red paisley design. That paisley pattern reminded me of tiny red caterpillars, bending to begin spinning their cocoons.

I used to daydream and hope that one day those caterpillars would turn into beautiful crimson butterflies and carry me off into the sky—a mighty accomplishment for a humble feed sack!

—*Susan I. Katz
Phoenixville, Pennsylvania*

An Embarrassing 'Slip'

MY MOTHER made a number of things out of feed sacks, including undergarments. She always bleached the sacks until they were white, but once in a while she'd have trouble getting the printed words out of them.

One day, she was dressing for a meeting of her church circle and put on a thin voile dress—over one of her homemade feed sack slips.

I looked at her, all dressed up, and said, "Mom, you can't wear that dress over that slip. You can read the print right through it." It read: "100 lbs. Net Weight." We sure got a laugh out of that!

—*Dorothy Kyes, Valparaiso, Indiana*

Remember Bleaching Those Feed Sacks?

ONE DAY my mama showed me how to bleach feed sacks so we could make them into clothes, and I helped her from that day on. Most sacks had only names printed on them, but some came in colors, and red dye was always the hardest to get out.

We'd rub Fels-Naptha soap into the sacks, scrub them on a washboard, then boil them in a big tub on the stove. After a thorough rinsing, we soaked them again in bleach and soap. Sometimes even that wasn't enough, and they had to be boiled again to get out the last hint of color.

Once the color was gone, the cloth was stamped with designs and embroidered for tea towels or tablecloths. The first year I was married, I embroidered and appliqued 12 flour sacks into luncheon cloths for Christmas presents.

—Mrs. C.R. Leonard
Ridgecrest, California

FEED SACK FAVORITES: Wanda Yates of Fontana, California (left) and her cousin Dorothy made their own dresses from floral-print feed sacks when they were in junior high school. "We had several dresses made from feed sacks, but these were our favorites because we made them ourselves," Wanda recalls. "We were so proud of them!"

Daughter Wore 'Designer Original'

BACK DURING those "hard times", sewing with feed sacks was part of our way of life. We raised only a few chickens, so I had a limited number of sacks from which to choose. But a chicken farm a few miles away had more sacks than its owners could use, and they sold extras for 25¢ each—not bad for more than a yard of material!

Once, I found two sacks with tiny red flowers sprinkled on a white background. I used these sacks to make a dress for my youngest daughter. It was quite a sight, trimmed with red rickrack, small red buttons and a sash that tied in back with a big bow.

One day I had to go to an office in town on business and my daughter came

BERRY GOOD GARB: Dorothy Paterick (front right) and her sister (holding pail) donned feed sack aprons before going on a berry-picking expedition. The three other young ladies are neighbors who joined them for the outing. "Feed sacks were strong, useful and durable," says Dorothy, who's from Shawano, Wisconsin. "Some pillowcases made from them are still being used today!"

with me, wearing her new dress. A lady in the office commented on how pretty the dress was. When I said I'd made it from feed sacks, she could hardly believe it. She repeated her compliment and then said, admiringly, "It is remarkable what some folks can do."

I was so pleased that I walked out feeling as though I'd created a "designer original" from those two lowly feed sacks! —Beulah Sutton Waite
Sullivan, Illinois

Worn with Pride

MY FOLKS raised hundreds of chickens, so we had plenty of feed sacks, and my mother used them to make most of my clothes. She used the prints for items like dresses, and saved the white ones or those with lettering on them for undergarments.

One day at a family picnic, we kids were turning somersaults on the grass. Suddenly, everyone began laughing!

I stood up, wondering what was going on. An uncle asked me, "So you're the Pride of the Rockies?" I didn't understand what he meant until he explained, "That's what it says on your underpants!" Embarrassed? You bet!

—Joyce A. Coleman
Hotchkiss, Colorado

Feed Sacks Dressed Family in Style

AS A MOTHER of nine children—six of them girls—my sewing machine was constantly running. Using it, I was able to completely outfit my daughters for school with the aid of those pretty feed sacks.

I really felt like a designer—although I'd use the same pattern over and over, each dress was a little different, with changes to the necklines, sleeves and trimmings. And the variety, color and designs of those feed sacks seemed limitless!

I don't think our daughters ever felt

deprived, or that they weren't dressed as well as their classmates. In fact, some of the feed sacks could even be used for more fancy attire.

The one I remember best was a floral design with a gold thread running through it. I used that pattern to make a party dress for our oldest daughter, and she felt it was the most beautiful dress in the world. —Melba Bender
Sidney, Ohio

LIKE MOTHER, LIKE...: Verna Olson of Montevideo, Minnesota made matching dresses for herself and her daughter. Marge. "We wore them everywhere, except church," she recalls. Like many of her neighbors, Verna used chicken feed sacks for her creations. "It was fun comparing prints and dresses. Those lucky enough to have a lot of chickens had quite an assortment of dresses."

Mom Held the Answer to a Little Girl's Prayer

DURING THE Depression, we lived on a small farm along the Illinois River, so we knew what feed sack dresses were all about. All our dresses and skirts were made from that material—and *only* that material!

We went to town once a week to exchange eggs for groceries, and to buy whatever else we needed for the week. The highlight of the trip was always the stop at the feed store. We were delighted to see all the pretty material, and my sisters and I usually got to choose which print we wanted.

On one of those trips, I found a rose-patterned print I will never forget. It was the most beautiful thing I'd ever seen. To my disappointment, only two sacks were available in that print, and my

By Jalie Boulware
Auxvasse, Missouri

mother would've needed at least three to make what I wanted—a new dress. We took the two sacks anyway. All the way home I kept hoping that my

---

"I hoped my mother could 'stretch' two sacks into three…"

⚛

---

mother could "stretch" those sacks somehow, or that a miracle would turn the two sacks into three.

As I lay down to sleep that night, I prayed for a new dress out of those two small pieces of cloth, but I knew my

prayers wouldn't be answered. It just couldn't be done.

Next morning, when I went downstairs, hanging there in the kitchen doorway was a beautiful rose-patterned jumper! Without saying a word, my mother had made it for me after I went to bed.

The design was plain, but to me it was the most beautiful dress I could have ever imagined. I was proud to wear it to church on Easter Sunday.

SEWING MACHINES like the vintage Singer in photo above were vital to most Depression-era households. Some women became so skilled at creating clothes for their families that they made their own patterns.

'Making Do' Was Way of Life for Her Family

By Mary Ann Kunselman
Longmont, Colorado

OUR FAMILY of five moved to Colorado from Missouri just before the Depression started. Money was always scarce, but we got by thanks to the food and animals we raised, and thanks to my mother's thrift. I don't know when I first heard the phrase "Make over, make do, or do without," but it must have been during the Depression!

Our clothes were usually hand-me-downs from friends and neighbors, but Mother made them over to fit us, and they always looked like they were our very own clothes, not someone else's.

One winter a neighbor gave Mother

> ● ─────────────────────── ●
>
> *"Our clothes were hand-me-downs, but Mom made them over to fit us..."*
>
> ● ─────────────────────── ●

several old coats, skirts and men's suits made from wool, corduroy and other heavy materials. Mother ripped them all apart, pressed the fabric, cut the pieces into squares, and made quilt tops, half of which she returned to the neighbor. (She believed in "share and share alike"!) Those quilts sure made warm covers on cold winter nights.

Mother taught my twin sister, Martha, and me how to sew, too. We used her basting thread, which she saved for us by pulling it out in one long, unbroken piece.

Years later, a childhood friend told me that she and her sisters always liked coming to our house because we could sew doll clothes. They couldn't do that because their family couldn't afford to buy any extra thread. I just assumed that *all* mothers saved their basting thread for their daughters' sewing projects!

Occasionally Mother was able to buy some new material—usually an inexpensive cotton print. If Martha and I were lucky, we each got one new dress in the fall, and our brother got one new pair of pants. We always changed clothes immediately after school, because those new clothes had to last the whole year.

Another way we got by during those years was to collect our own firewood. In the summer Daddy would hitch up the horses to the wagon, and we'd pack a picnic lunch and head for the river, about a mile away. While Mother and

Daddy sawed up big limbs and dead tree trunks, we kids collected all the smaller pieces of wood we could find.

When we got too hot and tired, we'd take off our shoes and socks and go wading in the cool, clear water. We were all tired by the time we got home in the late afternoon, but it was always a great day, and we'd have enough firewood to last a long time.

I believe those of us who grew up in those times were richer than we realized. We learned to cope with almost anything, and we learned some valuable lessons.

Those experiences have stayed with me, too. I've always shared my quilt scraps, magazines and books with others who might enjoy them. I still save every scrap of sewing materials, make scratch paper from junk mail and stash away all my plastic grocery bags and cottage cheese containers. (I'm very glad that many of these items can be recycled now!)

Sometimes my children and grandchildren kid me for saving so many things, but they never went through the Depression. Those of us who did will never forget it.◗

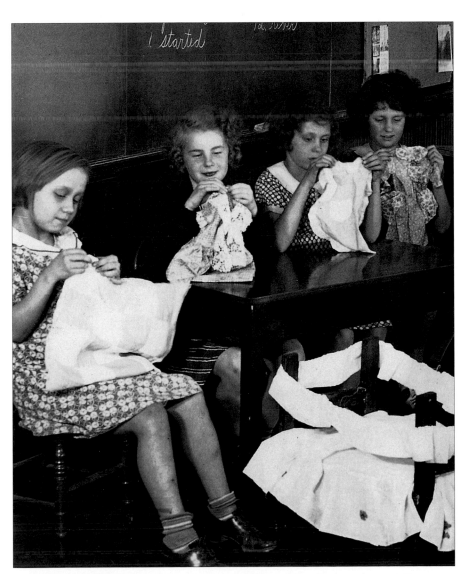

LITTLE SEAMSTRESSES found many opportunities to hone their sewing skills. Joyce Burke of Huntington, West Virginia (second from left) and three classmates stitched doll dresses and a doll-sized bedspread for a school project.

She Grew into Her Winter Coat...for 8 Years

By Barbara Faber
Lamar, Colorado

"MAKING DO" without complaint was a universal characteristic of families who lived through the Dirty Thirties. But really, what choice did we have? There was very little money.

Our family lived in southeastern Colorado, and I remember making do even as a child. My grandmother sent me a coat when I was 2-1/2 years old. It was so large that my fingers didn't reach the edge of the cuff until I was in third grade. It was a perfect fit by the time I reached fifth grade.

Having been swallowed up in that big coat for 8 long years, I just didn't like it anymore. My older brother had a

---

> *"My brother had an old coat like mine. He didn't like his either..."*

---

coat just like mine. and just as oversized. I don't think he liked his coat either.

The outer shell of those coats was made of a material called "oil skin." It was slick and looked like plastic; my coat was red, and my brother's green. Though they weren't much to behold,

ROLLED-UP SLEEVES were a common sight on kids' clothes during the Depression. If a hand-me-down coat didn't quite fit and couldn't be altered, children knew they'd just have to "grow into it"! Barbara Faber of Lamar, Colorado shared the photo.

our coats were lined in sheepskin and were very warm.

We never complained about our old coats because we didn't know any different. And complaining wouldn't have done much good anyway—there was no money for new coats.

Finally Spoke Up

As I was entering fifth grade, however, I did make one comment. Mother was taking out the winter clothes when I happened to see my coat. "Do I have to wear this again?" I asked.

I did have to...but not for long.

A few months later at Christmas, I was overwhelmed to open a package and find a beautiful blue *cloth* coat! The rest of the gifts were the usual Christmas fare: some pecans, an orange in our stockings, and maybe a pair of mittens. I hardly noticed those gifts at all because I was so *thrilled* with my new coat. Finally, I had a coat I didn't have to grow into!

As I look back through the years, that blue coat remains the highlight of all my Christmases. My parents couldn't afford a new coat, but somehow they made the sacrifice for me. It was that kind of sharing and love that saw us through the Dirty Thirties.

Homecoming Queen Made Her Own Gown for $1.20!

I MADE many of my own clothes when I was in high school, but my senior year in 1934 posed a special challenge!

As graduation time approached, the high-school and seventh- and eighth-grade students cast votes for a senior girl as homecoming queen. I had made no special plans for homecoming, thinking I didn't have a chance. But when the votes were counted, I had won!

Naturally, I was excited, but when I told my parents I would need a special dress for homecoming, they said we just couldn't afford one. I was disappointed, but I couldn't stop thinking about it. I knew I could make the dress myself if I could just find the money for material!

I sometimes worked in the principal's office, answering the phone and helping with paperwork, and I knew there was a petty cash fund used to buy supplies for needy students. One day I got up my nerve and asked the principal if the school could give me just enough money to buy material for my homecoming dress.

He said anyone who received such an honor should be willing to buy her dress. When I explained that I couldn't

afford it, he asked, "How much money are we talking about?'" I replied, "I think I can make the dress for $1.20."

The principal just smiled and said, "Anyone who thinks she can make a homecoming queen's dress for $1.20 deserves a chance to try!" And he gave me the money!

A friend drove me to the nearest village, where I bought 7 yards of cheesecloth for 70¢, three packages of white crepe paper for 45¢ and a small spool of thread for 5¢.

I made a foundation garment from part of the cheesecloth, hand-stitched crepe paper to the bodice, ruffled a piece of paper for a collar, and then cut the rest of the paper into strips for ruffles, which I stitched in tiers from the waist to the floor. The rest of the cheesecloth was used to make a train.

My crown was a piece of cardboard covered with gold foil, and I carried a bouquet of fresh apple blossoms from my parents' orchard.

The highlight of my reign came when the mother of a younger student said, "My daughter thinks you're beautiful, and she wants to look just like you when she graduates!"

—*Mildred Gilliam, Tipp City, Ohio*

Extra Help on Washdays

NOT ALL feed and flour sacks were taken apart for sewing. Some were left intact for carrying or storing things. On washdays, many women would put their undergarments inside a bag and hang it in a sunny spot. That way, the underwear got dry—but without being seen by all the neighbors!

—*Mary Alice Pope*
Pocahontas, Arkansas

Creative Mom Turned Drafty House into Cozy Home

IN THE DEEP Depression days of the early 1930s we lived in a drafty old tenant farmhouse. My mother worked hard to make it a home, and even at age 6 I knew that she was unusually creative.

We had no running water, but thanks to Mother we did have a "sink"! She punched a hole in the bottom of an old dishpan, attached a funnel underneath, and hooked that up to a rubber hose that ran through a hole cut in the floor.

That's just one example of how Mother learned to "make do." Here are a few more:

In our front room, she covered the bare wooden walls with a combination of burlap feed sacks and three different patterns of wallpaper a friend had given

her. She worked the wallpaper scraps into an attractive design, affixing them with a flour-and-water paste.

Mother even made a sofa for us! She cut some old bedsprings in half with an ax and placed the springs on a wooden frame she had built herself. She made the seats and back from a chintz fabric backed with flannel, and stuffed the cushions with "unginned" cotton

she had picked with her own hands.

The central room of our house was covered with wallboard, and Mother took care of that, too. She went to the creek bank and brought home tubs and buckets of clay, which she spread over the walls. When the clay dried, it was a pale buff color—much more attractive than the wallboard had been!

—*Jonnie Gregory, Mathis, Texas*

Thrift Didn't Pay on Bank-Closing Day!

IN EARLY 1930 I was about to enter nursing school, and I needed a raincoat. Like all country folks at that time, we had very little money.

Most of the raincoats I had seen were very cheap and tacky looking—at least to my young tastes. I had my heart set on a "French style" coat that I had seen in one department store. That coat cost the unheard-of sum of $14.98. I had all of $15.77 in the bank.

I begged my father to let me withdraw the money, and after some time, he finally relented. *The next day,* our local bank in Newton Falls, Ohio closed.

Daddy never again saw the money he had in that bank. But I had my raincoat, and it lasted for years and years!

—*Mary Frances Evans*
Ocala, Florida

GOOD-BYE, OLD PAINT: Home improvement projects were a do-it-yourself proposition for many homeowners during the Depression.

Mom Gave New Life to Worn Sheets, Shirt Collars

MY DAD worked in construction, building new homes, but when the Depression hit, there was no new construction. After searching for work for several weeks, he finally found a job driving a cab.

Dad worked long hours and barely made enough for us to live on, so there was no money left for things like linens. But my mother was thrifty, and used her sewing machine to help us economize.

When our sheets wore out, the material would be threadbare in the middle. Mother would rip the sheet right down the middle, sew the outside edges together, then hem the worn sides. The sheet now had a seam down the middle, but we got extra use out of it.

When the sheets became too worn to use on the beds, Mother used the least-worn parts to make pillowcases. She even used the scraps to make pot holders, which she trimmed with red stitching. No one could stretch the life of a common white sheet like my mother!

She also put her skills to work on my father's shirts. When a collar became frayed, she'd carefully rip it out, turn it around and reinsert it into the body of the shirt. The collar looked almost like new!

When I outgrew a dress, Mother let down the hem, which invariably left a worn white line. Mother had a solution for that, too. She covered the old hemline with tape or rickrack, which not only disguised the old hemline but gave the dress a "lift."

Our family got through the Depression just fine, thanks to Dad's cab-driving and Mother's thrift!

—*Ruth Tvedten, Grand Rapids, Michigan*

Our Clothing Taught Us About Recycling

IT MAY be surprising to youngsters, but the jeans we wore through the Depression were very much like the ones in style today—faded and wrinkled from repeated washing.

I'll admit our jeans didn't fit like those of today, but we certainly got more for our money!

We called jeans "bibless overalls" back in the '30s, though Levi Strauss sold them as "waist overalls."

I bought my jeans through the Sears catalog and there was nothing glamorous about them. They were actually men's pants, as no jeans were made specifically for women until about 1935. I wore them cinched in at the waist with a leather belt. High fashion didn't matter around the house or farmyard.

When I wanted to go to town I had two dresses from which to choose. One morning I was putting one of them on when I found that a grasshopper had gnawed a big hole in the front of it!

I was reduced to one "good" outfit, just like my husband, who had one pair of pants and one sweater (besides the jeans and shirt he wore every day). Our kids' clothes were strictly "make-overs."

Relatives gave us their used clothes. Though these articles were old, they were constructed of good material, and when "made up," they really looked nice. I made pants for our son from a pair of his grandpa's corduroys. And I made his coat from an old coat of mine. Used coats normally looked just like new when they were turned inside out.

We'd never heard of recycling back in the 1930s—but we were practicing it. Everyone was making do. It wasn't so bad having to wear cheap clothes if all your neighbors wore the same kind.

—*Rose Van Schaack, Mesa, Arizona*

'We Invented Our Own Dish Soap!'

THERE WAS no such thing as liquid soap in the 1930s, so we used salt sacks to invent our own!

The sacks were 6 to 7 in. wide and 10 to 12 in. long, and we used them as dishcloths after carefully removing the "pull thread." To make "liquid soap," we'd put a bar of Crystal white soap in the sack and soak it in dishwater. In a few minutes, the soap was soft enough to make a lather inside the sack.

Once the soap had softened, we'd open the top of the sack just enough to blow a little air inside. Then we'd close the sack and squeeze. The result was plenty of bubbles, much like the ones we get today by adding a little liquid soap to dishwater.

The convenience of today's dishwashing liquid is nice, but it was lots more fun to make our own!

—*Margaret Berlien*
Great Falls, Montana

A.M. Wettach

SOAP-MAKING is all but a lost art today, but during the 1930s many farm families (left) helped keep expenses down with homemade soap.

"WATCH IT, MOM!" Clothing was mended, patched and then re-patched to make it last as long as possible. A few mending jobs, like this one (right), just couldn't wait!

'We Made Tracks with Home Shoe-Repair Kits'

WHEN I graduated from high school in 1931, the only job I could find was as a helper in a sign shop. The job paid $7.50 a week for 60 hours of work.

At that time, many thousands of people were unemployed and they spent their days walking the streets to look for work. In doing so, they wore out a lot of shoe leather. The five-and-dime stores came up with an economical answer to that problem.

The stores sold stick-on rubber shoe soles for 20¢ per pair, complete with a tube of rubber cement. Such do-it-yourself shoe repairs were messy but very practical.

So many miles were put on shoe soles that it inspired some wry humor. Whenever a person met a friend on the street, he would ask the friend, "Are you working now?"

"Yes," the friend often replied, "for Walker & Turner."

This meant he was *walking* the streets and *turning* the corners!

—*R.S. Croom, Norfolk, Virginia*

'I Made Shoes from Hats!'

BOTH MY daughters were born during the Depression, and we had to make do with whatever we could. I was a proud mother and I wanted my little girls to have shoes, so I cut patterns to fit their feet and made shoes from secondhand felt hats. Our relatives and neighbors

STURDY SHOES were often in short supply for families on tight budgets; Many people received needed footwear from charitable organizations that collected secondhand shoes by the boxful.

helped out by giving me hats they no longer needed.

The shoes were made in a moccasin style, so I'd stitch designs or sew beads on them to make them prettier. The felt would wear out quickly, so I'd make new shoes from that heap of old hats every Friday or Saturday.

That way, my daughters would have "new shoes" for church on Sunday.

—*Mrs. W.F. Clark Valley Head, Alabama*

Straw Stuffed Under Rugs Saved on Heating Costs

LIVING THROUGH the Depression helped us grow and made us better folks. It gave me a strength I'd never had before.

My aunt kept our old farmhouse warm and saved on fuel by stuffing straw beneath rugs. All of us kids would drag the rugs outside and beat them on the clothesline to remove the dust. Then we'd fill buckets with soapy water, wrap towels around our feet, dip them in the water and waltz over the floors!

Our aunt played marching music on the old Victrola to urge us on, and we'd skid over the floors and laugh and have a marvelous time!

After we'd soaped the floors, my oldest brother would wrap burlap sacks around his feet and carefully go over the floors to remove the water. When the floors were dry, we'd scatter fresh straw over the floor, paying special attention to the corners and any cracks. Finally, the big rugs were

brought back inside and placed on top of the straw and tacked down. After about a week, the stuffing would flatten out and we had nice, warm floors.

Electricity in rural areas was expensive then, but our aunt had a way to save money on that as well. During the summer, when the fans were running, she'd hang wet sheets across the doorways of our bedrooms to help keep us cool and comfortable.

We also saved money by storing our food in the cool springhouse. Milk, cream, butter, vegetables, fruits and some meats were all placed in and around the stream. Sometimes we kids sat in the springhouse to cool off, too!

Although those were grim times, we had many bright moments, and I believe the lack of money actually brought our family closer. The days I remember most vividly are those when we did things *together.*

—*Juni Dunklin, Sandersville, Georgia*

CHAPTER SIX

Cherished Photos

FOR MOST OF US, family photos are the possessions we treasure most. During the Depression years, cameras were a luxury and photographs were taken only rarely, making pictures from that era even more precious to their owners.

WHEN OTTO Wesolowski bought his first car (at right) around 1933, his friends and family just couldn't wait to pile into it! "The car ran occasionally on gasoline, but mostly it was pushed by our friends," report's Otto's wife, Thelma. The couple lives in Cincinnati, Ohio.

FANCY DRESSES of silk and satin were made for Sarah Gross and her sisters (opposite page) by their Aunt Frances. Sarah, of Orland Park, Illinois, later learned the fabrics were casket-lining remnants from the company where their Uncle Leo worked. Aunt Frances saved the small pieces until she had enough to make each girl a dress.

Welcome to America's Family Photo Album of the '30s. A photo is a moment in time, frozen forever. Just a hundredth of a second out of a lifetime—the blink of an eye—but long enough to capture a memory or a moment that can be savored again and again, and then passed on from generation to generation.

You have, of course, heard the saying that a picture is worth a thousand words. Sometimes it is even the equivalent of a book. There's so much to see. The pride of a parent. The joy of children. The optimistic happiness of a bride and groom. A lifetime of living in the eyes of a grandparent.

Photos tell us where we've been and who we were. Nothing else can do it as well.

Our Past Pictured

That's how we know so much about the Depression years. They were superbly documented on film by men and women, many of whom later became internationally famous. Most were funded by various government agencies, including the WPA and the Department of Agriculture. Their work provides a remarkable national treasure, recording in great detail the devastation of the Dust Bowl years, as well as the grinding hardships of the Depression.

Doubtless you've seen many of those photos. But most in this book are of a different sort. They were taken by folks just like us, usually with cheap box cameras and no special photographic skills. Today their prints are faded and cracked with age.

What did they choose to photograph? Not the miseries of the era, but the intimate family moments and occasions. The happy times they shared. The homes they lived in. The places where they worked, the cars they owned, the rare holidays they enjoyed.

So here is America's Family Photo Album of the '30s. We hope you enjoy these pictures contributed by your friends and neighbors and relatives.

—*Clancy Strock*

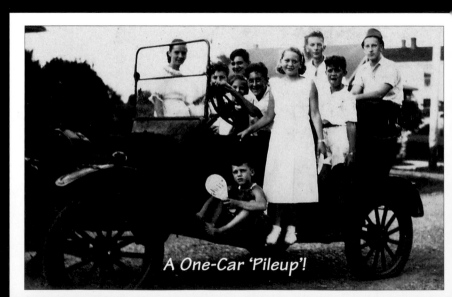

A One-Car 'Pileup'!

Dresses of Silk and Satin

1. Strike Up the Band!

2. Tea for Two

1. **BAND DIRECTOR** Gordon Tetzlaff (standing left of banner) led a sharply dressed group of high school musicians in Mukwonago, Wisconsin during the 1931-32 school year. His granddaughter Lisa shared the photo.

2. **DAINTY DAUGHTERS** of Irene Beck of Harold, Kentucky were photographed "having tea" in 1939. The girls' grandfather built the table and chairs.

3. **TRAVELING PHOTOGRAPHER** snapped Gerald Gappa, 6, and brother Warren, 2, in a goat-drawn wagon in 1930. Gerald's wife, Jean, of Wausau, Wisconsin, says the photographer provided the goat and wagon, which was quite a thrill for a couple of "city boys"!

4. **FOUR FRIENDS** took a break from sunbathing to show off their stylish swimsuits. Gretchen De Kiss and pals were from Milwaukee, Wisconsin.

3. They Got Their Goat!

4. Bathing Beauties

5. On Top of the World

6. The Ladies of the Court

7. 'Coffee Ready Yet?'

8. Special Delivery

5. NEW CAR OWNER Alex Meyers perched proudly atop his automobile at his parents' home in Luxemburg, Iowa in the mid-1930s. His daughter, Julie Habel, says this was a popular pose among first-time car owners during the '30s.

6. "VICTORY" was often the cry of the 1929 women's basketball team from the YWCA in Milwaukee, Wisconsin, reports Mary Ann Koebernik of nearby Franklin. The team was virtually unstoppable and did a lot of traveling to play other women's teams. Mary Ann's aunt, Betty Chetik, is the player at far left.

7. LITTLE CAMPERS Mari Jo and Margaret Norlin of Fort Collins, Colorado helped on a 1931 camping trip in the mountains by brewing a pot of coffee for their parents. Like many farm families of that era, the Norlins took few vacations because of the heavy workload at home.

8. BREAD WAGONS were a common sight in the 1930s. Mrs. Fulton Hallowell Jr. of Thomasville, Georgia cherishes this photo, which depicts her younger sister and brother. Their mother took the snapshot in Drexel Hill, Pennsylvania in 1933.

9. Five Generations—
With a Stand-In!

9. **WHEN JUNE COX** was born September 15, 1929, a five-generation portrait was scheduled. But her great-great-grandfather was ill the day of the photo session, so another man sat in for him (far right), and the family patriarch's head and feet were added later! June now lives in Boca Raton, Florida.

10. **SISTERS**, Blanche, Beatrice and Margaret Freischle of Duluth, Minnesota were photographed wearing dresses made for them by their grandmother in Germany. Both sets of grandparents lived in Germany, so the girls' parents also had many formal portraits taken at studios to send home to relatives in the "old country."

11. **ALL SIX** of Paul Mitchell's children climbed on the family horse for this portrait by J.C. Allen and Son in Battleground, Indiana. From left, the youngsters are David, Carol, Frances, Jean, Marjorie and Floyd.

10. 'Great Dresses, Grandma!'

11. Ride 'Em, Cowpokes

12. All Dolled Up for World's Fair

13. Grandma's Confirmation

14. Studious Students

15. Thelma's First Car

12. *RINGLETS AND RUFFLES* were show-stoppers when Pat Squire and her favorite doll participated in the Baby Doll Parade at the Chicago World's Fair in 1933. "My mother and grandmother spent hours making my dress and the crepe-paper rose petals for the carriage," recalls Pat of Alexandria, Virginia.

13. *LINDA CARVER* of Franklin, Wisconsin provided the photo of Grandma Evelyn Kolek's confirmation class in Watertown, Wisconsin. The priest was ill when the photo was taken, so his photo was added to the upper left corner later.

14. THE NINE PUPILS at Tillie Johnson's one-room school near Hastings, Minnesota pored over the day's lessons. Tillie, who was the youngest child in a large family, says she was so lonely when the last sibling went off to school that she was allowed to start classes early—at age 4!

15. *THE WHOLE FAMILY* was excited when Thelma Huovinn of Oregon City, Oregon bought a car in the early 1930s, because it was the first automobile anyone in the family had owned! From left are siblings Margaret, Doris, Esther and Chuck, and Mom Ida Carlson.

16. Wedding Day

16. NORRIS AND LORRAINE
Beno posed for a formal portrait in their wedding finery in Green Bay, Wisconsin in October 1930. Lorraine is wearing the necklace and earring set Norris gave her as a wedding gift. Grandson Mike says she's worn that jewelry on each of their anniversaries since!
To see the poster the Benos distributed inviting everyone to their wedding dance, turn to page 125.

17. "HEALTH IN EVERY BOTTLE"
was the slogan of the SD Sanitary Dairy, and it was displayed prominently on the business' "float" in an "old-timers' parade" in Fillmore, California around 1930. Riding the float were Dorothy Nickerson and sister Betty Jean, and Dorothy's friend Olive Brown. Dorothy, who provided the picture, now lives in Santa Barbara, California.

18. BOATING ENTHUSIAST
Betty Chetik (center) rounded up a few relatives for a leisurely ride in the 1930s in Iowa City, Iowa.

17. They Loved a Parade

18. Ahoy, Ladies!

19. What Could Be Slicker Than Knickers?

20. Puppy Love

21. Say 'Cheese'!

22. On the Road to Yellowstone

19. *SNAPPY DRESSERS* gathered for a portrait in the early 1930s. Betty Martin of Hagerstown, Maryland says her dad is at far right; the other children are his cousins. "I just love the boys' knickers," Betty says.

20. *WINSOME THREESOME*—Theresa K. Ross (at left), 7, sister Mary, 5, and devoted terrier "Tootsie"—was photographed at Fairview Farm in New Windsor, Illinois. Theresa now lives in Pueblo, Colorado.

21. *APPLE-CHEEKED* brothers Homer and Warren Bottemiller were more than happy to smile for the camera in the late 1930s in Oregon City, Oregon. Their sister, Gail Denham of Newberg, Oregon, shared the photo.

22. *FAMILY TRIP* to Yellowstone National Park in the early 1930s began after Lydia Seifert of Milwaukee, Wisconsin was photographed resting on the car husband Henry bought for the vacation. Neither drove, so daughter Gertrude Mulhern did all the driving, and the Seiferts sold the car after the trip! Gertrude's daughter, Patricia Sloane of Sun City, Arizona, provided the picture.

23. Audrey Mae's First Portrait

24. It's Patsy's Birthday!

25. Have Buffalo, Will Travel

26. Bare Feet and Bib Overalls

23. *HAPPY BABY* Audrey Mae Bowers' cheerful smile was captured by a traveling photographer who visited her home near Richmond, Virginia. "Remember those old itchy mohair sofas?" Audrey adds. "I was sitting on one!"

24. *NEIGHBORHOOD* youngsters donned unique party hats to help Patsy Lovell celebrate her fifth birthday in West Lafayette, Indiana. J.C. Allen and Son provided the photo.

25. *VERNON PATTERSON* of Wichita Falls, Texas says his mom snapped this photo after a man traveling from Wyoming to the East Coast in a buffalo-drawn wagon spent the night on their Missouri farm. That's Vernon on the buffalo and his brother, E.J., holding the lines.

26. *GROUP PICTURE* of third- and fourth-graders was taken at Stotts City, Missouri in the early 1930s. All the boys wore bib overalls, and a few came to school barefoot! Christine O'Brien of LaRussell, Missouri, who was a member of the class, shared the photo.

CHAPTER SEVEN

How We Got Around

How We Got Around

T he Depression made everyday activities just a little more complicated. Take, for example, the simple act of "getting around." You had your legs, of course, and that's what most folks depended on. It was the cheapest way to go, and what could be more reliable? When a trip got too long for a person's legs, town folks were drawn to the *click-clack* of streetcars and trolleys (when they had the nickel fare). And "interurban" trains carried people between towns.

But just as today, for all-around gettin' around, you couldn't beat the good old automobile.

These days, cars are regarded as necessities. My neighbor owns *four*— one for each member of the family! But of course! How could a 16-year-old girl live if she didn't have her very own fire-engine red car?

Perhaps you've noticed, too, that there are only two kinds of autos today: those made in the U.S., and those produced in faraway places across the Pacific or Atlantic.

There Were Many Models

Things used to be a lot different. Every make of car had its own unique look and personality. Doctors and bankers drove Packards. A Packard was indisputable evidence that you had become a success in life.

Farmers preferred Dodges. They had the power and high clearance you needed to plow through winter snowdrifts and navigate the muddy, rutted roads of spring. Lawyers owned LaSalles. Factory owners drove Buicks. Fords were both affordable and easy to work on—two traits that made them favorites with working-class folks.

Every car had its individual idiosyncrasies. I especially remember a 1930 Willys we owned for 10 years. It had been designed with a tiny gas line that clogged shut every time a piece of sediment flowed downstream from the gas tank.

The car would gasp to a dead stop, Dad would get out, pull off the gas cap, take a deep breath, put his mouth over the opening and blow into the tank. When enough pressure built up, the obstruction would be dislodged and work its way down the line. Gas would finally flow to the carburetor. Generally this would keep the engine running for another 3 to 5 miles. Then it was time to blow the gas line again. We referred to this routine as "Dad blowing us to Rockford".

Car Had More Quirks

That Willys had another idiosyncrasy. The horn button served a variety of functions. Push down and the horn blew. Pull up and the automatic starter kicked in. Turn the button clockwise and the lights came on.

This sounds convenient, but I vividly remember the day the entire mechanism worked loose, and all the gizmos and springs stuffed into the steering column flew up into my mother's face. It was the last day she ever drove that car, on the perfectly sensible grounds that she would not drive anything that physically attacked her.

The big event of every year came in September, when the new models were introduced. Showroom windows were blocked with brown paper. The new models arrived off the car transports draped in tarps. The anticiation was almost more than you could stand.

When the big day finally arrived, throngs crowded the showrooms. The dreaded "new car fever" hit every man in town. Those were the days when "demonstrators" were actually demonstrators, not just perks for car salesmen. A salesman would come to your home and urge you to take the car for a day or two. "Drive it in to Chicago," the salesman would beg. "Go wherever you want to."

No matter how much owners might cuss their cars in private, they were fiercely loyal in public. Every man lied about his gas mileage, of course. It was the first thing you heard when visitors arrived from a long trip.

Before the owner got out of the car, he had gas receipts in hand and was doing calculations in his notebook. "Got 24 miles to the gallon!" he would boast. And while no one necessarily believed him, everyone would nod and act impressed.

As you read the stories that follow, you'll quickly notice that auto owners had special relationships with their cars, whether they were purchased or laboriously put together with parts from the junkyard. The car was *part of the family*. And like a family member, it had a personality all its own.

Those cars didn't have heaters or radios or cruise control or turn signals or six-way power seats. You couldn't hook them up to a computer to find out where they were ailing. Tires blew out so often that you had to carry a patch kit and pump. Belts often broke. And cold air leaked in through every crack and cranny.

They weren't perfect.

That's what made them seem part of the family.

—*Clancy Strock*

GET A HORSE! Though the automobile age had long been a part of the American scene by the time the Depression hit, real horsepower was still depended upon in many sections of rural America. It was a good thing, too, because many a Hudson or Packard was pulled from muddy ditches in the spring by a friendly farmer and his dependable team.

The Model T Was Symbolic of Simpler Times

By Joyce Urrutia
San Antonio, Texas

ANTIQUE CAR shows or a parade of restored automobiles always inspire tender memories of my dad's old Model T Fords. To me, any Model T is more than just a symbol of my Depression-era youth in Texas; it's a reminder of family love and togetherness.

When we moved off the farm. Dad found work as a carpenter in the city and left horsepower behind, moving up to bicycles and trolleys and then to his first Model T. That skinny old Ford Express truck with the canopy and wooden bed opened up whole new vistas for a married man with five kids!

With gasoline 10¢ a gallon, Dad could drive to work all week and church on Sunday for $1. For another dollar, we could visit relatives in the Texas hill country or go on family outings.

The Model T took us fishing and swimming in warm green rivers, and to family weddings and shivarees. At harvesttime. Dad would drive us to his family's farm, where we'd play with our cousins while he helped with the threshing, sorghum-making or hog-butchering. Daddy was a gifted storyteller who entertained us with tales of cattle drives, Indians, ghosts and buried

treasures while the Model T puttered along.

At night coming home, we kids would stretch out in the truck bed on layers of quilts while katydids and crickets added their sounds to the Ford's rattles and squeaks. We'd fall asleep

---

"Sometimes we repaired flat tires by lantern light..."

---

watching the moon rise majestically into the star-stippled sky.

Sometimes we repaired flat tires by lantern light, or bumped home on a steel-rimmed wheel. Other times we got mired in sand or mud and everyone was awakened to help push. Occasionally we ran out of gas and would flag down another traveler, who usually had a running-board gas can or would let us siphon off a gallon or two.

On one trip, we had to patch several flats on the hot summer pavement. Before we got home. Daddy spotted a

small bakery and stopped to buy us two hot 5¢ loaves of crusty French bread. He broke off chunks and slathered them with butter with his pocketknife while Mama used a crust to dribble the bread with sorghum. Nothing ever tasted so good!

On cold winter mornings, Daddy would jack up a rear wheel to make cranking easier. There were always two cast-iron teakettles waiting on the wood stove; Daddy would pour one into the radiator and the other onto the motor.

I have sad memories, too. Model T's were easy prey for thieves, and that's how we lost our truck, along with all of Daddy's carpentry tools. It was a sickening blow for our impoverished family. Through the years, Daddy lost a total of four Model T's plus batteries and two sets of tires to thieves. Each time it meant starting all over again. We always did, and we always got along.

But most of my memories are pleasant ones. Daddy's affection for his Model T's gave all of us a sense of comfort and familiarity with cars. I'm glad he was one of the pioneers of that first "mobile" generation!

Novice Needed Tips to Drive Three-Pedal Ford

By Russell N. Fraser
St. Petersburg, Florida

IN 1934 I'd just left the Civilian Conservation Corps and was clerking in a grocery store. I earned $15 for working 12-hour days, 6 days a week. The money wasn't great, but it turned out to be enough to buy a used car!

One day on my lunch break, I spotted a 1925 Model T Ford coupe at a used-car lot. It was clean and appeared to be in good condition. The price—$15—was painted in white numbers on the windshield. Over the next few days I went back to look at it several times.

Finally I convinced myself I had to have it, even if it did cost a whole week's wages!

On payday I took my $15 to the car lot. As the salesman completed the transaction, he asked, "Do you know how to drive one of these?"

"Oh, sure," I lied. I knew how to drive a regular-shift car, but I'd never driven a three-pedal Model T.

The salesman gave me the keys, I pressed the starter button to the floor ...and it started! "Wow," I was thinking, "My own car, and it *runs!*" I released the hand brake and the Ford jumped ahead and began chugging down the street.

I thought I'd better pull into a filling station to check the gas, oil, water and tires. As I pulled up to the gas pump, I pushed down on the brake pedal and what I thought was the clutch, and the car promptly bucked and died.

The station attendant came over and said, "You sure you know how to drive

Photographic Design

this Ford?" I had to confess that I didn't. The attendant proceeded to give me a quick driving lesson. Here's what he told me:

"When the hand brake on the left side is all the way back, the parking brake is on and the engine is in neutral.

"To start driving, push the left foot pedal halfway down and release the hand brake. Then give it some gas and press the left pedal all the way down for low gear. After gaining enough speed, let up on the pedal for high gear.

"To stop, push the left pedal halfway down, into neutral, and use the right pedal as the foot brake.

"To back up, push the left pedal halfway down or the hand brake halfway back, then press the center pedal all the way down.

"If the car can't make it up a steep hill, turn around and go up backward!"

After all that, I still had a question: "Where's the gas tank?"

The attendant said, "You're sitting on it." Sure enough, the seat was divided, and under the right-hand cushion was the gas cap.

After that, I became an expert and did a lot of the maintenance myself. I wish I could own another one—or at least drive one again. ◗

'Every Trip Was an Adventure...'

By Robert Taege, Cape May, New Jersey

A TRIP in my dad's first car was always an adventure. After we moved from Brooklyn, New York to Hillsdale, New Jersey during the Depression, Dad bought a 1928 Dodge. We relied on that old car to get us back to Brooklyn to celebrate Christmas with my Uncle Harry.

We made the trip about a dozen times, and there was a tale to tell about every trip. We'd start preparing a week ahead of time by giving the car a tune-up and a complete going-over. After all, this was a *big* trip—35 to 40 miles! When everything was loaded up, Dad would get behind the wheel and we'd head down the road flat-out, at 30 miles per hour.

We could usually expect some trouble after we'd taken the Hoboken ferry and gotten onto the Belt Parkway. You could see the thermometer on the radiator starting to rise after we reached the parkway. Before long, the radiator would boil over and we'd have to stop.

After about 3 hours we'd finally limp into Brooklyn,

and I'd empty any remaining water from the radiator so it wouldn't freeze. Then we were free to enjoy a great turkey dinner, exchange presents and visit with relatives.

When we were ready to return home, we'd pour hot water back in the radiator and put hot wet rags on the manifold. I'd have to crank the car, too, because it was too cold for the starter to turn the motor over. (Dad had lost a leg and couldn't do the cranking himself.)

Once back on the ferry, we always had trouble starting the car again. That meant Dad had to pay some longshoremen $10 to push the car off the boat. By that time it was usually late, and I was too tired to do any more cranking, so Dad would pay a tow-truck operator another $10 to jump-start the car or push it to get it going.

If it weren't for the great family gatherings we enjoyed at Uncle Harry's, I don't think we would have put up with that heap! But God blessed our old car, and I'll always have fond memories of the good times we had with her. ◗

Hard Work Turned a Junk Car Into a Reliable Jewel

By Gerald Braatz
Kandiyohi, Minnesota

I GOT my first car in an unusual way. I built it from scrap parts!

I started with a junked 1925 Model T, which I got in exchange for 3 days of digging postholes near our home in South Dakota. The car hadn't been driven in some time; the body had been removed, and some of the parts had been cannibalized to repair another car. I had to pull it home with a team of horses.

When my father saw it, he asked what I was going to do with that piece of junk. I replied, "I'm going to build a car!" He had his doubts about that.

I spent the little free time I had getting the engine running. After that, I started looking for a body and found one that had been removed from another 1925 Model T. The owner said if I could haul it away, I could have it.

Once more, I hitched the horses to the wagon. I brought the body home and it needed a lot of work. Some parts were missing, like the fenders and headlights. One of my father's friends had several junked Model T's and he gave me a few parts. The rest I had to buy from a junkyard.

As the work progressed, my mother started taking quite an interest in the project. She lent her own touch to the remodeling by buying material and sewing new upholstery for the car.

By this time, a year and a half had passed. My father no longer doubted I really was going to make a car out of all the junk I'd brought home.

When I was a senior in high school, my parents moved some distance away. I stayed behind to finish school, moving in with the school janitor and helping him with his duties to earn my room and board. He was a mechanic, too, so he ground the valves and did some other engine work on my car. I did extra work after school to pay for his labor.

By the time I graduated in 1936, the car was running well. Times were hard, though. We had 2 years of drought, and extra jobs were difficult to find. I decided to move to Minnesota and look for work. My father and I built a two-wheel trailer, loaded it with my few belongings and hooked it up behind the Model T.

Before I left, my father gave me a wonderful gift. To show me how proud he was of what I'd done, he painted the car a beautiful black and bought new tires for it!

All that work paid off in Minnesota. I not only found work on a farm, but got a job as a mechanic. And I drove that old Ford for a long, long time.

'My First Car? I Still Drive It!'

MOST PEOPLE think of their first car in the past tense, and they wish they still had it or are glad it's gone. Well, I *still have mine*!

My dad bought the car, a Ford Club coupe, when it was new in 1937. All six of us children learned to drive in that car, and since I was the youngest, it was promised to me for my 16th birthday. It served me through high school and 4 years of college.

My travels 70 miles to college in winter remain memorable because that car didn't have a heater! Although heaters were available when Dad bought it, he figured he wouldn't need one just for driving to work and back.

I'm sure he never dreamed one of us would still be using the car so many years later! I decided to have the

By David Higgins, Littleton, Colorado

IT'S A KEEPER: This Ford has been in David Hugins' family since his dad bought it new in 1937. This photo was taken in 1960, when the coupe had been on the road a mere 23 years!

engine rebuilt when I was a junior in college. It cost more than I'd expected, but was still cheaper than buying a used car I'd know nothing about.

After completing college, I got a job teaching elementary school and drove the Ford to work every day. All the kids knew me by that car, and many of them waited around after school, hoping I'd ask if anyone needed a ride home. Once I bought a newer car, hardly anyone waited around for a ride!

After fixing the car in bits and pieces for 20 years, I found a family-run restoration business and let them redo it properly. The car still serves me well today. I'm certain our family has gotten our money's worth out of the $870 my dad paid for it!

Winter Trolley Rides Always an Adventure

By Virginia Leaper
West Kingston, Rhode Island

DO YOU remember trolley cars? I sure do! The cars were closed and stuffy in winter, open and breezy in summer. I can still hear the bell clanging, the cord you pulled when you wanted to get off, and the sign in front that said, "Spitting is Unlawful!"

The conductor wore an outfit with a high collar, a visored cap, and a coin holder around his waist. He always looked hot and a little distraught—probably with good reason. He had to cope with the occasional cranky passenger, people who forgot their money, and kids who got carsick.

The motorman's life was no bed of roses, either. In winter, ice would form on the overhead wire, and the pole would slip from it. He often had to get out to put the trolley "back on line."

One of those "freeze-ups" happened when I was a teenager. A boy had taken me to the movies to see *It Happened One Night*. When we went into the

theater, it was snowing lightly, but when we came out, there was a foot of white stuff on the ground, and more was falling.

My date and I managed to catch the last trolley car to our neighborhood, but it was slow going. The overhead wires had iced up and the car would move

only a few hundred feet, then stop. Each time, the motorman and my date would get off the trolley to put it back on the wires.

That trip took several hours! When I finally got home it was nearly 2 a.m. and my parents were waiting up. I sure had some quick explaining to do.'

New Drivers Needed More Than 'Horse Sense'

IT MAY HAVE been 60 years ago, but I still remember my dad's first solo drive in our old Model T! He'd only had a few lessons in starting the car, but decided he was capable of handling it alone.

After Dad started the car, he headed down the driveway for his first spin in his Model T. The car began picking up momentum, and he quickly realized he wasn't going to be able to make the turn onto the street.

Dad was used to driving old "Jerry," our horse, so he began yelling, "Whoa, *whoa*, WHOA!" and pulling on the steering wheel the way you'd pull on reins.

Of course, four-wheeled Lizzie didn't respond the way four-legged Jerry did, and the car flew across the street and up an embankment and bounced into a stone wall. Luckily, Dad wasn't hurt; amazingly, neither was the car!

—*Mrs. Preston Townsley, Ashfield, Massachusetts*

Model T Took Pals on Coast-to-Coast Trip

By Ed Simpson
Clemson, South Carolina

ONE OF the more memorable trips of my life was in 1932, right after I graduated from high school. Three buddies and I drove from East Orange, New Jersey to Long Beach, California in a 1925 Model T touring car. We bought the car for $15, then loaded it down with four collapsible cots, eight blankets and the clothes we'd need for about a month's trip.

We didn't have a single flat tire on the 14-day drive west, but we had a few other mishaps. First the generator burned out in Utah's Wasatch Mountains, and we couldn't replace it until we found a junkyard 30 miles down the road in Salt Lake City.

When we climbed the steeper roads through the Rocky Mountains, we sometimes found that our Tin Lizzie didn't have enough power to top the rises. So three of us would get out and walk as the driver turned the Ford around and backed it up the hill! For some reason, it had more power in reverse.

One of our stops was Las Vegas, which in those days consisted of a store, a few houses and a gas station. The station owner advised us not to cross Death Valley in the heat of the day, so we waited until nightfall to get back on the road.

By the time we arrived in Pasadena, the Model T was huffing and puffing. We stopped at a Ford garage, where the mechanic cleaned the carbon out of the valves and cylinders, adjusted the plugs and replaced a bad coil.

The mechanic also pointed out that we'd had the choke set improperly the whole trip, which explained why we were only getting 14 miles to the gallon. The mechanic showed us how to reset it, and our gas mileage improved to 20. After those adjustments, we felt like we were driving a new car!

Our final stop was Long Beach, where we found a furnished cottage on the beach for only $40 a month—$10 each, or 33¢ a night. We took turns fixing breakfasts of cold cereal or pancakes, making enough to keep us full until suppertime. In the evenings we went to a restaurant in town where we were served all we could eat for 40¢. (I'm sure the owners were glad when we finally left town!)

Then I received some welcome news: I'd been hired as an usher for the Olympic Games at the Coliseum in Los Angeles for 2 weeks, at 50¢ a session. My post was right at the finish line for the running events, so I had one of the best seats in the house!

Before long it was time to start back for New Jersey. We were on the road most of the time, stopping only every other day for a rest. And we needed it. We made the trip in only 10 days, but we had to stop for *30* flat tires and 10 of those blew in a single day.'

Snappy Sayings Spruced Up V-8

By John W. Keller
Lititz, Pennsylvania

WHEN I WAS a high school junior in 1934, a classmate offered to sell me his Model T Ford V-8 phaeton. The only money I had was from my paper route, but the price was right—$5—and he assured me the car was in perfect working order. I couldn't pass it up, so I thought I'd better just buy the car before telling my dad about it.

Of course, the car ended up costing more than just $5. Dad said that before I could drive it I had to get insurance (not for *my* protection, but that of the other drivers on the road!). The insurance cost $17, the license was $10 and tires were $2.

I also wanted to have a car that was different from everyone else's, so I paid a friend $8 to paint it with various sayings. The sides read: "5,000,000th V-8 Ford Going West" and "Watch This Ford Go By." One of several sayings on the hood was "Old But Paid For." And on the back, my friend re-created a Ford billboard that showed a greyhound telling a terrier, "No Use,

FLASHY PHAETON: John Keller had an artistic friend who lettered snappy sayings on his Model T Ford (above).

Mac; It's a Ford V-8." I can't begin to tell you how much fun my friends and I had with that Ford. Those were the good old days!

J.C. Allen and Son

Car Drove Family Back to Horse and Buggy

THE FIRST car I remember my family owning was Mr. T., a second-hand Model T Ford. Although Mr. T. was a car, he wheezed, bucked, spat and kicked just like a mule whenever anyone tried to crank him up.

Mama didn't much like Mr. T. She still preferred to ride in the buggy pulled by our horse, "Bill." But one day Daddy had business in town, and he talked Mama into going there with him in Mr. T.

The trip went well until just before they got home, when Daddy dozed off behind the wheel. Mama was thinking about the things she had to do when she got home, so she didn't notice Daddy had fallen asleep—until she saw the car was headed straight for our fence!

By Elizabeth Bowman Good
Mt. Vernon, Washington

She quickly woke Daddy, who groggily pulled on the steering wheel and yelled, "Whoa, Bill!" That approach might have stopped Bill, but it didn't stop Mr. T., and the car plowed down two sections of our picket fence.

After that experience. Mama refused to ride anywhere with Daddy unless he took Bill and the buggy.

Mr. T. became the property of my two older brothers, who used him to go "courtin' in style." This arrangement worked fairly well until one night when my brother Joe apparently kept Mr. T out past his bedtime. When Joe tried to turn down the lane leading to our house, Mr. T. simply dropped his

steering wheel into Joe's lap and took off across a neighbor's pasture through a herd of beef cattle!

Joe raced home and roused the other boys to help him retrieve Mr. T., round up the neighbor's cattle and mend the pasture fence. Much later, as the boys pushed and pulled Mr. T. to his spot in the barn, they decided he could stay there forever!

From that day on, as Mr. T. sat collecting dust, he became the sole property of my sister and me, and we were glad to have him. We used him to sit in and dream, or as a private reading room, or as a favorite spot to cut paper dolls from the Sears and Ward's catalogs. He might have disappointed the rest of our family, but Mr. T. served *us* well for years. 🍃

Picnickers Got Quite a Ride in Three-Wheeled Model A

By Harold J. Dow
Outlook, Montana

MY DAD'S 1929 Model A Ford boasted neither a trunk nor spare tire, because those things were considered luxuries in the '30s. Instead, tools were stored under the backseat, along with a tire patch kit and a coffee can full of water in case the radiator boiled dry.

One memorable summer, my aunt came to visit at our northern-Minnesota farm. We decided to take her on a picnic, and I still don't recall how we fit three adults, five kids and a lunch hamper in that little car.

We were pulling up to Jay Cooke State Park, a beautiful spot that had been built by the CCC, when we heard a loud noise. With a hard *jolt,* the rear end of the car fell onto the pavement and our right rear wheel went bouncing merrily down an embankment toward a swiftly flowing river!

Auntie let out a scream and the car ground to a stop. Fortunately, my two older brothers clambered down the hill and caught the wheel before it landed in the river.

During the 1930s it was not infrequent to see a wheel fall off your car. Our picnic, by the way, went on as planned.

'Goofus' Gave Owner Lifetime of Memories

By Bob Hutchings, Wadsworth, Ohio

I PAID just $7 for my first car, a Model T Ford, in 1931. I didn't really take stock of it, though, until I was driving it home. That's when I realized the engine was running hot because the radiator leaked. From that day on, I always carried five 1-gal. cans of water with me, and whoever was riding along would have to periodically climb out onto the running board to pour it in.

As time went on, I made a few improvements. First I installed a starter motor (bought for $1 at the junkyard) so I didn't have to crank the car to start it. All I had to do was press my heel on the starter button. What a luxury!

Once the starter was installed, I had to devise a better way to *stop* the car. There were three pedals on the floor—for forward, reverse and braking. (The accelerator, a lever just under the steering wheel, was operated with the right hand.) To stop, I had to raise the gas lever and jam down on all three pedals with both feet. I corrected that by installing new bands in the transmission. After that, instead of driving over curbs and onto people's lawns, I could stop just like everyone else.

Traffic wasn't too bad in those days, but after a few close calls I realized I needed a horn. That problem was solved with a doorbell from my father's storeroom. It not only cleared traffic, but got the attention of girls on the sidewalk, so it soon became the most frequently used accessory on the car!

Car Had Personality

The car acquired even more personality when a friend painted it in red, brown and green checks. Girls' portraits were painted on the hood and doors. We named the car "Goofus," after a tune whistled by a popular singer of that era, and painted the name on the front of the radiator.

By the time summer vacation rolled around, Goofus was in great shape, and a friend and I decided to show it off. After planning a trip that would allow us to stay with relatives wherever possible, we left the Chicago area with a full tank of 18¢ gasoline, a case of Montgomery Ward oil and 5 gal. of water for the radiator.

The water cans soon were empty; our reckless speed of

"GOOFUS" is what Bob Hutchings named this Model T after he and a friend painted it in an eye-popping checkerboard pattern with portraits of pretty girls. He bought the car for $7 in 1931.

35 miles an hour was making Goofus run hot. We replenished our supply from creeks running underneath the roadways. We reached Indianapolis about dusk and rented a tourist room overlooking a park for $1. Goofus was quite a hit with the other guests, and the owners let Goofus rest in their garage for the night.

We drove on to Cincinnati and Springfield, Ohio, then north to Detroit, bemoaning the fact that Goofus didn't have a top. It rained on us for much of the trip.

But Goofus' lack of a top had some advantages. As we crossed the border into Canada we were stopped for a customs inspection, then were immediately waved on. When I asked the officer why they didn't want to check our belongings, he just laughed and said he could see everything in the car!

Once we were back home, someone offered me $15 for Goofus. Since that was more than double what I'd paid, a deal was struck and Goofus was gone. But it's a part of my life I'll never forget.

It Was High Time We Learned About Life

I WAS all of 19 years old in 1939, and living in Long Island, New York. That summer, my father decided, it was high time my 18-year-old brother and I learned something about the world.

So, over our mother's strenuous objections, he put us in a 1938 Chevrolet coupe, laid out a map and told us to drive to Los Angeles! He said that when we got there we should swing north through Oregon and Washington, then head back to New York across the northern-tier states.

With that, he handed over $150 to cover the trip and wished us good luck. While that was quite a bundle back then, it *did* have to carry us all the way across the continent and back. Could we really make it by ourselves?

My brother and I had never driven out of New York State before, but we were eager to try. The first leg of the Pennsylvania Turnpike was just being completed that summer, so we had smooth travel for quite a distance west. Once we rolled out of Pennsylvania, however, we found no more "freeways" as we were accustomed to. The rest of the trip would be on two-lane roads, many of them dirt.

Had Crude Lodgings

Motels, as we now know them, did not exist then. So the first night out we stayed in a "tourist cabin"—and the dingy little building was a *cabin* in every respect.

As we continued west, our food costs

By Phelan Beale
Oklahoma City, Oklahoma

were running about $1 per day—we never spent more than 25¢ for breakfast or lunch. And gas cost only 11¢ per gallon in those days, so our bankroll was holding out quite well.

We rolled into the Midwest, and had our one and only accident while driving through Illinois. A farmer pulled his old pickup truck out from a side road and right into our lane! We hit him broadside, but at the speeds we traveled back then, very little damage was done to either vehicle.

When we asked the man why he had driven right into moving traffic, he replied, "Well, I just got plumb tired of waiting!"

Realized They Were Lucky

We picked up old Highway 66 in St. Louis and it was a straight shot all the rest of the way.

Driving through Oklahoma, we saw firsthand the devastating effects of the Dust Bowl. For mile after mile down Route 66, we passed whole lines of "Okie" caravans heading for the promised land of California.

While my brother and I were traveling to learn about life, they were traveling to find any life at all. It was then that we truly began to realize just how lucky we were.

In Albuquerque, New Mexico, we saw our first real motel. We stopped

there but they wanted to charge us $2.50 a night. We decided that was too much and drove on further, finding another that charged only $1.50.

The next day we hit the California state line—and were promptly stopped by the Highway Patrol! The officers would not allow us to cross into California unless we could prove that we had enough money to support ourselves while we were in that state. Luckily, our bankroll had not dwindled too far.

We stayed in Los Angeles 4 days and then continued on to San Francisco. There we visited Treasure Island, an attraction which at that time was competing against the New York World's Fair. From there we headed to Oregon and then Washington.

I'll never forget the waitress in Oregon, who, no matter how hard she tried, could not understand our New York accents. Problem was, we were ordering our hamburgers with no "*my*-onnaise" instead of "*may*-onnaise."

All too soon, we turned east for New York. The money finally gave out in Ohio and we had to wire our father for enough to get us back home.

Even though our mother was horrified that her 18- and 19-year-old children (she still called us that) were sent off on a cross-country trip all alone, to this day I remain grateful to my father for making us do it.

He gave my brother and me far more than a summer trip on Dad.

First Dune Buggies Were 'Doodlebugs'

By Niles Eggleston
Milford, New York

DUNE BUGGIES and recreational vehicles aren't a new idea. We had our own versions of them in the '30s and '40s. But ours didn't roll off an assembly line, and they didn't cost a fortune. They were converted hand-me-downs called "doodlebugs." Younger folks loved them; older folks hated them. And in my father's case, he had good reason!

A doodlebug was the reincarnation of a worn-out automobile that had been big and powerful in its glory days. It was stripped of all unnecessary gadgets—like the body, muffler and fenders. The drive shaft was shortened to make a vehicle about the size of a small tractor, but the similarity (unfortunately) ended there. These beasts had no practical application; they were little more than an engine and bench seat mounted on a short platform that rested on four wheels.

The teenage members of our family watched enviously as other folks' doodlebugs tore up turf all over the neighborhood. We never dreamed we'd get one of our own. During the Depression we never bought anything unless it was essential to making a living on our farm. We couldn't even afford to buy some things that *were* essential, like a tractor.

Then we discovered our favorite mechanic had built a doodlebug with a short platform behind the driver's seat. Now *there* was a doodlebug that could actually be useful!

"THE GREEN HORNET": Niles Eggleston's brother Oz loved taking the family's temperamental "doodlebug" out for a spin. This contraption was intended for use on the farm, but The Green Hornet didn't always cooperate with those plans.

We tallied up the selling points for our father. We could use it to transport fence posts, bags of feed or potatoes, or use it to pull the hayfork into the mow. Our arguments *actually worked,* and we soon had our very own doodlebug!

We named her "The Green Hornet" after a radio thriller that featured a loud, speedy automobile. The name was appropriate, because our doodlebug was a stripped-down Hudson "straight eight." Although they were heavy and built like tanks, those old Hudsons ran fast—they were a favorite of moonshiners who wanted to outrun "revenuers." In fact, it was said an eight-cylinder Hudson could pass anything on the highway except a gas station!

Unfortunately, by the time we got her, our old Hudson had been stripped of most of her weight and her dignity, and she demonstrated her resentment in a variety of ways. When asked to pull the hayfork or some other heavy object, The Green Hornet could dig a hole and bury herself quicker than a badger.

When pulling only her own weight, she threw huge gobs of dirt and mud into the air, most of it raining down on the driver. And the platform turned out to be so small and the springs so weak that anything we hauled would fall off right in the path of the rear wheels.

But The Green Hornet could roar in righteous indignation. Oh, how she could roar! Our hired man and the younger members of our family seemed to associate noise with power, and we all loved her.

My father, on the other hand, always felt that he'd been stung by The Green Hornet!

Photo courtesy of Lisa Tetzlaff

TWO-WHEELERS weren't just for kids. Teens and young adults, like the three women shown here, often relied on bicycles for trips around town.

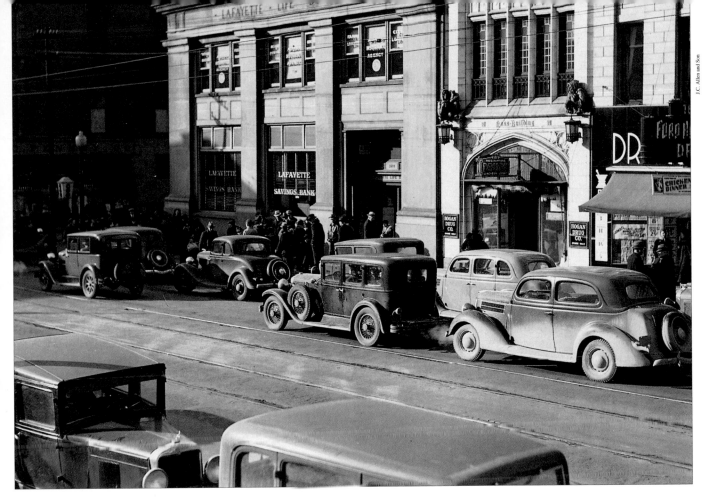

J.C. Allen and Son

Magnificent Marmon Made Travel Thrilling

*By Ford Charlton
Gulfport, Florida*

OUR FIRST family car was a beauty, a true aristocrat in the automobile world of the early 1920s: a Marmon sport phaeton. As a young boy I marveled at its glamour, decked out as it was in a deep olive green with red stripe, red wire wheels, big nickel-plated drum headlights, and a rear-mounted spare. The body and fenders were made of heavy-gauge aluminum, so dents could be ironed out easily and scratches didn't rust.

The long hood swept back to a slanted windshield flanked by two beveled-glass wings that gave the "cockpit" a touch of splendor. The dashboard was solid walnut, and the interior was upholstered in deep black leather.

Acquiring this car was a giant step for us. We'd gone from bicycles to public transportation to the Marmon, and we loved it. We kept that wonderful car for a long time.

The Marmon did get me in trouble once, though. While I was driving some friends to a neighboring village, the police stopped us and wanted to know why four "young blades" were

cruising around in a car like that. They thought we'd stolen it!

After a few more years, the grand old car was handed down to me. I got

---

"I hated to think of letting it go…"

---

married, and my young wife and I enjoyed the Marmon, even though it had begun to show signs of wear.

The touring top went first, and by then the Depression was in full force. When I found out what it would cost to repair or replace the top, I just removed it. Sheepskins and raincoats became standard equipment aboard the Marmon.

In the following months, other expenses developed. It looked like we'd have to say farewell to the Marmon. My wife and I discussed keeping the car and restoring it gradually, as money became available.

"Let's hang onto it," Ginnie urged. "I know I'll never get tired of driving and riding in it."

I hated to think of letting it go, but common sense prevailed.

"I'd like to keep it, too," I said, "but a complete overhaul would be too expensive for us right now, and if we put it in storage we'll probably wind up with a junk car no one will want. By selling it now we may be able to get a couple of hundred dollars for it." And so we said good-bye to the Marmon.

Recently, I saw a newspaper item about an antique car show. I called to Ginnie, "It says here a 1922 Marmon will be displayed."

"I'd love to see it," she said excitedly. "Our old Marmon gave us lots of happy memories. I sometimes wish we'd made more of an effort to keep it. A car like that might be worth a little something now."

I read on. She was right. "Yes," I said, unable to stop the catch in my voice. "It says here that this Marmon is now valued at $308,000."

Car Enriched Young Couple's Life in More Ways Than One

By Betty-Jane Heitz, Savannah, Georgia

WHEN I became pregnant I quit my job, so my husband and I moved from a modern high-rise apartment to the first floor of an old-fashioned frame house.

Though it was 1941, the effects of the Depression still lingered where we lived and we had to make do. But we had each other and we were happy.

The one thing that was missing was a car. We turned out our pockets, shook out my purse and combed the used-car lots until we found a 1936 two-door Ford with a stick shift. The $150 price tag ate up most of our meager savings, but at least we had wheels! We rolled to a nearby park on Saturday afternoons to let the baby smell the roses. After weeks of scrimp-

POWERFUL PACKARD: Veronica Ososki, Bay City, Michigan, loved the sturdy 1931 Packard. Once a Model T rammed into it, and the Packard didn't even move!

ing to pay for the gas, we drove across town to eat with our parents.

Then came the bombing of Pearl Harbor. War was declared, and rationing began. One startling day a letter came for my husband…he had been drafted!

Now what? We were already living from paycheck to paycheck, and a private's send-home pay was about $35 a month. Our rent alone was more than that!

We started selling our possessions

—bric-a-brac first, then even some wedding gifts, and finally, with great regret, our collection of books. But none of this brought very much. The car would have to go. Our 1942 license tags were long overdue anyway.

"What do you think we can get for it?" my husband asked. "You're lucky to get half the purchase price of anything used, and most times only a third."

"Not *our* car," I said. "We'll ask $165."

I ran an ad that described the car in glowing terms, but didn't mention the price.

While my husband was at work, a potential buyer came by the house. He walked to the curb, kicked the tires and ran his hands over the body. Then he came back inside and offered $95!

"$165," I said.

"$100," he countered.

"$165," I repeated.

"$125—my last offer."

"One-six-five," I said, trembling.

The man looked around. He couldn't miss the boxes of books, the framed pictures removed from the walls, the small statues—all with price tags attached. The baby wailed in her bassinet. He sighed and rifled the bills in his wallet.

"I can't go over $130," he said.

I felt tears rising in my eyes, but fought them back. I knew I had lost, even though $130 was much more than 1/2 or 1/3 of what we'd paid for the car. I picked up the keys and held them out to him. He took them and pressed some folded bills into my outstretched hand.

As the man dashed outside, I slowly unfolded the bills and counted them through my tears. There was a $50 bill, and a $20 bill or two, and then I came to see…he had given me *165 dollars*!

Streetcars Offered Cheap Transportation

By Margie M. Frank, Washington, Pennsyvania

WHENEVER my family wanted to go somewhere in the 1930s, we took the streetcar. My father couldn't afford an automobile, but streetcars would take you across Cleveland for a nickel or a dime. Sometimes we had to transfer several times, but many transfers were free. Those that did carry an extra charge were only a penny.

How well I recall walking to the streetcar stop with Mother! There were stops every two or three blocks along Main Street. During the day, a car would come along every 15 or 20 minutes, and more often during rush hour.

The streetcar office printed schedules, but the cars were so seldom on time that few people paid attention to them. Sometimes, though, you'd catch a ride on a streetcar that was actually running ahead of schedule. When that happened, the motorman would run the car as slowly as possible—about 5 mph. On those trips, it would have been faster to walk!

If no seats were available on the car, riders would stand in the center aisle, clutching an overhead strap or holding a handle on the back of a seat.

You quickly learned that if you were standing, you'd better hang on; the car swayed from side to side as it moved, and it often stopped abruptly. Those who didn't hold on often found themselves thrown into the laps of other passengers when the car made a sudden stop!

Two men were always in charge of the car—the conductor, who usually sat in the middle of the car next to the fare box, and the motorman, who sat on a small stool in front and operated the controls. The motorman had a loud, clanging bell he used like a horn if cars were blocking the track ahead.

I wouldn't want to go back to traveling by streetcar, but it was cheap and dependable at a time when people were more willing to put up with a few inconveniences.

Trips took a little longer—it took us about 45 minutes to travel 8 miles. But then, we weren't always in such a hurry in those days. 🖋

Trips to School Were Never Dull!

By Virginia Hearn Machir, St. Charles, Missouri

THERE WERE no big yellow school buses to transport students during the Depression. But my friends and I figured a surefire way around that problem!

The year was 1932. I lived 12 miles from the Missouri high school that I would attend as a freshman, and I had no idea how I would get to school every morning.

Including me, there were six high-school age students in our rural neighborhood—three boys and three girls. We all faced the same problem, so one day we got together and decided to do something about it. We would buy our own car!

Pooling our few meager dollars, we bought a much-used Ford sedan. One of the boys knew how to drive, so he was automatically appointed chauffeur. It didn't matter that Joe was only 14 years old—no driver's license was required in those days!

Each passenger was levied a tax of $13 per month to pay for gasoline, which was about 10¢ a gallon.

It was often tough to get to school on the rutted roads we had to travel. But if *those* roads seemed impossible, my family's old farm lane was downright impassable! So every morning I had to walk a mile out to the end of that lane to meet my friends at the main road.

I'll never forget the misadventures we had in our old Ford. That's because I kept a diary of our Depression-era trips! Here are some entries:

Tuesday, January 12: The three boys sit in the front seat of the car and we three girls sit in back. They tease us a lot. Tiny brought a lap robe and we spread it over our legs to keep us warm because there is no heater.

The car wasn't running right so it was slow going today. Once we even had to get out and push it up a hill! We were late getting to school and Professor Dillenger wasn't too happy about

that. He said it was the fourth time we had been late this month.

The car ran out of gas on the way home, so we girls walked the railroad tracks back home. The boys had to walk the roads to get a can of gas, then walk back to the car. I was very late and Dad was mad. Even after I explained, he was still mad.

Thursday, January 21: We got to school on time today! We are having equations of the first degree in algebra and they aren't easy. We performed an experiment on a pig's bladder in science, but it didn't work.

I wish that our high school had an indoor bathroom—it is so cold to walk to the outhouse in this weather. Mom, Dad and I played rook tonight—it was so much fun!

Tuesday, January 26: The car nearly turned over when we were going to school this morning. We girls were screaming so loudly you could have heard us for a mile! The car got too far over on the shoulder in loose gravel, and we were fishtailing from one side of the road to the other. Joe finally got it under control, though.

The close call even stopped Russell from teasing us in the car— but he made it hard to study in school. He has very large ears, and today he took some matches and propped his ears out from his head. He sure did look funny and had everyone laughing. But then Mr. Dillenger made him stand up in front so that everyone could laugh at him—then it didn't seem very funny.

Monday, February 29: It was warm today and we played outside at noon and jumped rope. On the way home a spring broke on the car, and we had to stop to have a new one put in. We waited until 6 o'clock, and then we girls got a ride home with a neighbor.

By the time we got to my lane it was very dark and I was afraid to walk down the lane alone. I went to another neighbor's house and called Dad, and he came after me on horseback. I had to ride behind him on the horse. He was mad again.

Tuesday, April 12: It is warm today and the fruit trees are in bloom. We were late for school again today.

Friday, May 13: This is the last day of school—for once we didn't have car trouble and arrived on time.

We didn't have lessons today, just had to get our report cards. Next year I will be a sophomore!

Purchase of a 1927 Chevy Fulfilled His Lifelong Dream

By Dick Gardner
Scotts Valley, California

I HAD WANTED to drive for as long as I could remember. I spent most of my first 13 years waiting for the day when my dad would let me sit in the driver's seat of our 1923 Star milk truck and guide it along the wagon ruts of our dairy farm. And once that dream was fulfilled, I moved on to a bigger one: having my own car!

That time came during my summer vacation from high school in 1930. Although the Depression was well under way, I managed to get a summer job at the local cannery, making fruit cocktail. I saved my wages and made almost daily tours of used-car lots. Finally, I had enough cash in my pocket to talk business.

I chose a 1927 Chevy cabriolet with a rumble seat—a must for a young fellow trying to be a "sport." The car was in good shape, and I paid $150 for it.

For once, I was actually looking forward to the first day of school. I pictured myself cruising to my old streetcar stop and picking up all the kids I knew until my car was crammed full. We would whoop it up and have a good time.

The Sunday before school started, I was lovingly going over the Chevy one last time, checking for any smudges I might have overlooked. Just then my dad strolled over.

"Richard," he said, "let me see that rumble seat again."

"Sure," I said, raising the lid. I was proud of that car, and I didn't mind showing off any part of it.

"Uh-huh," Dad said, peering inside.

"Yup, it'll work. Plenty of room. Tomorrow, early, we'll dump in the calf I just slaughtered and you can take it to the butcher's on your way to school."

My heart dropped to my beloved car's hubcaps. Surely he was joking! I waited for Dad's bellowing laugh, but I soon realized he was serious.

"Dad," I objected, "I can't do that! It'll leave blood all over the seat!"

"Throw in some gunnysacks first," Dad replied.

"But Dad. I was going to take some kids...".

"Take 'em. That carcass won't make any passes at your girlfriends." He bent over double, laughing at his joke.

"But Dad—"

"Mind you, get up early tomorrow," he said, walking away. "I don't want you to be late for school."

I was crushed. It wasn't fair! What if the kids saw me with the calf in the rumble seat? I'd worked all summer to buy this car, and now I couldn't even enjoy it. I kicked one of the front tires. Why had I even bought this car?

Then I picked up the polishing rag again and wiped the rubber where I'd kicked it. Gee, I thought, get a load of how this car sparkles in the sun! My spirits started to lift. So what if I couldn't drive my friends to school on Monday? There was always Tuesday!

HEAVY TRAFFIC marked Chicago's business district even in 1932. Elevated trains ran above the street, with freight trains beneath and tunnels underground.

CHAPTER EIGHT

Love and Marriage

Love and Marriage

How I adore the girl next door," sang the boy in the movie *Meet Me in St. Louis*. Once in a while, that was how it happened. One day you looked up and that nasty little brat next door had become a young woman and made your heart skip a beat. Then again, maybe she was the carhop at the A&W root beer stand. Or even (terrible predicament!) your best friend's girlfriend.

If you were female, maybe he was the boy from the corner grocery who made deliveries to your back door. Or a face in a streetcar window. Or the clarinet player in the high school band. Or someone else's date at the high school prom.

However and whenever it happened, you knew something both agonizing and tantalizing had just occurred. *You'd fallen in love!*

Now what? Pass a note across three aisles during homeroom? Send a valentine? Deliver a May basket to the front porch? Ask a friend to hint that you were smitten?

Temporary Insanity?

Meanwhile, you couldn't sleep or eat or even think sensibly. You paid endless attention to how you looked. You schemed over the best way to arrange an "accidental" encounter. You carved initials into trees or painted names on overpasses.

A young man had it tough in those days. If your house was equipped with a party line telephone, you agonized over whether or not to make that call to the girl who'd turned your head.

Once you'd finally screwed up enough courage to pick up the receiver and ask her for a date, a jolt of fear surged through you like electricity. *What if she says no?* On top of that, what if someone on the party line *overhears her saying no?*

While the men were squirming, the young ladies had it even worse. Because it was considered "unladylike" to make the first move, you had to sit…and hope…and wait for the call to come.

When Jack Met Jill

Who can explain why we fall in love? "There's a Jack for every Jill," my grandfather would say. Sometimes the right Jack met the right Jill in kindergarten. Other times it didn't happen until both were middle-aged or even older.

This chapter is about how Jack found Jill (or vice versa)—and the agony and ecstasy in the finding.

It's about how they courted, how they married, how they were "shivareed," how they honeymooned on a budget and how they lived happily ever after.

Because it is about love and marriage in the Depression years, you won't find stories of pricey receptions at the country club. There are no rented tuxedos, no custom-designed bridesmaids' dresses, no videotaped ceremonies and no cruises to Bermuda afterward.

Generally weddings weren't expensively staged pageants. Instead, they were celebrations of love. Maybe it's just a coincidence, but people seemed to stay married a lot longer, too.
—*Clancy Strock*

DEPRESSION WEDDING was far from depressing for Pauline and Gordon Tetzlaff, who wed June 9, 1934 in Madison, Wisconsin. Pauline's mother, who owned a bakery, prepared all the food, including the cake, for the reception in the church parlor.

Her Beau Proved He Was No Stick-in-the-Mud

I MET JIM in the spring of 1936, just after he returned from 6 months in a Civilian Conservation Corps camp. I was a schoolteacher, boarding with a lady who had rented her farm to Jim's parents. The house was divided so Jim's family had separate quarters.

I first noticed Jim working on the family's battered 1932 Chevrolet in the farmyard. Even from a distance, he looked handsome!

Once Jim had repaired the car, his mother suggested he give me a ride home from school, which wasn't far from the farm. I was surprised and thrilled when he came to pick me up, and rushed to finish my work.

When we got outside we realized we had a problem: how to get the car turned around. This was in early spring, when Wisconsin's gravel roads often turned to a sea of mud. There was just such a sea right in front of the schoolhouse. Since Jim couldn't turn around, he drove me home in reverse!

After that, Jim began to drop in at suppertime, entertaining me with his funny stories. I loved his visits, but

By Thelma McCann
Kent, Washington

TIRED OUT: That's how Thelma McCann and her husband, Jim, felt after their long-awaited first date. They went to a movie in this 1932 roadster, which had three flat tires on the trip home!

couldn't understand why he didn't ask me out. I later learned there were two reasons.

First, he didn't have a suit to wear, and in those days a man wouldn't think of wearing casual clothes on a date! Second, the car needed new tires, and

the family just couldn't afford them.

Jim eventually saved up $12 and bought a beautiful suit, but there still wasn't enough for those tires. He finally threw caution to the wind and asked me to a movie. I lost no time accepting! We dressed in our best clothes, enjoyed the movie, shared a few kisses and were on top of the world.

We were heading home when—whomp! A flat tire! Poor Jim had to change a muddy flat in his new suit. Luckily he had two spares in the trunk. Unluckily, we needed them both.

Then disaster struck. Just before we reached the mud hole in front of the school, we had a *third* flat tire. We'd used both the spares, so we had no choice but to try driving through the mud. Of course, we ended up hopelessly stuck…in ankle-deep mud!

Now we'd have to walk. To my surprise, Jim came to my side of the car, picked me up and carried me the whole way home!

After an exciting summer and many more adventures, we were married on Valentine's Day 1937.

Tough Times Delayed Wedding

By Marie Jenkins
Porterville, California

I WAS "courted" during the Dust Bowl days. While the billowing black clouds hovered overhead, my husband-to-be and I went to dances, rode horses, worked the fields and enjoyed life. We planned our wedding for the autumn of 1932. But it was not to be.

The Depression worsened, and our parents begged us to wait another year.

My father wanted to give his only child a nice wedding.

So we waited. In March of 1933, all the banks in the country closed, and I knew without asking that there would be no wedding that year, either. At the end of the crop season, my fiance and my father divided their profits. Each had made $17.

Times were hard, but we were happy. I made clothing out of gunnysacks, and stitched a stylish skirt and jacket set on my old treadle sewing machine. On Dec. 23, 1934 my fiance stopped by to see me with a somber expression on his face.

"I'm going to ask you just one more time," he said. "Are we ever going to get married, or do you want to call the whole thing off?" I looked long and hard into his honest blue eyes and knew he was serious.

Before I could answer, he went on. "I have $8. That's all I could get to save my life. I love you and will do the best I can."

I didn't have to think very long about my answer. "Let's try it," I said.

A happy smile came over his face. "When?"

"Now," I replied.

"Do we tell our parents?" he asked.

"No," I said firmly.

I rushed to my room and jumped into my knee-high lace-up boots and gunnysack suit, and we headed for town. We were married in the courthouse. The license and the ceremony cost $2 each, so we started married life with $4 to our name.

The hard times of the 1930s may be legendary, but those years also gave me some of the most beautiful memories of my life.

Bidding Was Often Fierce at Box Suppers

BOX SUPPERS were very popular in our area during the Depression. They usually were sponsored by schools or churches to raise funds, and they always raised a lot of money even in those lean years.

Most of those who attended were couples who were dating or singles *looking* for someone to date, so the bidding on those boxes was fierce!

Many times, a young man would bid as much as $5 or $6 for his girlfriend's box to prevent an "outsider" from buying it. A boy who had an eye on a certain girl in the crowd would do the same.

Since the young ladies knew their boyfriends would outbid everyone else, they made the foods the boys would enjoy most, particularly cakes and pies. A few sandwiches, usually made of home-cured ham, were included for good measure, and sometimes a piece of fruit.

Each girl would prepare the box in a manner that her boyfriend could readily identify. However, there were mix-ups from time to time. The boy who bought the wrong box would be embarrassed, because tradition required him to eat with the girl who'd prepared the box, and sometimes it was a young lady he hardly knew—or even one that he didn't particularly like!

On an average night, about 25 boxes would be prepared for sale, decorated in all the colors of the rainbow. Shoe boxes made ideal containers, wrapped in colored paper and topped with a ribbon.

Many of the boxes resembled Christmas gifts, but that wasn't what sparked a young man's bidding; it was the fact that the girl of his dreams had prepared what was inside.
—*Albert McGraw, Anderson, Alabama*

Some Bids Thwarted Young Love!

WHEN I was in junior high school, box suppers were "in". We girls would go off to the dime store to buy crepe paper and ribbons and then find a suitable box to decorate. When the box was decorated to our satisfaction, we'd pack it with two pieces of chicken, some potato salad in a fruit jar, and some cookies or a piece of cake we'd made ourselves.

At the supper, the boy who bid the highest amount of money on a particular box got to eat with the girl who had brought it. Of course, we hoped the boy of our choice would bid enough to get our box, but it didn't always turn out that way. Once my brother bid on mine by mistake and we had to eat together! He still teases me about that!
—*Edna Lewis, Escalon, California*

Trip Took Honeymooners 100 Miles from Home

By Doug Emerson
Bend, Oregon

MY WIFE, Lois, and I were married June 18, 1938—my 20th birthday. We had known each other since seventh grade and gone all through high school together in Painesville, Ohio.

While I was a high school senior, I bought my first car, a 1929 Model A Ford coupe, for $95. I paid $10 down and $10 a month until the car was paid for, plus a yearly insurance premium of $12.

By the time we started planning our wedding, I was working for $17 a week at the local newspaper. My pay had just been increased by $2, and the business manager made quite a production over giving me such a big raise —the usual was $1 a week.

A Brash Idea?

Still, when I told the boss Lois and I planned to get married, he chided me for being so brash as to think we could pay $25 a month for a home, plus taxes and insurance. "Not possible," he said.

But he was wrong! We paid $50 down on a $2,650 home that had three bedrooms, a living and dining room, kitchen and bath.

Then there was the honeymoon to plan. Despite the high price of gasoline at the time—15¢ a gallon!—we planned to drive to Cook Forest State Park in Pennsylvania, more than 100 miles away. Since neither of us had ever been even 50 miles from home, this was a truly epic undertaking that was not to be taken lightly!

First we purchased a 6-ft. by 6-ft.

NEWLYWEDS Doug and Lois Emerson posed for this photo the day after their wedding in 1938.

floorless umbrella tent for $1.98 plus tax. Then we found some used army blankets, which were as good as new, for 50¢ each. We had never heard of sleeping bags, but we probably couldn't have afforded them anyway.

To say we were both apprehensive about embarking on such a long trip would be an understatement. We were both *very* nervous!

At the beginning of our trip, we encountered hills more than a mile long in Pennsylvania. To save precious gas, I did what most drivers did in those days—I shifted into neutral and coasted whenever possible.

But as we coasted down one hill,

we became more than a little concerned; even though we were going downhill, our trusty car kept slowing down until it almost stopped. I shifted back into high gear, hit the gas, and we kept going. We learned the front wheels were badly "toed in," which not only slowed down the car but wore the tires badly.

Fortunately, I was able to buy some used tires with plenty of tread on them for 50¢ each. We also bought a new battery for $2 and the trade-in of the old one.

When we finally arrived at our campground, we nailed the tabs of our tent to a huge wooden platform big enough to hold a 20-ft. by 20-ft. army tent. The sight of our small tent on that big platform provided plenty of amusement for our campground neighbors!

The next day, Mother Nature provided us with beautiful weather. We hiked along paths and streams past gorgeous pines, rhododendrons and azaleas.

Spent Night in Car

That night, though, it poured, and our little tent leaked like the proverbial sieve, drenching everything inside. In desperation, we fled to our car and huddled here until daylight.

The sun shone brightly the next day, and we hung our wet blankets out to dry while we hiked along another forest trail. Our blankets were dry by nightfall—but then it poured again, dampening not only our bedding, but our spirits. We packed up and started for home, where we could hang the blankets on our own clothesline!

HONEYMOON HIKING through Cook Forest State Park made a tired young wife of Lois Emerson (left). Wet gear was hung out to dry after the Emersons returned home to Ohio from their soggy camping trip.

FREE! WEDDING DANCE

AT Du Jardin's Palm Garden
CHAMPION

WED. OCT. 15

MUSIC BY HARMONY KINGS

Given By Lorraine Doyen and Norris Beno
Both of Green Bay

Come Out And Have A Good Time
EVERYBODY IS WELCOME

A FREE DANCE meant a jammed country dance hall during the Depression! That was the result of this post announcing the 1930 wedding of Lorraine and Norris Beno of Green Bay, Wisconsin. The wedding nearly didn't happen, they recall, because their fathers refused to sign legal consent forms (he was 19 and she was 17). The conflict was resolved when their mothers secretly signed the permission papers!

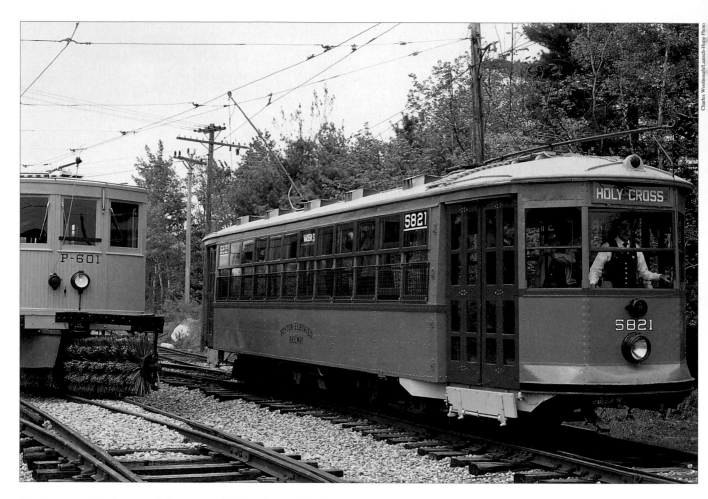

Her Trolley Trip Was a Ride to Romance

By Sylvia Roberts
Escondido, California

WHEN I WAS growing up in the 1930s, my mother was a young widow, struggling to support herself and me on a small income. We didn't have any money to spare, but for a nickel and a transfer, we could travel all over San Diego on the trolley.

The trolley was a central part of our lives and it even played a role in my first romance—but that's getting ahead of the story!

Mother and I took the trolley downtown to shop, to have lunch or to see a movie. Sometimes we took it to Balboa Park to visit the zoo or museums. It was only because of this cheap transportation that we could afford such luxuries.

When I wasn't riding the trolley with my mother, I was riding it with my best friend, Norma. Norma and I logged hundreds of hours traveling from one end of San Diego to the other. Once we rode the trolley to the ferry landing and took the ferry across to Coronado Island.

We took another trolley to the elegant Del Coronado Hotel. Curious to see this place in all of its splendor, we peeked into the luxurious dining room. How we longed to be seated at the linen-covered tables—but we dared not linger.

On the way home we were feeling sorry for ourselves, so we treated each other to candy bars and cherry Cokes.

Date Was Right on Track

I discovered romance on the trolley when a handsome young man asked me to a dance. After a week of feverish preparations, the magical evening finally arrived.

My date and I, dressed in our fancy formal attire, boarded the trolley and immediately became the embarrassed center of attention.

I was wearing a long, flowing pink gown and white high-heeled shoes. My mother had loaned me a stole, a

silver handbag and a string of pearls. I had begged for some silver slippers to match the handbag, but the gown was all Mother could afford.

Everyone stared and smiled and whispered as we walked down the long aisle to the back of the trolley. We looked straight ahead and tried to act grown-up and debonair.

My escort and I survived the ride to the dance, and once there, we had a wonderful time. As the evening progressed I kicked off my high-heeled shoes, and the silver slippers were long forgotten.

Coming home on the nearly empty trolley, we snuggled in the backseat and exchanged a few warm kisses. It turned out to be one of the most romantic evenings of my life.

SIMPLE DATES that cost little or no money were popular with couples during the Depression. Canoeing seemed to especially please the young woman relaxing in the photo at right!

HAPPY COUPLE: Florence and Anton Sedlak were married July 9, 1938 in Milwaukee, Wisconsin. Few couples used caterers; Florence's mother and other relatives prepared all the food for the reception.

Most Weddings Were Simple, Inexpensive

WEDDINGS WERE seldom elaborate during the 1930s. There were no bachelor parties, rehearsal dinners or expensive wedding dresses.

Most couples were married in a private ceremony before a judge or clergyman, with one person to "stand up" with them as an attendant.

It was always a great day when one of our Bohemian-Polish neighbors got married, as their celebrations sometimes lasted as long as 3 days! Everyone got together, brought food and danced. Sometimes the male guests paid a dollar—*a whole dollar!*—to dance with the bride.

But most of us celebrated with a shivaree. The ladies would bring food and shower gifts. My own gifts included 13 tablecloths! When my husband and I opened a restaurant years later, we used those cherished cloths many times for special occasions.

—*Marcia D. Bloomfield*
Adams, Wisconsin

'An Illinois Farm Girl Won My Heart'

IN THE SPRING of 1937 I was starting to think about settling down, but most of the girls in my Michigan hometown were either already married or had moved to the city to look for jobs. I asked my cousin's wife if she knew any girls back in her hometown in southern Illinois.

"Why, yes," she said. "I know a nice farm girl you might like."

I wrote a letter of introduction, which the girl answered politely. We corresponded until September, and then I decided we should meet in person so I traveled 550 miles to her home.

I was met at the door by a very pretty young lady and her family, and we spent several days getting better acquainted. It didn't take long to realize I wanted her to be my wife. After I returned home, I wrote her a letter asking her to marry me.

The night before I expected her answer, I dreamed a rattlesnake bit me! With such a bad omen, I expected the worst, and when her letter arrived I kept it in my pocket all day, afraid to open it. When I finally did, my hunch

MESSAGE IN BOTTLE brought James and La Vina Kindred together! La Vina, from Laguna Hills, California, found a bottle that sailor James threw overboard while stationed in the San Clemente Islands. Inside that bottle was a note asking the finder to let him know where it washed up. The two wrote for a year and a half before meeting in person, and married 2 years later! They're standing exactly where La Vina found the bottle, in Sunset Beach, California.

SMILING GROOM Chester Johnson posed for this photo after he and his bride, Gertrude, were married October 31, 1937 in Algoma, Wisconsin.

was correct. "Stop wasting your paper," she wrote. "I am not interested."

I courted other girls, but I never got that Illinois farm girl out of my mind. Three years later, I was walking past the drugstore and saw a Valentine's Day display. Suddenly, I knew just what to do. I bought her a 5¢ valentine with a little bear on it and the words: "I couldn't bear it if you won't be my valentine."

To my delight, she replied that if I was still interested in her after all that time, she'd be happy to correspond again. I went to visit her that May, and we were married in September.

My wife turned out to be a rare jewel, and we raised two fine children. In 1991 we celebrated our 51st anniversary and have our sights set on many more.

—*Harry J. Steiner*
Bellaire, Michigan

Couple Met on Scavenger Hunt

WHENEVER someone asks my husband how we met, he always says, "I found her on a scavenger hunt!"

It was 1937, and we were freshmen at a small college in Iowa. The scavenger hunt was organized to help the new students get acquainted, and it certainly worked for us! My future husband and I were paired off and instructed to request a clerical collar from the minister. We got the collar, and we were married 5 years later.

—*Veda Wilson Fatka*
Muskegon, Michigan

Ride Became Lifelong Journey

WHEN WE were in high school, most of us didn't have cars, so we rode our bicycles around in the evenings. One night I boldly asked the prettiest girl in the neighborhood if she'd like to take a ride with me. She accepted, and we've been riding through life together ever since!
—John Bedner
Colonia, New Jersey

Pen Pals Had 'Write Stuff'

I WORKED in our small town's telephone office, and one night when business was slow, a co-worker and I found a magazine with letters from people looking for pen pals. We'd never seen that before and thought it would be fun to send in letters of our own. I wasn't looking for a boyfriend; I was already engaged. I was just curious to see what would happen!

I got many responses, including one from a lonely young man who lived about 3 hours away. We exchanged snapshots and I told him I was engaged. "When you get married," he wrote, "I'll send you a high chair."

He didn't need to, though. Not long after that, I decided marriage wasn't for me and broke off my engagement.

When it came time for my vacation, my sister and I went to a beach town with an aunt and uncle. I was walking on the boardwalk with a young man

SWINGIN' TIME: Hazel and Fritz Franke relaxed on a swing in a park near their home in St. Paul, Minnesota.

I'd met there, and got sand in my shoes. As he knelt down to clean my shoes, he muttered. "If that guy doesn't stop following us, I'll fix him!"

I hadn't noticed anyone following us, so I turned to look. When my companion pointed, I saw none other than the man who'd promised to send me a high chair!

My pen pal and I spent the last few days of my vacation together, and I was sorry when it was time to leave. As my sister and I were returning home, she handed me a tin egg my pen pal and I had won at the penny arcade. "Your friend asked me to give this to you," she said.

When I opened it, I found a note inside that said: "Why don't we get married?" Two weeks later, we did! And he bought me the high chair, too!
—Evelyn Sudduth, Fresno, California

Caroling Brought Couple Together

IN DECEMBER 1934 our youth group was going Christmas caroling and gathered at the church to load up in cars. One girl had brought a visitor, a young man named Robert Miller. As we piled into the cars, it turned out I had to sit on Robert's lap! Fifty-seven years later, he still claims I "made an impression" on him.
—Mrs. Robert F. Miller, Fresno, Ohio

She 'Roped' Her Husband—Literally!

MY HUSBAND and I met on horseback! My family lived on a ranch along the White River in South Dakota, and my brother and I broke horses to make our spending money. When I was 15, we heard new neighbors had moved in about 2 miles up the river with a son around my age.

One evening I rode my horse to the river to bring the milk cows home, and I heard a noise in the bushes. When I moved closer to check it out, a young man, also on horseback, came tearing out and rode upriver as fast he could!

Well, my horse was pretty fast, too, so I took off after him. I not only caught him—I roped him! He was embarrassed, but I couldn't help noticing how cute he was. Five years later I married that neighbor boy, and he became a good roper himself. In fact, he won many roping events in local rodeos.
—Frances Jensen
Kimball, South Dakota

WEDDING PORTRAIT of Leon and Frieda Steffens was taken in Wilmette, Illinois on October 5, 1935. Frieda Alexander had moved to Illinois from Coats, Kansas to work, staying with relatives in nearby Winnetka. The Kansas clan couldn't afford a trip to the wedding—so the couple went to Frieda's hometown for their honeymoon!

TENDER MOMENTS: Gretchen De Kiss took a cozy stroll with a beau in the late 1930s. Lisa Tetzlaff of Wauwatosa, Wisconsin, who shared this photo, said Great-Aunt Gretchen left Wisconsin on her own to become a stewardess in Los Angeles around the time this photo was taken.

WOODEN SHOES were traditional garb in some parts of the country on a couple's fifth, or "wood," anniversary. Mrs. Eugene Meier of Wakefield, Nebraska shared this photo of her parents, Art and Hertha Schleusener.

Valentines Lasted A Lifetime

I MET my husband-to-be at a neighborhood Easter egg hunt. I was 4 and he was 6. I had left my basket unattended for a moment, and when I returned, the eggs were gone. When I began to cry, a handsome little blond boy comforted me and gave me his eggs!

When I started school in 1933, this same boy sent me the first of many valentines, a big lacy heart that said, "Be my valentine." We were together all through grade school and high school and never dated anyone else.

From 1933 until my husband's death, he never failed to give me a valentine every February 14. We were married 25 years, but in my heart we had been together for 39—from the moment he gave me that first valentine.

—*Jeanette D. Blount*
Paris, Kentucky

Trip to Heal the Body Also Opened His Heart

I CONTRACTED tuberculosis as a youth, and even after I recovered, the Indiana winters were hard on me. In an effort to regain my health, I moved to Arizona. Money was scarce, so I rode the bus only part of the way and hitchhiked for the rest of the trip.

While attending church in Tucson,

I met a wonderful girl, and we fell in love and decided to marry. My health improved, but there were no jobs for me in Tucson, so I returned to Indiana to look for work. Employment was all but impossible to find; the only jobs I could get were temporary ones. Without steady work, there was no way Emma and I could be married.

Since we couldn't be together, Emma and I kept our love alive by writing to each other every day. Hundreds of letters passed between Indiana and Arizona as I kept searching for work.

Finally, after Emma and I had been separated for 16 months, I became assistant manager of the F.W. Woolworth store in Frankfort, Indiana. The long, lonely wait was over. My father, a minister, performed the wedding ceremony, and our 53-year marriage has been a joyful journey.

—*Hillary Howell, Phoenix, Oregon*

Their Courtship Was Letter-Perfect

WHEN A new girl came to sing in our church choir, she and I became friends. One day she told me she had a brother in Oregon who was lonely and needed someone to write to. I wrote my first letter to him in October of 1935. He wrote a beautiful letter in return.

Before long I was writing to him every day, and he answered each letter the same day he received it. This was getting interesting!

The first week in December, he wrote that Christmas was going to be lonely without his sister. I suggested he

TWENTIES-STYLE headpiece was a focal point of this bride's finery. Martin and Helen Dix were married in their hometown of Ripon, Wisconsin. The reception was held in the farmyard of Helen's girlhood home.

come for a visit so he could see her, and meet my parents. He agreed, and he arrived 3 days before Christmas. We had a wonderful time.

On Christmas Eve, he gave me a diamond ring and promised to send me a train ticket. I arrived in Portland 3 months later, and we were married 4 weeks after that.

I'd always known my future husband would "sweep me off my feet"—and he did! We had 48 exciting years together and were blessed with three beautiful children. I thank God for giving me such a beautiful life.

—*Mabel Meola, Salem, Oregon*

JUST MARRIED: Ferne and Bill Vance posed happily after their wedding April 30, 1938. Ferne's dress cost a whopping $15, and she not only still has it, but wore it at their 50th anniversary celebration! This photo was taken at the couple's reception, on Ferne's sister's farm in Fulton, Wisconsin.

Couple Danced Away Their Doctor Bill

RECENTLY, I chanced to see a program on television that discussed the staggering cost of having a baby.

"Why, the diapers alone would cost over $1,000 the first year!" the man proclaimed.

My mind immediately took me back to 1929. My husband and I were young newlyweds living in eastern Colorado then, during those desperate days of dust storms and the Depression. I was 6 months pregnant and believe me, I wasn't worried about $1,000 for diapers—I was sweating the doctor's fee of $25!

Money had almost vanished from our lives. Roiling black clouds dumped hail on our neighbors' wheat crops and brought furious dust storms that blew out the seeds when the farmers tried to replant. My husband and I kept our little repair shop operating by bartering for our food and rent.

But that didn't help when it came to having a new baby—there just didn't seem to be a way to pay off our bill.

By Mrs. Vern Berry
Bettendorf, Iowa

Then, one day, an idea came to me! In the depths of such dark times, would folks be willing to spend a dollar to attend something as frivolous as a *dance?* The dollar would include a ham sandwich and coffee at midnight.

Dancing for Dollars

I asked my husband about the idea and he thought it was a good one...but then again, what if no one came? We decided after much worry and discussion to go ahead with it. Maybe the risk wasn't so great after all. We'd at least make enough money to pay for the music...wouldn't we?

We hired a band and set a date to use the school gymnasium. Next, we notified the folks in all the little surrounding towns. And we were surprised to find that the idea of having a little fun really caught on!

When the big night came, folks arrived in droves, bringing their chil-

dren. The little ones slept on the benches surrounding the gym—we had no "baby-sitters" then.

All through the night as I worked, I breathed prayers of gratitude. When the long evening was finally over, my husband and I sat down at our kitchen table, shades drawn, and counted the stacks of silver dollars.

We paid the band. We paid the rent on the gym. And we had enough to pay the doctor when our baby girl was born. We even had a little left over to purchase some things for her care. (But it wasn't $1,000 worth of diapers, either!)

How times have changed. I'll never forget those downtrodden people in desolate times, trying to forget their troubles for only one night. They danced and swirled to *My Blue Heaven* and *Sleepy Time Gal.* They smiled and socialized and enjoyed each other's company. And they helped us pay for our baby when we didn't know where else to turn.

Remember Shivarees?

SOME called them "bellings," others referred to them as "horning bees." But no matter what you called these memorable gatherings, shivarees were downright noisy!

A shivaree was a loud, mock serenade often held in tribute to a newly wedded couple.

It usually happened after dark when the honored couple was in bed. A group would gather outside their home; then, when the signal was given, those outside would do *anything* to make a racket! They'd beat kitchen utensils against pots and pans, ring bells, blow car horns or even set off fireworks.

When the "lucky" couple was finally roused, the gathered group held a small party in their honor. Sometimes, as part of the honor they would even parade the couple down the street in their nightclothes!

The word "shivaree" is derived from the French word *charivari*, which loosely translated, means "headache." As you'll see in the following passages, many Depression-era newlyweds suffered this kind of late-night "headache."

But it was all in good fun!

'I Had to Bake Biscuits For My Own Shivaree!'

WE GOT BACK from our honeymoon late on a Friday afternoon, but had only a few minutes in our new home. My husband's employer was hosting a fish fry that evening and we were expected to attend.

We had a good time visiting with our friends at the fish fry, but we'd had a long drive and were impatient to get back home. We were the first couple to leave.

When we got home, I made our bed and we turned in, exhausted. Just then we heard cars and laughter outside. We were going to be shivareed! We pulled on our clothes just as our friends walked in through the unlocked front door.

To my surprise, they announced, "We've come to stay with you until you make us biscuits!"

My husband opened our empty refrigerator and apologized, "We haven't had time to go to the grocery store." "No problem,'" our friends said. "Just tell us what you need and we'll get it."

I'd made biscuits before, but I'd never cooked for such a crowd. I was only 19, and it made me nervous 10 have so many excellent, experienced cooks looking over my shoulder!

Despite my nervousness, the bis- cuits were perfect, and I was just as surprised as everyone else! When we'd eaten them all, our guests wished us a happy life together and went home.

—*Gypsy Damaris Boston Shreveport, Louisiana*

Shivarees Offered 'Homemade Fun'

SHIVAREES were an integral part of rural amusement when I was growing up. This was well before anyone had televisions, and few of us could afford radios or movies, so most of our fun was "homemade"!

Once a newlywed couple had settled into their new home, they prepared themselves for a shivaree. But such events were supposed to be a surprise, so the neighbors sometimes put out a false alarm or acted as though nothing was being planned. When the time seemed right, the news would be passed in person from household to household. We never used the telephone for that; it was too easy for word to leak out over the party line!

After darkness fell, the group would gather some distance from the couple's home with washtubs, kitchen pans, cowbells and anything else that would make noise.

On one occasion a man brought a bugle he had used during World War I. When it was time to descend on the couple's house, the bugler sounded a "charge," and pandemonium broke loose! I was only 5, but I did my part by using a claw hammer to pound on a circular buzz-saw blade!

In a few minutes a light came on inside the house, and the noise let up for a bit. We waited for the couple to come out, but nothing happened. No one came to the door or even pulled aside a window shade for a peek outside!

One bold member of the group, thinking the couple wasn't ready for us, decided to take matters into his own hands and yanked open the screen door. To his surprise, the couple had rigged a poultry-watering trough over the door, and he was rewarded with a deluge of water on his head!

I often think back to those days, when life seemed less complicated and fun really was *fun*, even when it was "homemade."

—*Irvin A. Pogue Chillicothe, Illinois*

Kids Had Special Roll in 'Bellings'

SHIVAREES, or "bellings," were an important tradition in our neighborhood. Before the wedding, we children would hunt for an "instrument"; an old washtub or bucket was considered a treasure. After the ceremony, we followed the wedding party home and "serenaded" them. Then the groom led us to the general store for our reward— a 5¢ ice cream cone.

This was at the height of the Great Depression, and that simple hand-dipped cone tasted as good and meant as much as a meal at a five-star restaurant would today.

—*Mrs. Harry Coine, Oregon, Ohio*

SHIVERIN' SHIVAREE: Margaret Van Haaften of Pella, Iowa recalls that any time a member of her church group got married, they could count on having their friends surprise them with a shivaree. The celebrants had to bundle up for this one!

'Cash Stash' Bought Sweet Treats

WE WERE married in 1933 at the height of the Great Depression. I had a dental practice in Skagway, Alaska (population 600), but money was still very tight.

The night we returned from our wedding in Juneau, we heard a terrific noise outside our window. When we peered out, we saw the street filled with young people beating on washtubs and garbage can lids and shouting "Shivaree!"

We were flat broke and had no treats to hand out. Then I remembered the $20 bill I'd hidden in the apartment for emergencies. That was a lot of money in those days! We used the money to take everyone to the town coffee shop for ice cream cones.

By the way, my wife was wearing house slippers, and one husky young man carried her the whole three blocks so she wouldn't have to walk through the snow!
—*Clayton L. Polley*
Juneau, Alaska

She Helped 'Bell' Astronaut's Parents

WHEN I WAS about 5 years old, I attended the "belling" for astronaut Neil Armstrong's parents!

The belling started during the wedding reception, with people banging on old pots and pans, ringing bells, shooting guns off in the air—anything to make noise! The couple let this go on for a while and then went outside to invite everyone in for food and drinks.

We never dreamed that night that the Armstrongs would be the parents of the first man to walk on the moon!
—*Dorothy Merger, Naples, Florida*

He Could Dish It Out, But...

ONE FRIEND of ours loved planning shivarees for others, but when *he* got married, he boldly announced that no one would be able to convince him and his bride to take the traditional ride in the neighbor's dump truck. A few nights later, we gave him a sensational shivaree. We didn't get him into the dump truck, but we *did* take him on a ride in a cleaned-out manure spreader!
—*Joan Griffith*
Smicksburg, Pennsylvania

Revelers Descended On Wrong House

WE HAD been married a couple of days when we saw a long string of cars coming down the hill toward our house, so we knew it was our shivaree. The tradition was for the couple to provide treats, and we just didn't have enough for that many people, so we hid outside.

As it turned out, someone took a wrong turn and the revelers not only went to the wrong house, but pulled the couple who lived there out of bed! It took several hours for the group to find us. By that time most of them had given up, and only two couples were left!
—*Thelma Farris, Winchester, Kansas*

The Haunted Shivaree

IT'S EASY to say which shivaree, or "serenade," I remember best. It's the one where I thought I saw a ghost!

The newlyweds were a very young couple who had moved into a cottage just a few hundred yards from the groom's parents. Around 9 o'clock, when we figured they were asleep, we gathered at a neighbor's home carrying metal containers filled with marbles and pebbles. On a signal, we rushed toward the cottage, shaking our noisemakers with all the fury of soldiers charging to battle. The noise was deafening!

As I was making my third lap around the cottage, something white zipped past me at the speed of light. I stopped dead in my tracks. Could it really have been a ghost? Several others had seen the same thing, but none of us could explain it.

Then someone noticed the back door of the cottage was standing open and stepped inside. The newlyweds were nowhere to be found. We placed the wedding presents on a table and left, disappointed that our fun had been so short-lived.

Later we found out the couple had been so frightened by all the noise that they didn't even take the time to dress. The groom simply grabbed his bride, threw a sheet over the two of them and

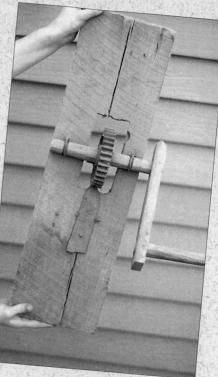

HORSE FIDDLES like this one were commonly used in some areas to wake up newlyweds at "bellings." Priscilla Gresser of Orrville, Ohio says this noisemaker was used at her grandparents' belling and many others. When the crank is turned, the cog strikes the saw blade, and "the resulting vibration is enough to rattle all the windows in the house!" Priscilla reports.

fled to the safety of his parents' house. The "ghost" was the very couple we'd been trying to serenade!
—*Albert McGraw, Anderson, Alabama*

I'll Just Take One Bite...'

AFTER MY sister was married in 1934, she and her husband stayed with my parents for a few days and stocked up on candy bars and cigars for their shivaree. The temptation of having all that candy around the house was just too much for me to resist. But I didn't want to get caught, either! So I took a bite out of just one bar, rewrapped it and put it back with the others.

When my sister and her husband celebrated their golden anniversary, a neighbor and I were swapping memories about them. "You know," he said, "the night we shivareed them, I got a candy bar that had a bite out of it. But since candy bars were hard to come by, I just ate it!" I started laughing and told him I'd waited 50 years to know who got that candy bar!
—*Otis Patterson, Melvern, Kansas*

They Took a Ride
In an Outhouse

ONE OF MY co-workers had to sit in an outhouse for his shivaree! His friends replaced the outhouse's front wall with lace curtains, put the structure on a wagon and drove it to his home. The newlyweds were informed they were going to sit on the outhouse seat, framed by the tied-back curtains, while they were driven the length of Main Street. The bride objected, but when she was told what the alternatives might be, she finally consented!
—*Ken Murphy
Royal City, Washington*

'Our Shivaree
Landed Us in Jail!'

AFTER VERN and I married, he warned me we'd probably be given a shivaree. I was a city girl and that word wasn't even in my vocabulary. But I learned!

Several weeks after our wedding, we went to town for the Saturday night movie. When we came out of the theater I told Vern there were too many cars on the street for that time of night, but he just laughed it off.

We got into our car, started it, put it in reverse—and nothing happened. Vern's friend Sparky, a mechanic, just "happened" to walk by, saw our predicament and knelt to look under the car.

"Well, here's the problem," Sparky said. "Somebody's jacked up your hind wheels. Who in the world would do a thing like that?"

After getting the wheels on the ground again, we started out of town, and every single car on the street fell in behind us! But Vern had a plan.

"We'll take another way home and lose them," he told me as he stepped on the gas. "Hang on to your hat!" But Sparky was a pretty good driver himself and managed to get us stopped. He ambled up to the car and said, "Vern, marriage must've addled your brains. This isn't the way to your house! Scoot over and I'll drive you home."

When we arrived, everyone was waiting for us. I handed out candy and cigars, naively thinking that would be the end of it. But the fun had just begun!

Sparky took Vern into the bedroom so he could change clothes, and then his wife, Joan, stayed with me while I changed. That was to make sure neither of us tried to run away!

Then the whole crowd drove us back to town, tied cans around Vern's waist so they hung to the ground, and put me into a wheelbarrow! Vern pushed me two very long blocks, with cans clanging and banging every step of the way.

After that, Sparky and Joan loaded us into their truck. Within minutes, the town police officer pulled us over and said it was illegal to have four people

in a pickup truck! Sparky drawled, "Officer, this is my pickup, so it must be Vern and Vorine who are breaking the law."

The officer—who, of course, was in on the plan—agreed, and took us to jail! We stayed there long enough for the town newspaper photographer to take our picture. We were on the front page the next week!

Finally, even Sparky could think of no further mischief and we were taken home. But even then we couldn't rest; alarm clocks kept going off every hour and we had to get up and hunt them down.

Our friends must have used up all their creative juices on that shivaree, because there haven't been any around here since!
—*Vorine Charter
Sterling, Kansas*

Pranks Part of the Fun

MONEY WAS SCARCE during the 1930s, but fun was plentiful. And some of the best moments were our shivaree pranks!

After our own shivaree, we discovered our bedroom no longer had a bed! We found the mattress on the porch roof, and the bedstead scattered throughout the house—except for the footboard, which was nowhere to be found.

After searching for an hour, we gave up and decided to sleep on the floor. When my sister-in-law turned down her bed in the next room, she found our footboard nestled neatly under the covers.

At another shivaree, the groom was thrown into a full horse tank. The bride jumped in with him, sat down and refused to come out! In later years, these two became ringleaders in other shivarees.

When our son got married, he and his wife were dunked in the river several times, then came home to find sand in their kitchen canisters and their sheets hanging from the windmill tower.

Those of us who participated in this mischief sometimes got paid back, too. After almost every shivaree, my husband and I would find corncobs on the floors, chairs turned upside down or beds taken apart. But it was all in fun, and those evenings are among the most hilarious I can recall!
—*Rose Schmidt, Taylor, Nebraska*

BAND AID: Henry and Jean Schiesser were serenaded by the high school band at their shivaree! Henry found his uniformed students waiting in the street after the wedding, playing the *Wedding March*! The police chief drove the couple through the streets of Glasgow, Montana with the band following. The parade ended at the dairy, where the newlyweds scooped free ice cream cones for everyone. The Schiessers' daughter, Karen Rachels, shared the photo.

CHAPTER NINE

HowWe
Had Fun

How We Had Fun

There were lots of bad things about the Great Depression. But let's not overlook one wonderful thing: entertainment didn't cost a lot. Some of the best was free.

Without spending a penny you could sit on the grass and enjoy the Wednesday night band concert in the park. Or you could just relax in your car with the windows down and honk the horn to show your approval when the band finished *Poet and Peasant Overture* or *Semper Fidelis*.

You could bring your own popcorn from home and, for a nickel, buy a bottle of pop at the stand the American Legion set up with two sawhorses and four 2-by-12 planks.

If you left home early enough on Saturday night and drove downtown, you might get a choice parking spot in front of Sears and Roebuck. That was the one place where you *knew* all your friends and neighbors eventually would turn up.

Radio, Marvelous Radio

At home sat the marvel of the ages—the family radio. Our first one ran on storage batteries housed in the basement. The radio itself had more dials than the cockpit of today's 747s, and it was a technological mystery that only a parent was qualified to handle. Atop that old radio sat a grand "tulip horn" speaker.

Below-zero winter nights were the best, because the radio stretched out and brought in signals from far-off cities: KDKA, Pittsburgh; WLW, Cincinnati; WCCO, Minneapolis; a station in New Orleans that broadcast from "high atop the Roosevelt Hotel"; and even a renegade station operated by the legendary Dr. Brinkley just across the Rio Grande in Mexico. Most families kept a log of the stations they heard and proudly compared notes with friends and relatives.

Later we were able to afford an imposing 10-tube radio housed in a piece of ornate furniture. It's strange to recall, but the whole family intently watched the lit dial just about the same way we watch the TV screen today. Now here's the great part about radio. Someone referred to it as "the theater of the mind." It beat television by a long shot because *you created your own pictures!* When Fibber McGee opened his closet door and the noisy avalanche tumbled over him, *you* decided what was in that closet. For some of us, it was fishing tackle boxes and golf clubs. For others, perhaps brooms, mops and a vacuum cleaner. It was whatever *you* wanted it to be.

When Jack Armstrong and his friends, Billy and Betty, dared to venture into the abandoned silver mine, the scene was just as spooky as you could invent. Was the ceiling low and rickety? Did the shaft twist and turn? Were there deep shadows beyond the torchlight, hiding heaven-only-knew what sort of monsters? It was up to you.

Our villains were as menacing as our minds could conceive. The leading lady was short or tall, blond or brunette, buxom or slim, each man to his taste. And the hero was the man of milady's dreams, without flaw or blemish.

That was radio. And after you paid for the radio, the entertainment didn't cost a cent.

Movies were a different matter. They cost a dime. But from the moment you walked in the door, you entered a fantasy world of plush red carpets, gleaming brass railings and moody lighting. To recapture the ultimate in movie houses of the era, promise yourself to visit one of the restored movie palaces back in operation today, such as the Fox Theater in St. Louis.

Many theaters—even in modest-sized towns—housed one of the mighty Wurlitzer organs made expressly for theaters. Often the program opened with the Wurlitzer and organist rising grandly out of the floor, rattling the

---

MONEY may have been scarce during the Depression, but there was no shortage of fun. It was the Golden Age of Radio. Movies provided wholesome family fare. And when there was no money for a radio or a Saturday matinee, kids and adults alike made their own fun.

seats with an up-tempo show-opener, followed by a 20-minute program that showcased the organ's infinite variety of sounds.

Then you settled back for a dazzling few hours of entertainment. You'll learn all about its infinite variety in this chapter, and perhaps wonder if today's dinky, sticky, smelly strip-mall "Cinema Fours" don't represent progress in the wrong direction.

Anyhow, 3 or more hours after entering, you stumbled out into the world, blinking at the sunlight, satiated with thrills. All for a dime.

Not to close on a dour note, but there was another form of Depression entertainment that honesty must include. It was the "marathon dance contest," a bizarre entertainment never seen since those dark days. Perhaps it was popular because it truly captured the misery of the times—bone-tired people shuffling, shuffling to nowhere, and mostly winning nothing at all when they finally collapsed in defeat.

But it was free.

—*Clancy Strock*

COUNTY FAIRS were big social events across rural America during the Depression years. This crowd had lined up to sample baked goods at the Tippecanoe County Fair in Indiana in August 1936.

Family Outing Brought Shower of Blessings

By Corinne Kolen
Evanston, Illinois

FAMILY OUTINGS were rare events during the Depression, especially if they cost money. But I vividly remember one fall evening in 1936 when our family went to the movies.

We lived on Chicago's northwest side, and my brother and I were playing outside, keeping an eye peeled for Dad. We always started watching for him around 5 o'clock, looking for a short, stocky figure with a newspaper under one arm and a broad smile on his face. We didn't own a car then, so Dad walked home.

Suddenly, there he was! He came toward us, his brawny arms outstretched so we could hurl ourselves at him and be scooped up for a hug.

"Come on, kids," Dad said. "Let's make the early movie at the Crystal."

We squealed with excitement and pulled Dad to the house as fast as we could. Admission was 25¢ for grown-ups and 10¢ for children if we got there before 6:30. If we got there any later, we couldn't afford to go in.

Ran to Tell Mom

I ran on ahead, through the long courtyard and up the two flights of stairs to our apartment to give Mom the news. Her reaction was predictable.

"Willy, we can't go to the movies," she told our dad when he came in. "There's not enough money for food tomorrow. We just can't go!"

Dad laughed and said, "Oh, come on. Tomorrow we'll worry about tomorrow!"

"What a great dad," I thought, hugging him. "Mom's such a spoilsport!" Only after I grew up did I realize Mom

needed to try to keep Dad's extravagant nature in check if we all were to have enough to eat during those lean years. But Dad's mind was made up.

While we ate, she said, "Maybe I can get two more soup bowls tonight." With each admission ticket, movie patrons received part of a dinnerware set. Mom had slowly been collecting pieces during the past year.

"And tonight is Bingo Night," Dad added. "We've never been there before on Bingo Night." I didn't know what that was, but it sounded like fun!

We ate quickly, finishing at 6:10,

> **"Come on! Tomorrow we'll worry about tomorrow..."**

and I danced around impatiently as my parents checked their keys and money before we started out. The fallen leaves swirled around us as we walked the six blocks to the theater. It seemed to be taking forever to get there, and we *had* to arrive by 6:30!

We made it—but just barely. The cashier was changing the admission price sign just as we reached the window. Mom quickly selected two soup bowls, my parents were each given a pencil and a bingo card, and we hurried to find seats in the dark theater.

I have no idea what movie we saw. All I remember is that when the film was over, the lights came on and a big glass container resembling a fishbowl was carried on stage. Inside were slips

of paper with numbers on each one.

Then a big wooden easel was rolled out, its front covered with 12 large cardboard squares. Behind each square was a number representing a sum of money, from 50¢ all the way up to the jackpot, which was the huge sum of $10! Whoever got a bingo first would go up to the stage, choose one of the 12 squares and win whatever amount of money was revealed.

Suddenly, *Bingo!*

A lady on stage picked one slip of paper at a time from the bowl and called numbers. Mom and Dad were quiet, intensely marking their cards. I was leaning over Dad's shoulder, watching his progress, and almost flew out of my seat when Mom yelled, "Bingo!"

Dad grabbed her arm and whispered: "Pick the square in the top left-hand corner. I have a hunch!"

Mom hurried to the stage and pointed to the square Dad had suggested. The lady pulled it off and revealed, to our amazement, "$10" in large red letters! Mom screamed so loudly that she put both hands over her mouth!

People in the audience clapped and stamped their feet. Dad hugged my "brother and me, saying, "Can you believe it? Ten bucks!"

Mom practically danced back down the aisle to us. "Ten dollars!" she said. "And I didn't want to come!"

We left the movie house, all of us talking at once. Then Dad laughed loudly and announced, "Come on, kids, we're all going to the ice cream parlor for sodas."

Mom started to object, then smiled and said, "Well, maybe we can have ice cream cones."

"No," Dad said. "Ice cream sodas, or maybe hot fudge sundaes. And no splitting! Everybody gets their own tonight."

I had a sundae all to myself, and can still remember how the gooey fudge stuck to the roof of my mouth.

Later, as we walked home in the dark, Dad's hand firmly enveloped mine. and we marveled at the Big and Little Dippers illuminated in the clear autumn sky.◗

LINED UP: Patrons waited outside the Mosinee Theater in Mosinee, Wisconsin to see Give Me Your Heart, starring Kay Francis, in 1936.

Movies Were 'Reel Life' for Theater Owners

By June Lassack Jens
Sheboygan Wisconsin

WHEN I WAS growing up, I was the envy of all the kids because I could go to "the show" all the time. That's because my dad owned the movie theater!

While I got to see lots of movies, I had jobs to do, too, as most of the business was run by our family. My mother was the cashier. Dad was the projectionist, and when my sister was old enough she worked as an "usherette." We all helped sweep the floors, clean the restrooms and scrape bubble gum off the seats.

Times were very hard then and nothing that could be used was thrown away. When there was leftover popcorn, Dad brought it home for us to eat the next day. It was usually tough by then, but it was a real treat!

Dad's first theater was the Elite, in Milwaukee, Wisconsin. He would show a cartoon, a newsreel, a "short subject" such as an *Our Gang* comedy, a serial, and then the feature—all for a dime!

Every Wednesday was "Dish Night," when a piece of pink dinnerware was given away with every admission. Now those dishes are known as Depression glass. We still had quite a bit of it around our house in 1945, but Mother was so tired of it, she threw it all out. When I see the prices those dishes bring now, I could cry!

Dad eventually replaced "Dish Night" with something he called "Payday Night." Everyone who bought a ticket got to select a manila envelope containing money. Most contained pennies, but others held nickels, dimes, quarters, and even a few $1 and $5 bills. It was a lot easier than handing out dishes!

Dad also drummed up business by sending his right-hand man to all the local merchants on Tuesdays to drop off "stills" of coming attractions. Anyone who brought a still to the theater received two free passes.

Over the years. Dad bought four other theaters, in Wautoma, Hancock, Mosinee and Plainfield, Wisconsin. My favorite was the Park Theater in Wautoma. The light fixtures on the side walls had colored light bulbs that could be adjusted to show either a single color or a whole rainbow. There was a curtain on the stage, which the usher opened just before the show started. Once you saw the usher coming down the aisle, quiet prevailed—or else!

These days, there's talk about films being "realistic," but back then we didn't need realism. Going to the movies put us in another world, which was just what we needed. We got plenty of realism once we walked out of the theater and back into those tough times.

ELITE TREAT: When the Elite Theater in Milwaukee, Wisconsin hosted a special promotion in 1932, it seemed as though the whole neighborhood showed up, including a band! On this special day, patrons could watch two feature films for 10¢. The owner, Bernard Lassack, is standing next to the horse.

A Day at the Movies...for Just a Dime!

By Blanche Collins
Redford, Michigan

DURING the Depression, the Saturday movie matinees were one of the highlights of our lives, and we waited for them all week with eager anticipation.

After breakfast, Mama would pack lunches for us in waxed Wonder Bread wrappers and send us on our way to the 10 a.m. show. She always encouraged us to stay for the second show if we wanted. It occurred to me later that those matinees were the "baby-sitters" of the Depression era!

When Sis and I reached the neighborhood picture palace, we'd join the long line, our dime admission safely knotted in a handkerchief pinned to our clothing. When we reached the cashier, I had to slouch; my height made me look older than I really was, and we could only afford the child's fare.

Inside the jam-packed theater, there was bedlam until the lights dimmed and the Movie Tone News appeared

on the screen. After that came "coming attractions," a nerve-tingling cliffhanger, scores of cartoons and then the double feature. One movie was usually a Western; the other might be a tearjerker, a musical, or a film featuring one of the many child stars of the 1930s. We all adored Shirley Temple, but my favorites were Fred Astaire and Ginger Rogers, who ignited my girlish hopes and dreams.

Of course, the movie projector broke down several times during each show — usually at the most crucial moment. We reacted by clapping, stomping our feet and shouting, "Put a nickel in it!" We were convinced that this made the repairs go more quickly, because the big screen always came alive again within minutes!

After we sat through everything twice, memorizing as many lines as we could, we left the theater, starry-eyed and usually in love with a new screen idol. By then it was suppertime, and we were famished!

At our first opportunity, Sis and I would gather some pals and re-create parts of the films we'd seen. The backyard was our theater; the stage was under Mama's clothesline. Since I was the oldest and bossiest, I was the director and star. Once we perfected our routine, we'd round up all the neighborhood kids and charge a penny admission. We usually earned enough for the next week's matinee!

The movies were a vital lifeline during the Depression. They entertained us, sparked our imaginations and gave us something to reach for. In short, they were an unforgettable part of our childhood.

COLORFUL POSTERS depicted the Stars of *Gone with the Wind* and *The Wizard of Oz*, two of the most popular films of the era. Both are now considered classics.

Movie Ticket for a Tire

IN THE late '30s, our town's only theater burned old car tires for heat. If you didn't have the dime for the ticket, an old tire would get you into the matinee for free. Every Saturday afternoon I'd buy a tire for a nickel at the junkyard, roll it up the hill to the theater and present it to the ticket taker. To this day, the sight of an old car tire reminds me of those days!
—*Betty Warne, Pierre, South Dakota*

Matinees Provided Cheap, Clean Fun

WHEN TODAY'S kids go to the movies on Saturday afternoons, it must be a completely different experience than it was for me way back in the 1930s!

I recently paid $7.50 to see a movie; in the '30s, we could go to the Amendola Theater for a nickel on Saturday afternoons. Admission to Sunday movies was a dime until you turned 12 —then it was a quarter. One of the most traumatic moments in my life was when the cashier refused my dime, saying I obviously was 12 years old (I was, by about 2 months). I had to go home and get another 15¢ from my mother, and movies were never quite the same for me after that!

When *Gone with the Wind* opened in 1939, people were shocked by the ticket price—an unbelievable 75¢! No one had ever heard of such outrageous prices. If only prices were still like that today!

Parents never had to worry about what their kids saw in those days, either. There was no need for a movie rating system then; everything would've just had a "G" rating. Anything that was even slightly suggestive was always edited out before the film made it to the theaters.   —*Elio Desiderio New York, New York*

Merchants Provided Free Outdoor Shows

IN THE 1930s, the residents of our little town could watch movies on Saturday nights for free, thanks to the town merchants. They'd provide the movie, which was shown in a vacant lot next to the grain elevator. The projector was set up and the images were projected onto a large white sheet.

Everyone brought a quilt or comforter and sat on the ground under the trees. There were always some black-and-white cartoons for the kids, and then a movie for the adults. When the show was over, we'd walk or take the trolley the half-mile back to our home.
—*Waydella Hart, Bartlett, Kansas*

MOVIE NIGHT in some communities offered patrons a choice of several films. One street (opposite page) boasted three theaters within a block of each other! Previews of "coming attractions" (left) tempted moviegoers with a glimpse of the films that would be playing in their towns next.

Parents Sacrificed for Kids' Favorite Show

WHEN WE WERE kids on the farm, long before the days of rural electrification, we owned a battery-powered Philco radio. It was a prized possession, and we cared for it with tenderness.

I have no idea what a battery for such a radio cost, but I seem to remember Mom saying that it was over $4. That was an awful lot of money in those dark Depression days, especially with nine children and two grandparents sharing our little house.

Our favorite program was the hour-long *Lux Radio Theater* on Monday nights, and we had to have all our chores and homework finished to listen to it. At the end of each program, the announcer would talk about the movie or play that would be performed the following week, so we spent the whole week looking forward to the next show.

One Monday afternoon, Mother warned us not to turn on the radio. "Dad wants to hear the weather forecast and Lowell Thomas with the news, and the

By Joy Higgins
Warsaw, Kentucky

---

battery is very weak," she told us. Our hearts sank. We knew that night's Lux Theater performance would be *Magnificent Obsession* with Merle Oberon. Oh, how we wanted to hear it!

We finished our chores and homework, laid our schoolbooks on the old library table in the parlor, and waited. Dad listened to the news and the weather, and then the radio was turned off. No one said anything about our program. We watched the clock, waiting and praying for permission to turn on the radio when the time came.

Would They Get to Listen?

At the appointed hour, Dad rose from his rocker and switched on the radio. "I know you've waited for this and want to hear it," he said. "The battery may run out of juice before it's finished, but we'll try."

We hovered close to hear every

word. Sometimes the voices faded and we feared the battery had lost its last ounce of power. To save as much energy as possible, we'd turn the radio off as soon as an advertisement began, then turn it on again when we thought the play was about to resume.

Well, we heard the whole story—and what an inspiring story it was! We could picture that lovely blind woman and hear every bit of her heartache. Such programs were wonderful entertainment for children in those innocent times.

Of course, the battery was shot after that, but our parents never expressed any regrets. We had no radio for several weeks; I'm sure Mom and Dad were saving during that time to buy a new battery. What a keen sacrifice for them to make for their children!

RADIO DAYS: After the evening meal, many families gathered around the radio to listen to their favorite programs.

One Radio Entertained a Whole Community

By Albert McGraw
Anderson, Alabama

WHEN MY favorite aunt moved from Texas to Alabama in 1930, she brought along the first radio most of us had ever seen. It had a separate speaker on top and was powered by at least three batteries, one of which looked a lot like the batteries used in cars.

When the neighbors heard about this fascinating contraption, some traveled more than 25 miles to see it! My aunt said it was like having her radio on display in a public meeting house!

At first, some were just curious about how the radio worked, but before long people were flocking to "sit for a spell" and listen to this astonishing invention.

Many of our visitors came on Saturday afternoons, and most of them were uninvited, but that didn't matter to my aunt. She loved company, and she certainly enjoyed showing off the area's first radio.

The biggest crowds came on Saturday night for the 4-hour *Grand Ole Opry* program. The groups were so large that my aunt couldn't accommodate every-

one! She kept the radio in the back bedroom, and there simply wasn't enough room for all her guests to sit down. But she came up with a solution!

Every Saturday afternoon for at least 3 years, my aunt and uncle would move every stick of furniture out of the bedroom and pile it in another room. Then they'd move every chair in the house, along with the kitchen table bench and a few nail kegs, into the

---

"As many as 75 people crowded to listen..."

---

bedroom. Those who showed up first got those seats, and everyone else sat on the floor.

At times there were as many as 75 people in my aunt's house just to listen to that country-western music show! Many were there for the whole program, which started at 8 p.m. and ended at midnight.

After everyone had gone home, my aunt and uncle would put all the furniture back where it belonged. It often was well past 2 a.m. before they retired for the night, but they didn't

mind. They both seemed ecstatic at having made others so happy.

I know there are many people today who enjoy going out of their way to be helpful to others, but I think few would go to such lengths to entertain those who were less fortunate.

Rural Folks Tuned in To 'Grapevine Radio'

BACK IN the early '30s we had no electricity, but we did have a "grapevine radio." It was a box with an on-and-off button and no dial. Music came through it, and here's how it worked.

A fellow who lived about 12 miles from us had a private network rigged up to provide weather and stock market prices to the farmers.

The signal was sent out over telephone wires for about 30 miles. We had to buy the speaker box, and then pay a small monthly fee.

Only trouble was, we had to listen to whatever programs the provider chose. Still, we enjoyed it, and we heard lots more than weather and market prices!

We started each morning with a devotional program, followed by *The Breakfast Club.*

Next was Arthur Godfrey's music and talk show. In the afternoon we listened to soap operas like *Ma Perkins,* and, of course, we all enjoyed *The Lone Ranger.*

At night we'd rush through the evening meal so we could listen to *Amos 'n' Andy,* and we always listened to the news because we couldn't afford the newspaper.

We enjoyed so many other programs, too—the comedies, the scary shows like *Inner Sanctum* and all the music programs. How I would love to hear some of those shows again!
—*Era Vaughn Bonds*
Simpsonville, South Carolina

ALL EARS: **Some radio owners used headphones to listen to their favorite programs. The headphones required less power, thus conserving precious energy in the radio's battery.**

Even Politics Stopped for 'Amos 'n' Andy'

TO APPRECIATE my favorite story about the days of radio, you first must understand my father. He was head of the household with a capital "H".

Daddy worked hard and had no hobbies; he thought recreation and games were for the idle, and he had no use for radio except as a source of news or to determine the correct time. He also was a politician who'd served several terms in our state's House of Representatives and Senate before becoming a newspaper correspondent.

Daddy's newspaper was published in the morning, so he worked in the afternoons and evenings and came home for dinner. His routine was always the same. He'd eat dinner, retire to the living room, listen to the news on the radio, and then spend some time politicking on the telephone before returning to work.

In 1930, when I was 4, my maternal grandmother came to live with us. I don't remember much about her, but everyone said she was a pleasant, easygoing lady with a marvelous sense of humor. Her one "vice," as she called it,

was her love of the *Amos 'n' Andy* broadcasts. Unfortunately, that program followed the news and was in direct conflict with Daddy's phone calls. After she moved in, she ended up missing most of the programs.

One evening Daddy came home for dinner all excited because our congressman was home from Washington, which meant Daddy would be talking to him on the phone later. Daddy followed his usual routine. He ate, listened to the news, turned off the radio and called the congressman.

To his surprise, the congressman told him, "Charlie, we'll have to talk later. *Amos 'n' Andy* just came on the radio, and I wouldn't miss that program for anything." End of conversation!

Daddy hung up, stunned. Without saying a word, he walked into the living room, turned on the radio and quietly went back to work—never realizing that the congressman's booming voice had been heard by Mother, who, of course, told Grandma everything he'd said!

After that, Grandma never again had to forgo the pleasure of listening to *Amos 'n' Andy!*
—*Dorothy T. Dishon, Union, Kentucky*

Guidance of 'Capt. Tim' Led to Lifelong Hobby

FOR ME, one of the most entertaining radio programs was *Capt. Tim Healy's Stamp Club of the Air.* I can still remember the show's introduction:

"Listen now to a story told to you by Capt. Tim Healy, who fought in World War I, who tells a true story and the history of the events leading to stamps printed and issued by different countries, thousands of miles away in a strange land."

The story was aimed at children ages 6 to 12, and it was fascinating to hear the history of the various countries and then look in geography books to find out where they were located.

"Capt. Tim" started many of us in stamp-collecting. For a self-addressed stamped envelope and a wrapper from a bar of Ivory soap, which sponsored the program, Capt. Tim would send you stamps for free. As our collections grew, we formed stamp clubs at school and traded them with classmates.

Many of those young listeners— including me—continued collecting stamps through adulthood.

I was so sad when I read a few years back that Capt. Tim had passed away. I wonder if he ever knew how much he taught us, and how those lessons helped shape our adult lives.
—*William J. Anderson*
Los Angeles, California

TUNED IN: A rural woman relaxed in front of the family's prized electric radio in 1930 (top photo). Some youngsters, like the one at left, wouldn't miss their favorite programs for anything—including their buddies!

'Who Knows What Evil Lurks…?'

By Mario DeMarco
West Boylston, Massachusetts

"WHO KNOWS what evil lurks in the hearts of men? The Shadow knows!" Then the voice would trail off into sinister laughter....

This was the familiar introduction to one of the most spine-chilling detective dramas ever produced for radio. The Shadow, "the invisible enforcer of law and order," commanded a faithful following in the millions during the Great Depression, when organized crime was running rampant.

The first show aired August 30, 1930 on Street and Smith's Detective Story Magazine Hour.

At first, The Shadow was merely the

> ## "The invisible enforcer of law and order had a faithful following…"

narrator who read stories from Street and Smith's crime magazine. James La Curto was the first narrator, followed by Frank Readick, George Earle and Robert Andrews.

But listeners were so intrigued by the mysterious Shadow that he eventually became the star of the show, with his own stories to tell.

Street and Smith capitalized on The Shadow's popularity by publishing *The Shadow Detective Monthly* to complement the radio stories. It was a successful move; both the radio show's ratings and the magazine's circulation soared.

During the 1937-38 season, a 22-year-old actor named Orson Welles was hired to portray The Shadow. At the time, Welles was considered the hottest actor in radio, and the Shadow episodes in which he performed were later declared some of the best ever produced.

After Welles left the show, Bill Johnstone was awarded the part. Over the years, several women played the role of The Shadow's partner, Margo Lane, such as actresses Agnes Moorehead, Mar-

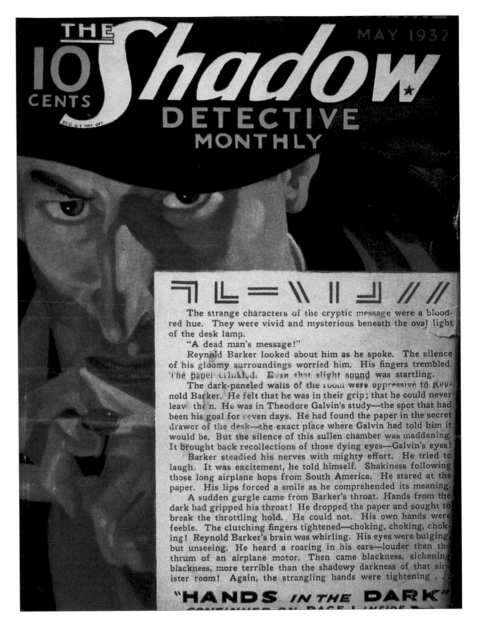

The strange characters of the cryptic message were a blood-red hue. They were vivid and mysterious beneath the oval light of the desk lamp.

"A dead man's message!"

Reynold Barker looked about him as he spoke. The silence of his gloomy surroundings worried him. His fingers trembled. The paper crinkled. Even that slight sound was startling.

The dark-paneled walls of the room were oppressive to Reynold Barker. He felt that he was in their grip; that he could never leave them. He was in Theodore Galvin's study—the spot that had been his goal for seven days. He had found the paper in the secret drawer of the desk—the exact place where Galvin had told him it would be. But the silence of this sullen chamber was maddening. It brought back recollections of those dying eyes—Galvin's eyes!

Barker steadied his nerves with mighty effort. He tried to laugh. It was excitement, he told himself. Shakiness following those long airplane hops from South America. He stared at the paper. His lips forced a smile as he comprehended its meaning.

A sudden gurgle came from Barker's throat. Hands from the dark had gripped his throat! He dropped the paper and sought to break the throttling hold. He could not. His own hands were feeble. The clutching fingers tightened—choking, choking, choking! Reynold Barker's brain was whirling. His eyes were bulging, but unseeing. He heard a roaring in his ears—louder than the thrum of an airplane motor. Then came blackness, sickening blackness, more terrible than the shadowy darkness of that sinister room! Again, the strangling hands were tightening . . .

"HANDS IN THE DARK"

jorie Anderson and Gertrude Wemer.

Over nearly 3 decades, Street and Smith's writers produced almost 900 radio episodes and more than 300 pulp magazines featuring The Shadow. Movie studios also made nearly 20 films featuring the mysterious masked avenger.

Perhaps there will never be another fictional character that will so capture a nation's imagination. The Shadow was created at a time when our minds were eager for something new and entertaining, and the "invisible enforcer" never disappointed.

Sounds of Radio Filled Summer Nights

THERE WERE so many gems in the early days of radio that it's hard to pick a favorite. Eddie Cantor, Red Skelton and Jack Benny were all good for laughs, and we also loved *The Lone Ranger, The Green Hornet* and the Lux Theater program.

We especially liked summertime, because we could walk all the way around the block, and every front door was open with the radio on. Even though we were outside, we never missed a word of the stories!
—*Mrs. Wayne Myers, Vestal, New York*

'Dramas Brought Stars into Our Living Rooms'

By Don W. Beeks
Long Beach, California

IN THE LATE 1930s and early 1940s our family had definite "don't-miss" radio shows.

On Monday evenings, we always had dinner out of the way and the dishes washed and dried by 6 p.m. Then my mom and dad, grandmother, brother and I would settle down in the living room and tune in for *Lux Presents Hollywood,* hosted by Cecil B. De Mille.

The best and newest films were dramatized, often with the top two stars from the films. At the end of the hour-long program, the stars were interviewed, and they always said they used nothing but Lux soap!

Then Mr. De Mille would announce the next week's fare and the studio audience would "ooh" and "aah"—and we usually did the same thing!

Right after the Lux program, we'd listen to *First Nighter,* which was a 30-minute drama. Mr. First Nighter would climb into a cab in New York City, and as the driver took him to the theater for opening night of a new play, he'd describe the route they were taking to the theater just off Times Square.

When Mr. First Nighter got out of his cab, you could hear the crowd buzzing about all the celebrities attending the show. You'd hear the doorman's greeting, which was always the same: "Good evening, Mr. First Nighter." Then he'd proceed down the aisle to his seat. He'd browse through the program, telling you the name of the play and its stars. As the overture began, he'd describe the dimming of the lights and the start of the first act.

I can still hear it all in my mind as though I just listened to it last night.

Radio was *the* big form of entertainment for us, bringing all the well-known stars right into our living room night after night. We couldn't see them, as we do today, but our imaginations provided the settings and costumes. While there's a lot to be said for some of today's television programs, I think the old radio shows were even more mesmerizing.

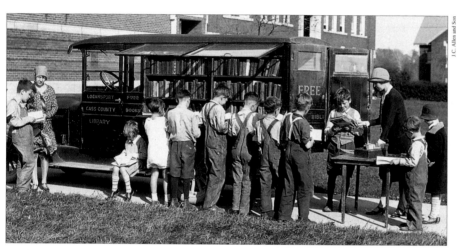

YOUNG READERS learned a love of books from their parents and through the "bibliobus," a library on wheels that traveled from school to school.

Orphan Annie's Decoder Pin Made Summer Memorable

THE MOST eagerly awaited package I ever received was the one that contained my Little Orphan Annie Secret Decoder Pin!

To get it, I had to mail in two seals from a jar of Ovaltine. That sounds easy enough, but you didn't know my mother! She considered milk the only beverage fit for children, and always said it didn't need to be "contaminated with that expensive Ovaltine." And during the Depression years, "expensive" was the operative word.

But my brother and I were not so easily discouraged. "Mama," we begged, "we *need* the decoder pin to understand Orphan Annie's secret messages on the radio!"

Without that pin, how could we know what trouble lurked in Annie's future? Annie always found herself in such deliciously dangerous adventures. Mama resisted our pleas for weeks, but finally realized how much that pin meant to us and bought the Ovaltine. We mailed in our seals and waited. Every day we asked, "Did it come yet?", and every day we got the same discouraging answer.

The weeks of summer dragged on like years. It was worse than waiting for Christmas! We worried that our stamp had fallen off, that Annie had run out of pins, that the postman had somehow lost our package.

But finally, the decoder pin arrived, and it was everything we'd hoped for. The pin was a glistening gold, with a clasp on the back so I could wear it forever, and there was even an official membership card signed by Orphan Annie herself!

At the end of each program we carefully wrote down the secret numbers and laboriously translated them with the pin. We learned, even before Annie did, that she shouldn't trust a certain sinister stranger, or that she soon would reach the hidden treasure.

The secret messages lost some of their luster when we realized that the same information was always revealed on the regular broadcast a few days later. We soon realized that having the pin wasn't nearly as much fun as waiting for it had been.

I no longer know what happened to the pin I intended to wear forever. But I will never forget that wonderful summer of waiting for it.

—*Mice W. Vail, Comstock Park, Michigan*

'Grand Ole Opry' Inspired Young Music Lovers

MUSIC WAS our main source of entertainment when we were growing up on a small farm in Tennessee, and our battery-powered radio played a major role.

The weekly *Grand Ole Opry* show was an event the whole community looked forward to. Each Saturday, after we'd finished our chores and prepared our clothes for church, we'd rush to finish supper, wash the dishes and wait for the neighbors who always stopped by to listen to the show with us.

My sister and I were fascinated by the banjo playing of "Uncle Dave" Macon and the singing of Roy Acuff and Eddie Arnold. We had hopes of one day playing the mandolin and guitar and began begging to own them. Papa thought it might be more ladylike if his daughters played the piano instead of stringed instruments. Somehow he found the money to order one from Sears and Roebuck, and we began our musical struggles.

The piano fascinated us. There was no one to teach us, but we managed to teach ourselves well enough to play church songs.

By A. Lee Hickman
Killen, Alabama

But we still longed for the stringed instruments we heard on our old Crosley radio. We wanted to listen to other music programs besides *The Grand Ole Opry,* but our radio time was limited. When the battery ran down it had to be driven to town and recharged, which cost *50¢,* and we didn't have a car.

My sister and I began sneaking in a little radio time when Mama and Papa went to milk the cows each afternoon. We'd listen to a country-music program and *The Lone Ranger,* my sister controlling the radio while I stood watch at the window. It didn't take Papa long to suspect something was going on when the battery needed to be recharged more often!

Our musical careers never got off the ground, but thanks to the inspiration my sister and I got from those radio programs, music has remained an important part of our lives.

Novelty Tunes Kept Spirits High

MONEY WAS the favorite subject of songwriters during the Depression, which was no surprise. Money was so scarce that even basic needs like new shoes often had to be put off. Those novelty tunes let us laugh at the hard times and became instant hits. Remember these? *Honey, Are You Making Any Money?... We 're in the Money... With Plenty of Money and You...No More Money in the Bunk...I Can't Give You Anything But Love...I'm Putting All My Eggs in One Basket...There's a Gold Mine in the Sky...* And then there was *Happy Days Are Here Again.* We belted that one out with gusto, even when we were still covering those holes in our shoes with cardboard!

Plane Kits Provided A Whole Day's Fun

WHEN THE Depression was in full swing, we'd run errands and do whatever other small jobs we could to raise 25¢ so we could go to the Palace Theater on weekends. The tickets were 10¢, which left us a nickel for popcorn and a dime to buy two hamburgers afterward.

But sometimes we'd forgo the hamburgers, and buy a model airplane kit instead! That gave us a *whole day's* entertainment.

The next morning, we'd get up early to cut out the balsa-wood parts before Sunday school. Later, after lunch, we'd lay out the pieces on a breadboard, stake down the stringers with straight pins, and attach the cutout pieces for the frame, wings, propeller, nose cone and landing gear.

After all the pieces were attached, complete with rubber bands on the propeller and the back end of the fuselage, we'd cover the frame, tail and wing with tissue paper. Next we'd spray water on the paper, using our mother's perfume atomizer, and let it dry. Once the paper was skintight, the great moment of flight was at hand!

Some of our planes survived their flights; those would be hung by a string from our bedroom ceiling so we could wind them up and watch them fly in a circle. Others were displayed on our clothes chest to show off our prowess as plane builders and pilots.

—*William J. Anderson*
Los Angeles, California

'We Staged Our Own Circus Parade!'

By Charlotte Augustin, Orange, California

WHEN I was a kid in Indianapolis, we didn't have television or video games to keep us entertained. We invented our own fun! Of course we had our favorite radio serials, like *Little Orphan Annie* and *Let's Pretend,* but for the most part we found our own ways to amuse ourselves.

All of the kids on Walcott Street played together, boys and girls, ages 6 to 14. The bigger kids showed the smaller ones how to skate, ride bikes, climb trees and whatever else caught our fancy. When we wanted dollhouses or clubhouses, we would make them out of large cartons discarded by the appliance store on the corner. During winter we'd build snow forts or lie spread-eagled in the snow to make "snow angels."

Our most creative effort was one summer when the circus came to town. We'd all watched the circus parade, with lions and tigers in wagons, elephants with women riding on their backs, trapeze artists, clowns and calliope music.

Those sights and sounds excited us

BATTER UP! Softball games (top photo) provided inexpensive entertainment for kids of all ages. Note the batter's bare feet, and the scrap of wood serving as home plate!

POPCORN cooked over an open fire (at left) was a tasty accompaniment to quiet nights spent at home.

so much we decided to have a parade of our own! It took days to put everything together, including appropriate costumes and signs.

When we were ready, we told everyone on the block that we'd be entertaining them on Saturday evening by hosting "The World's Largest Neighborhood Circus Parade." In those days, almost everybody had swings or gliders on their front porches, so we asked the neighbors to be there to welcome us.

They Loved a Parade

Musicians playing horns, drums, and combs wrapped in cellophane led the parade. Then came the "wild animals"—pet cats and dogs in orange crates that had been loaded into red wagons. Each "circus wagon" had a sign to explain which exotic beast the cat or dog represented.

There were other attractions, too: a trick bicyclist, a bearded lady, a boy on stilts ("The Tallest Man Alive!"), a girl being rolled in a tire ("The Trapeze Lady!"), a baton twirler and a clown or two.

Our efforts met with such overwhelming waving and cheering that we rewarded our audience by parading around the block a second time!

Everyone—kids and adults alike—remembered this event for a long time. Television and video games can't provide good times that are any more memorable than those we invented ourselves back in the '30s.

Trips to Town Were a Highlight of the Week

By Dorothy Daskam
Cresco, Iowa

THINGS WERE so much different during the Depression, but we still had a wonderful time, in a simpler way. For instance, we always looked forward to Saturdays in the summer, when our whole family would make the trip in to town.

First we'd take baths in a washtub out in the garage. Our mother would heat a teakettle full of water, adding just a little to the cold water in the washtub. After a good scrubbing, my sister and I would don our prettiest feed sack dresses, help load our eggs into the car and take off with our parents for a night in town.

I think those trips were just as exciting for Mother and Father as they were

for us. Everyone else came into town on Saturday night, too, to buy their staples, so our parents got a chance to visit with all the neighbors.

Once we arrived, my father would give me the 10¢ admission for the theater, if we could afford it that week. How thrilled I was whenever he handed me that dime! Sometimes there was

even an extra nickel for a bag of hot buttered popcorn.

When the show was over, my parents and sister would be waiting for me outside. My sister, who was 5 years older, wasn't interested in movies then, but she always enjoyed our trips to town. We all went home tired and happy after such an eventful evening.

Outings Kept Family Close

WHEN MY father finally got back on his feet during the Depression, he bought a secondhand car. We delighted in taking family drives for 5¢ ice cream cones or a picnic. Those trips often included parking to watch the sun set while we listened to our favorite radio programs. Every time I hear the names of those shows, I'm reminded of the contentment of those long-ago days of family sharing.

—*Patricia Collins, Bend, Oregon*

'Big Little Books' Offered Thrilling Stories for a Dime

By Ed Knapp
Three Rivers, Michigan

WHEN I WAS young, we didn't have comic books, roller-skating rinks, portable radios or television. But we had plenty of excitement—skinny-dipping in the old millpond, games of mumblety-peg, action programs after school on the radio, sand pit BB-gun "battles" and Saturday afternoon movie matinees. But the biggest change in our already exciting little world came in 1932. It was called "Big Little Books." These compact little volumes measured 3-1/4 in. x 4-1/4 in. and usually had no fewer than 350 pages. They were a perfect fit for small hands, and the price was just right for those of us with little pocket change to spare.

The first Big Little Book was *The Adventures of Dick Tracy,* followed by other comic-strip characters like Little Orphan Annie, Tarzan, Mickey Mouse, Skeezix and Buck Rogers.

As Big Little Books grew more and more popular, the subject matter expanded to include colorful characters from movies, literature and radio—Tom Mix, the Lone Ranger, Jackie Cooper, the Three Musketeers, the Count of Monte Cristo, Will Rogers, Shirley Temple, "The Shadow" and many others. Even Shakespeare was represented, with a Big Little Book based on *A Midsummer Night's Dream*!

Those books held a special place in the hearts and minds of kids trying to build their own "little folks' library," and they added a new element of adventure to our lives.

Now they are found only on the shelves of antique stores. What memories they bring back for those of us who loved them! ▷

KID-SIZE BOOKS opened up new worlds to young readers, with characters from comic books to classics.

Dances, 'Jam Sessions' and Library Kept Residents Busy

By Alice Schumacher
Great Falls, Montana

WE LIVED in a very small Montana town during the Depression, and for us it was a time of great fun!

We had free weekly dances at the school, with music provided by volunteers. The ladies made big pots of coffee on a two-burner kerosene stove, farmers donated fresh cream and everyone brought homemade doughnuts. Children of all ages attended. In fact, most of them learned how to dance from their grandparents!

My husband and I hosted musical gatherings, too. We ran a store and post office, with living quarters in back, and invited our musician friends to play there. They played the saxophone, trombone, accordion, guitar, piano, drums and even a tuba!

At midnight we'd take a break to turn the ice cream freezer or make waffles, and then we'd go back to making music. Most nights, we didn't stop until the sun came up!

We later turned our attention to starting a public library. The local high school had closed because of the Depression, leaving its large book collection unused. At the same time, there was a widow in town who desperately needed an income for herself and her son. We put the two problems together and came up with a single solution.

My husband and I donated space in our store to set up the library, and convinced the WPA to give the widow a special position as the librarian. All the WPA asked in return was a good circulation of books, so whenever people stopped in for their mail, we always encouraged them to take home some books, too! ▷

Moments When Life Was Truly at Its Best

THE DEPRESSION sometimes challenged our ingenuity, but it gave us plenty of warm, delightful memories. There were moments when life was truly at its best.

There were ice cream socials at the local school or church. There were spelling bees and quilting parties, ball games and board games. And, of course, there was radio; we had one of the first sets from Sears.

Most of all, I cherished the quiet, simple moments at the end of the workday, when we gathered on the porch to talk, sing to the soft strumming of a guitar, or just be alone with our own thoughts. Even today, I treasure the simplicity of those times.
—*Bonnie Lovell, Greenville, Kentucky*

CHAPTER TEN

Christmases We Remember

TRIMMING THE TREE: Tinsel
and cherished family ornaments were used to trim the
tree in the photo at far right
in 1929. As the Depression
deepened, many families
made their own trimmings
from cardboard, tinfoil, and
popcorn and paper chains.

Christmases We Remember

B efore you read this chapter, it might be a good idea to have a box of Kleenex handy. Not that our chapter of Depression-era Christmas memories is a sad one—quite the opposite is true! But the stories here may tug at your heart and bring a tear to your eye because they are filled with the *good* memories of people who often had little more to give than their love.

To understand what it was like to celebrate Christmas during the Depression, you must first realize that the people who lived through it weren't accustomed to joblessness and poverty. Many had owned their own businesses.

Life after World War I had been good to most people, no matter what they did for a living. Then the bottom dropped out of their world—stockbrokers and bankers now fell into line at the soup kitchens.

Christmas only magnified their misery. How could you surround the tree with presents for your children when there wasn't even money to buy coal for the furnace? For that matter, how could you afford a Christmas tree in the first place?

Waited for Their Tree

My dad solved the tree problem by waiting until a half hour before the Christmas tree sellers were ready to close on Christmas Eve. The trees that were left were the sorry ones that had already been rejected a score of times. They were the scraggly, ugly, lopsided ones with missing branches and bent trunks. The seller was happy to settle for 25¢ and close up shop.

Within an hour after the tree came into the house, Dad had transformed it into a splendid specimen, clipping and shaping it from top to bottom. Holes were drilled in the trunk, and branches were moved from hither to yon. True enough, only God could make a tree. But Dad saw nothing wrong in offering help.

The Depression established a tradition in our family: long after times got better, our Christmas tree still went up around 9 o'clock on Christmas Eve. And after an hour or so, during which everyone admired the lights and ornaments and agreed that "this is the prettiest tree ever," the children were packed off to bed.

In those Depression years, we knew that Santa Claus was hard up, too. We had been warned time and again not to expect much. About all you could do was include a small wish during your bedtime prayers for a miracle.

Would there be presents the next morning? Or would the tree be bare? With no money in the house, what could loving parents do? Each family found a different answer—as you'll discover in this chapter.

Made with Love

In 1934 my dad disappeared for long evenings into the basement, sternly instructing my sister and me to stay upstairs. On Christmas morning we learned why. He had constructed a miniature kitchen cupboard from an orange crate for my sister, and then painted it green. In another package my sister found a set of cheap doll dishes, pots, pans and utensils.

My gift was a checkerboard made from a piece of plywood, accompanied by a set of wooden chessmen in a wooden box with the price ($2.98) written in pencil on the bottom. We both received exactly what we wanted most and cherished our gifts long after we became adults.

The point of this story—and all those that follow—is not that we received handmade Christmas gifts. The point is that more than a half century (and hundreds of Christmas gifts) later, *these are the gifts we remember!*

But it isn't so much the gifts themselves that we recall, as the love that fashioned them.

—*Clancy Strock*

'Depression Christmases Meant The Most to Me'

IF I COULD go back in time, I would love to go back to the Depression at Christmas. Times were so hard, but our celebrations were always special.

Each year, we'd hike out to the timber to select our tree. The older boys would cut the tree, bring it home and anchor it in a milk pail. Mama would give us an old white sheet to drape around the pail as a tree skirt.

Then it was time to make our decorations. We'd settle in at the dining room table, with the kerosene lamp glowing in the middle. We'd start with paper chains, made from sheets of red and green construction paper we'd bought for a nickel. We held the strips togethr with glue made with a little flour and water. Then we'd string some popcorn.

When the tree was decorated, we always thought it was the most beautiful tree ever—even with the smeared paste that showed on our paper chains. The star for the top of the tree was made from cardboard and covered with tinfoil. It was lopsided, but to a small child's eyes, it was beautiful, too.

I remember one Christmas especially vividly. We were all looking forward to the program at our church. I put on a beautiful red-and-white dress, complete with matching bloomers, that Mama had made for me from flour sacks. When we were all ready. Mama told me that I was going to the biggest birthday celebration there ever was!

A Wonderful Walk

The walk to church was beautiful that night. The snow crunched under our feet as we walked, and the stars twinkled like fireflies.

When we arrived, the church was already full of people. The program started with our pianist playing songs like *Silent Night* and *0 Come, All Ye Faithful* while everyone sang. Then we little ones stood up in the front of the church, singing our little hearts out to *Away in a Manger*.

Then came the Nativity scene. Mary wore a halo made of cardboard and tinfoil, and Joseph knelt beside her. The Three Wise Men, their robes dragging on the floor, gazed down into the manger. I was so enthralled when I saw this rough, homemade crib and the baby Jesus lying atop the straw. After the minister read the Christmas story, the program was over. Just then, bells began ringing outside the church door and who should walk in but Santa Claus, with a big gunnysack full of gifts!

We could see a man's pant legs peeking out from below the Santa suit and some child yelled out, "That's my daddy!", but I knew it was really Santa. He gave me a little Bible, and it remains one of my most treasured possessions to this day.
—*Edna R. Hulon, Reading, Kansas*

Box of Gifts Filled Kids with Wonder

WHEN I WAS small, one of the best parts of Christmas was waiting for the box our grandmother would send us from Washington, D.C. What joy in waiting for it, and what suspense in trying to open it without our parents knowing!

That box was always placed at the foot of our parents' bed, and it was the first thing we saw in the morning and the last thing we saw at night. We would dream about what was inside.

On Christmas morning, when the box was opened, it never contained anything practical, much to our delight. Our grandmother made sure we always got something frivolous— something that Depression-era children could just play with and enjoy.
—*Warren Love, Fullerton, California*

Sweets for a Sweetheart

ON CHRISTMAS Eve, we would all wait in line for a couple of hours to get an orange and a box of hard candy from the people who worked at City Hall. One Christmas when I was waiting in line I found out that a friend was "sweet on me".

He stood in line with my family and gave me a box of chocolate-covered cherries. We never had money to buy candy, and those were the best chocolates I've ever eaten!
—*Adele Schaffer, Affton, Missouri*

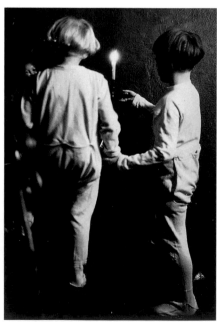

She Found Joy in Helping Others

By Mildred H. Ruddick
Marysville, California

I SHALL NEVER forget Christmas 1931, for it was the most memorable one of my life.

My family was very fortunate to have enough money for our four-person household. I was a cashier for the gas company, and my father, a retired Army officer, was our town's postmaster. With two jobs and my father's military pension, we had three checks coming in, so we were able to help many who were in need.

On this particular Christmas, a friend and I decided to take food and gifts to a poor family over the holidays. I already knew who many of the poor were, because they would come to the gas company office and plead with us to not turn off their gas, even though they couldn't pay their bills. They all kept hoping for some kind of job that would enable them to at least make a small payment toward what they owed.

The family my friend and I chose to help hadn't been able to pay anything, even a dollar, toward their gas bill for 5 months. My superiors had told me that we couldn't keep providing service to them indefinitely. Their gas was to be turned off right after Christmas.

My friend and I went out and bought a present for each member of the family—the mother, father, two girls and a boy—and wrapped them in colorful paper. We also bought them a Christmas tree and decorations plus a turkey, ham, potatoes, vegetables, cranberries and Christmas candies for a holiday dinner.

We drove up to the family's house on Christmas Eve. All the shades were pulled down tight. Their old car was parked at the side of the house, though, so we went to the door and rang the bell. No one answered.

We kept ringing, and finally we saw a child pull a window shade aside to peek out at us. When they saw we had presents and a tree, they opened the door to let us in.

Nothing could have prepared us for what we saw. The house had looked nice from the outside, but inside it was completely bare. There was no furniture in the living room or dining room. The bedrooms contained no beds, only

> ## "Nothing could have prepared us for what we saw."

mattresses with bedding on the floors. In the kitchen sat a table surrounded by orange crates the family had been using as chairs. The icebox was open and empty: There was no ice. No food was visible anywhere. Tears ran down the mother's cheeks as she helped me unload the groceries we had brought.

The father explained that he had sold all the furniture to buy food for his family. Now he had nothing left to sell, and no gas in the car. We had no idea they were so destitute.

As we walked back to our car, the father walked with us, thanking us over and over as tears streamed down his face. Before our visit, he had sunk deep into the depths of despair.

My friend and I immediately emptied our pockets of all the money we had and gave it to him. It was only $8, but it was enough for him to buy gas, ice and other things the family needed.

I told the father to come to my house the day after Christmas; I knew my parents would give him a job doing yard work. Perhaps some of their friends could hire him, too. We also promised to ask them if they had any extra furniture he could use to start refurnishing his home.

With that helping hand, the family got back on its feet. The father turned out to be excellent at yard work, and he built up a large clientele for himself.

That was a wonderful Christmas for me, and it quickly taught me the great joy to be found in helping others. I have done it every Christmas since.

'Uncle Jack's Box' Taught Us to Share

THE THING I remember most about Uncle Jack's box is that it always brought something for every child in the family except me.

There were six oranges, six apples, six packages of hard candy, six popcorn balls and six peppermint sticks, which usually were broken. There were, however, seven children in our family, and that's where I came in...or, more exactly, that's where I was left out.

Uncle Jack wasn't really our uncle. He wasn't any relation at all. His name was Jack Murphy, and he was a merchant in South Omaha. Sometime in the late 1920s, before I was born, Uncle Jack and a dentist friend found their way to our house in the hills of northwestern Nebraska on a hunting trip. Everyone got along well, and they stayed with our family for several days while they kept hunting.

Hunters Fit in

Uncle Jack and his friend liked biscuits in the morning, thick-cut bacon from a home-cured slab, and bird's-eye gravy. They were extremely compatible with our poor and crowded but exuberant household.

About a month after the hunters returned to Omaha, a Christmas box arrived. When my brothers and sisters opened it on Christmas morning they found six oranges, six apples, six popcorn balls, etc....and so an annual event was begun. Uncle Jack and his friend were back the next year. Again

By Robert Pearman
Holt, Missouri

their departure was followed by the arrival of the box.

They came the next year, and the next, and now the whole family looked forward to the arrival of "Uncle Jack's box." Even after they no longer came to hunt, the box was always waiting at the mailbox on the mail day just before Christmas.

The contents never varied: six oranges, six apples, six packages of hard candy, six popcorn balls, six pepper-

---

"We all looked forward to the box's arrival..."

---

mint sticks (often broken), a tin of peanut brittle, a package each of figs, dates, Brazil nuts, almonds and pecans, and, rolling loose as if for packing, English walnuts of various sizes.

Throughout the long decade of the 1930s, when the best Christmases meant new coats, caps and mittens, Uncle Jack's box appeared with unvaried contents and undiminished welcome. If Uncle Jack had fallen upon hard times, it didn't show in the contents of his box.

The box was there the year my oldest brother finished high school and when he finished college. In the first years of World War II, when Christ-

mas found not seven but two or three of us home, the box was there just the same. Mother often had tears in her eyes on those Christmas mornings.

We began to hear Uncle Jack was sick, but still the box came just the same. Then one year there was no box and we knew Uncle Jack had died.

Why Six Gifts?

I was there for the arrival of Uncle Jack's box in 1930, and for each one that followed. There were now seven children, not six, in the white frame house in a ring of cottonwood trees deep in the lonely hills. But in Uncle Jack's box there continued to be just six of everything.

One might suppose he never heard about me, but I discount that. Although he no longer came to hunt, we had contact with him over the years. He must have known.

Or one might think Uncle Jack merely made allowances, realizing that soon after I arrived the oldest would be leaving home. But that doesn't make sense, either, for Uncle Jack chose to ignore for almost 2 decades the inevitable facts of growth and maturity. From the first to the very last, each box was packed not for a family that was growing up and moving on, but for six runny-nosed youngsters living a long, long way from anywhere.

There were never any arguments, even when there were children young enough to argue over such trivial matters as the division of nuts and dates and hard candy. If there were six lots to be shared by seven, a little was given to each. It was given without question and without envy, something that is done because all know it should be.

In this, I think, is the secret of the missing portion in Uncle Jack's box—he knew there were seven but packed it only for six to teach us a lesson.

Packed in each box along with the good things was an invisible gift that a child's eyes, and those of some adults, could not see: the gift of learning to share what we have with others.

It was an object lesson, the spirit of Christmas personified, and Uncle Jack put it there as surely as he packed the nuts and dates, the figs and popcorn balls. He taught us all the true meaning of Christmas.

Gift Left on Doorstep Fulfilled Child's Dream

THE YEAR WAS 1939, not a good year for many people. My father almost never brought home a full week's pay and often was out of work completely. For my mother, it was a daily struggle just to keep her four children fed, clothed and warm.

I was the baby of the family, a quiet little girl who loved dolls, and I dearly wanted a new doll for Christmas. I was only 5 years old; I didn't realize we were living in poverty. And even if I had, I still believed in Santa, and Santa wasn't poor, was he?

On Christmas Eve, my mother was feeling sad because she hadn't been able to buy a doll for me, but I didn't realize that then. I was filled with anticipation. The tree was lit, and to me it looked like a wonderful fairyland sight with all the colored lights shimmering behind the tinsel.

Toward dusk, the doorbell rang. My mother and I answered it, but no one was there. On the doorstep, though, was a large flat box. We picked it up, brought it into the house and read the tag. It said, "Merry Christmas to Carol Jean from Santa."

When I opened the box, I couldn't believe my eyes. There was my very own doll, with the most exquisite hand-sewn layette a little girl could ever dream of. There were dresses, kimonos with embroidered trim, and crocheted sweaters, hats and booties.

We never found out who gave me that wonderful gift. Everyone knew my mother was very proud and would not accept charity, so the giver never identified herself to us.

But I think my mother may have had an idea who the giver was. She suggested I name the doll "Amy," which was the name of a woman who attended our church. I've often wondered if that was the lady who fulfilled a little girl's dream on that Christmas Eve so long ago. —*Carol Ulrich, Ashby, Minnesota*

Family Sleigh Ride Made Lasting Memory

I REMEMBER a Christmas shopping trip during the Depression.

We lived on a farm in northern Michigan, 9 miles from town. Early in the morning. Dad hitched the horses to the sleigh and filled it with straw. Then all four of us youngsters were bundled up and packed in the sleigh.

Of course, we were so excited we couldn't stay put for long. Soon we were out of the sleigh, running along behind it or sliding on the hard packed snow in the path left by the runners.

When we arrived in town, we went to the block-long "downtown" to shop. Each of us had 50¢ to spend, and we could always find a gift for a dime at the hardware or variety store.

Soon we all were loaded back into the sleigh for the trip home. Night fell, and the sky was filled with stars. All was quiet except for the horses' muffled hoofbeats...the squeak of the harness... the crunch of the sleigh runners in the snow. The whole family snuggled down in the straw and blankets, quiet and happy. The horses knew the way home.
—*Eleanore Van Zyll Wyoming, Michigan*

TURN THE PAGE FOR HOLIDAY CHEER: When the Journal-Courier newspaper in Lafayette, Indiana invited the unemployed to attend a Christmas party in 1936, the crowd was standing room only. Representatives of the newspaper distributed toys and other gifts to hundreds of needy families.

Lost Toys Rediscovered on Christmas Morning

IN LOOKING back over the years, I can remember many Christmases, some happy and some sad, but one stands out in my memory as very special.

It started out to be a sad holiday, as we were locked in the depths of the Great Depression. Our parents had told us not to expect a lot, as Santa had to spend his money on food for the poor.

My father was still working, but his salary had been cut in half and he was working longer hours. He was so tired when he came home that he would eat and go right to bed. I guess we knew—or sensed—the struggle both our parents were having just to make ends meet.

The day before Christmas, I was very sad. My doll had disappeared and I couldn't find her anywhere. Other toys were missing, too, and we had nothing to play with and nothing to look forward to.

On Christmas Eve, I was sent to the grocery store and the grocer told me I had just missed seeing Santa. If only I

By Lucy O'Leary
St. Peters, Missouri

had been there a few minutes earlier! I began to cry, and the grocer gave me a package of nuts to take home for Christmas. When I got home I had a

feeling that perhaps Santa had visited our house.

With my heart pounding, I ran inside and looked under the tree—but nothing was there. We children went to bed with heavy hearts. I didn't think I would ever be happy again.

I awoke early, walked into the living room and, lo and behold, my missing doll was under the tree with a new dress and a clean face! Our doll furniture was under the tree, too, now painted snow-white. In fact, every toy that had been lost was back, looking like new.

We shouted for joy as we picked up our lost treasures. We were the happiest children in the world! Then we gave our parents their gifts, calendars we had made for them at school. They were so glad to get them.

As we ate breakfast, laughter and joy enveloped our house. I remember thinking then, "If only I could keep this day forever." And I've done just that, in my heart. ✒

HOMEMADE CARD shows the kind of spirit that helped get Grace Brenner's family through the Depression. Grace, of Manahawkin, New Jersey, said her dad not only took the picture but processed it in his own "darkroom"—the kitchen pantry! "Our parents' attitude helped us grow up as normal children and adults," Grace says. "We never knew the economic crisis they were facing."

'Wish Book' Fueled Little Girls' Dreams

IT MAY HAVE been only mid-October, but when the Sears Roebuck catalog arrived, my sister and I were already thinking about Christmas! We couldn't wait to get our lessons and chores done so we could browse through that "wish book," looking at all the special toys. Since the Depression was upon us, we could ask for only one gift.

By mid-November, we'd decided what we wanted. My sister asked for a bright red Flyer wagon. My father, being a practical man, was pleased; after all, a wagon could be used to haul things, too.

He was less enthused about my choice—a new doll. At age 8, I was a little old for that, he thought.

But this doll was such a *beauty*. She had big, dark brown eyes like my sister's and was dressed in a hat, coat, leggings and black shoes. And she had real hair, not the painted-on kind my other dolls had. I had even picked out a fancy name for her to fit her beauty: "Babette."

I began checking the front porch every day for a box. When I didn't find one, I'd ask if anything had come in the mail. The answer was always "no." I'd sigh and think, "Maybe tomorrow." My sister offered encouragement, saying Mama would make sure I got the doll, even if Father thought it was silly.

By Christmas Eve, there was still no package. Maybe my parents had hidden the box. I held on to that hope.

On Christmas morning, the snow was so deep we couldn't tell where the sidewalk and curbs were. But there was my doll, all dressed for winter, sitting outside in my sister's new wagon!

I have always cherished Babette, and she now rests in a tiny carriage in my bedroom. She's a little worn from my play (and that of my children), but she survived the Depression very well!
—Dolores J. Bosley, Trinidad,

Woman Opened Heart and Home to Travelers

MY HUSBAND and I were the recipients of an unforgettable act of compassion in the winter of 1937.

We had joined the B.M. Goff Tent Show in Texas. In those days, traveling tent shows ran for a week at a time in each town, with a different show every night. Many tent shows went out of business during the Depression, but a few hung on, playing for an admission fee of 10¢, and sometimes taking chickens or garden produce in lieu of money.

Our show had a cast of only five people, and we did everything, from vaudeville routines to setting up and tearing down the tent.

Just before Christmas, we set up in the little town of Center, Texas. That week a flu epidemic hit the town, and everyone was either ill, had family members who were ill, or feared going to any public gathering lest *they* become ill.

At best, our show operated on a shoestring, so the flu outbreak spelled disaster for us. Nobody came to the show, and we didn't have enough money to buy gas to get out of town. We all were desperate.

By Lanya Bump
Greeley, Colorado

We'd been eating at the town's one small restaurant, usually getting just a bowl of chili or a 10¢ hamburger. On Christmas morning, my husband and I had a dime left. We went to the restaurant, thinking we could split a bowl of chili. But when we got there, we saw a sign on the door that said "CLOSED." The lady who owned the restaurant lived in the back, so we knocked, thinking she might at least let us have a cup of coffee, which was only a nickel then. By this time the other members of our troupe had arrived, too.

After a few minutes, the lady came to the door and we asked if she could let us have some coffee. She replied, "I'm sorry, but it's Christmas and we're closed for the day."

We must have looked as though we were facing the end of the world. Then, to our surprise, she smiled and said, "The restaurant is closed, but if you come in, maybe I can find something for you."

We walked in and saw a big table set with turkey and all the trimmings waiting for us. The woman told us she knew we'd have no Christmas, and from the way we had been eating all week, she also knew that we were broke, so she'd been planning all along to invite us in for Christmas dinner.

In addition to providing us with a meal, she had placed a small gift next to each plate. Mine was a little cedar chest filled with chocolates. I still have the box. Every time I see it, tears of gratitude fill my eyes.

Although I can no longer remember the woman's name, I will never forget her or the beautiful gesture she made for perfect strangers. She turned that bleak Christmas into one of the most joyful I have ever experienced.

And to top it all, the next night we opened our show to a full house! 🍃

FAMILY DINNERS remained a cherished holiday tradition even during the leanest Depression years. Those who couldn't afford the fixings for such meals often found the ingredients left anonymously on their doorsteps, or were invited to other families' homes to celebrate.

'We Heard Messages from Santa on the Radio!'

By Beverly Sheresh
Bonita, California

I'LL NEVER forget the thrill of hearing Santa's booming voice one snowy night before Christmas—especially since that voice came from our radio!

My brother and I, along with all the other kids in our neighborhood, had written letters to Santa and given them to my mother, who "forwarded" them to the North Pole. We were assured that Santa would not only receive our letters, but respond to them in person!

On the appointed evening, we all huddled in our front room in front of the radio. Santa called each of us by name and acknowledged receiving our letters, although he warned us that he might not be able to deliver everything we'd asked for.

When he asked if we'd been good, we all nodded vigorously. We were so caught up in the magic that we forgot Santa couldn't see us. Or could he?

In later years, I found out that my father, an electronics buff, had played Santa for us. He'd hooked up a microphone to the radio speaker and talked to us from the cellar, where he read our letters by flashlight.

My mother told us, laughing, that she thought he was just as nervous and excited as we kids were that night! ❦

One Special Gift Touched Many Hearts

TIMES WERE lean as Christmas approached in poverty-stricken Cochran County, Texas in 1936. The region had been devastated by dust storms that ravaged the earth, destroyed every living plant and rolled tumbleweeds against fences, breaking the posts and tearing them down.

The courageous people who lived there had little money and few possessions, and food was scarce. Growing crops or even a garden was impossible. Men trying to provide for their families would accept any offer of work, no matter how small the pay. Occasionally they would receive a dollar a day, but sometimes only 50¢ or even a quarter.

I taught at the one-room school, and the parents of my 12 students requested a Christmas program. Each child would have a part (some had two), and they would sing, tell the story of Christ's birth and welcome our visitors. We were all excited about having a gathering where we could share the joy of Christmas.

Since there were no trees to be found in our area, we stuck tumbleweeds together to make a Christmas tree. We wet the tumbleweeds and then sprinkled them with salt and flour to make them white and sparkling, then decorated them with paper chains, colored strips of cloth and a handful of buttons.

With donations of pennies, nickels and dimes, we managed to raise just under $10 to buy an apple, orange and a stick of candy plus a small gift for each child. A top or small doll cost a nickel, a ball could be bought for a dime and a little red wagon sold for a quarter.

A very special gift was purchased for one of my students. William was an undernourished but handsome 9-year-old with large, luminous eyes. His mother made his overalls by hand. They were faded and thin, but clean. His high-topped shoes had no soles. His parents put cardboard in his shoes each day, but it usually had worn through by the time school was out. He had no socks, and wore a thin coat that was much too large for him.

Despite his hardships, William was a happy child who spread joy to others. His favorite possession was "boughten bread paper." He had never eaten store-bought bread (it cost 9¢ a loaf), but the children whose families could afford it would save their bread wrappers for William. He would carry them and look at them until they were worn.

One of the best gifts I ever received was from William—a small handkerchief wrapped in his precious "boughten bread paper." For this child who had so little to call his own, this was truly a sacrifice.

William's parents brought him to the Christmas program in a mule-drawn wagon. As the boy entered the schoolhouse, he spied a red wagon next to the Christmas tree. He raced over and climbed into it, crying, "Oh, it's mine. I just know it is!" Just to be sure, though, he checked the tag to see if his name was on it. It was.

"Look, everybody," William called out excitedly. "I have a red wagon!"

From that moment on, William was not to be disturbed. He said that his part of the Christmas program was to sit in his wagon, and that's exactly what he did!

When his parents were ready to take him home, they simply picked up the wagon with William still in it. As he was carried out, he asked everyone he passed. "Did you see my red wagon? It is so pretty, and it's mine!"

Tears ran down many faces that night, and yet there was a feeling of joy in the air. We all shared in William's much-deserved happiness.

—*Myrt Young, Lubbock, Texas*